# The Gospel Mystery of Sanctification

## Growing in Holiness by Living in Union with Christ

By

**Walter Marshall**

A New Version,
Put Into Modern English

By

**Bruce H. McRae**

**Wipf & Stock Publishers**
Eugene, Oregon

The Gospel Mystery of Sanctification:
Growing in Holiness by Living in Union with Christ

© 2005 by Bruce H. McRae
Atlanta, Georgia
ISBN: 1-59752-054-3

Wipf and Stock Publishers
199 West 8th Avenue, Suite 3
Eugene, Oregon 97401

# Contents

## Contents

**Chapter 1**................................................................15
God in his law calls you to live a holy and righteous life. In order to do this, you first have to learn the only possible way you *San* live a holy life.

**Chapter 2**................................................................25
You have to receive certain qualifications to keep the law of God. There are four qualifications for living a godly life which you must receive from God: 1) Your heart has to be freely willing to live a godly life, 2) You have to be assured that you are forgiven and reconciled to God, 3) You have to be sure of a happy, eternal future with the Lord, and 4) You have to have sufficient strength both to will and to do what God calls you to do.

**Chapter 3**................................................................39
You receive the qualifications to enable you to keep the law of God out of the fullness of Christ, through fellowship with him. In order to have this fellowship, you must be in union with him. You must be in Christ, and Christ himself must be in you.

**Chapter 4**................................................................49
The Gospel is the way the Holy Spirit brings you into union with Christ, and into fellowship with him and his holiness. Through the gospel, Christ enters your heart and gives you faith. Faith is the way you actually receive Christ himself, and all his fullness, into your heart. Even this faith is a grace of the Holy Spirit. When you have faith, you believe the gospel with all your heart. When you have faith, you believe in Christ, as he is revealed and freely promised to you in the gospel, for all his salvation.

**Chapter 5**................................................................63
You cannot live a holy life, no matter how hard you try, if you still have your old nature. In order to live a holy life, you have to receive, by faith, a new heart and a new nature, through your union and fellowship with Christ.

1

If you try to obey the commands of Christ in order to earn your salvation, and to gain assurance of your salvation, you are seeking salvation by the works of the law. You are not seeking your salvation through faith in Christ, as he is revealed in the gospel. If you try to earn your salvation by your true obedience, you will never succeed.

Do not think that your heart and life have to be changed from sin to holiness in any measure before you are allowed to trust in Christ for salvation.

Make sure that you seek holiness of heart and life in its proper time. You can only live a holy life after you have come into union with Christ, have been justified, and have received the Holy Spirit. Once you have received these blessings, seek holiness by faith with all your might. It is a crucial part of your salvation.

In order to sincerely keep the law of God, you must first receive the comfort of the Gospel.

If you are going to obey the law out of the comfort of the Gospel, you must have complete assurance of your salvation. You obtain this assurance by believing and receiving Christ into your heart. Therefore, confidently believe in Christ without delay. Be assured that when you believe in Christ, God will freely give you a personal relationship with Christ, just as he has promised.

Believe in Christ without delay! Then, continue to build up your faith. When you do this, you will build your relationship with Christ more and more. You will also be empowered to live a holy life.

# Contents

In order to obey the law of God, earnestly live by your most holy faith. Do not walk according to your old nature, and do not put into practice anything that belongs to your old nature. Walk only according to the new nature you received by faith, and live the lifestyle of your new nature. This is the only way to live a holy and righteous life – as much as is possible in this present life.

Now that the Holy Spirit has renewed you, God calls you to live a holy life. To live this obedient life, you must continue to believe in Christ and walk in him by faith. To live this life of faith, God calls you to diligently use all of the means of grace he has given you in his Word.

I have been telling you up to this point that you must seek to live a holy life by believing in Christ, and by walking in him by faith. If you are going to do this, you must understand why living by faith in Christ is so important and beneficial to your soul.

The Doctrine of Justification Explained and Applied (Sermon)

The Gospel Mystery of Sanctification

# **Introduction**

I traveled a long, winding path to discover, and then to "modernize," this version of Walter Marshall's classic book, <u>The Gospel Mystery of Sanctification</u>. Several years ago, I heard one of the pastors under whom I grew up, Dr. C. John Miller, speaking of a book that had meant a great deal to him. He said that Dr. John Murray, late professor of systematic theology at Westminster Seminary in Philadelphia, had told him that it was the most important book on sanctification that had ever been written. The book was <u>The Gospel Mystery of Sanctification.</u>

Thus began my search to find a copy of the book. This was not an easy task, for it was long out of print. No used bookstore I checked had the book. Internet title searches in bookstores turned up empty. Therefore, my next stop was the theological library at the Candler School of Theology at Emory University in Atlanta. They had at least one copy, but there was just one problem – the book was in their rare book collection, and could only be read there in the library! The book was first published in 1692, and the version they possessed dated back to the mid-1800s. It was so fragile, I was not allowed to remove it from the library, let alone copy it!

The librarian at the Candler Library was kind enough to do an Internet library search looking for the book, and he was able to find several versions of the book in various libraries. The latest published date we found was 1954. One of the copies from a 1954 version was in the library at Covenant College, on Lookout Mountain, Tennessee, and I was able to procure it from there. It is that book which I have used to produce this new version of Marshall's classic book.

<u>The Gospel Mystery of Sanctification</u> has recently been republished in its old language version, but the book's relegation, for the most part, to rare book collections in dusty theological libraries, is something of a picture of what is happening in the church today. The great theme of Walter Marshall's book is that Christians grow in obedience by the power of the gospel, not by their own strength. Christians are in union with Christ, and their Christian growth flows from this union, not from their own efforts. The gospel is essential for growth in holiness.

In our day, however, this truth that power for growth comes from the gospel of grace seems to be long forgotten, relegated to the dusty, "rare book" room of the church. Why is this the case? Probably because it sounds too easy! "Surely," we think, "we must do something to pay God back for saving us by our diligent efforts to live holy lives!" Really?

The gospel says that through faith in Christ, you are completely forgiven of all your sins. Then, having been forgiven, you are called to sanctification by faith in Christ as well. Sanctification is the lifelong process of being conformed to the image of Jesus Christ. All Christians agree on this point: Christians are called to pursue godly, holy living. On this point there is simply no debate. However, confusion sets in as soon as the question is asked, "How do Christians become holy? Where does the power for godly living come from?"

This question has been debated for 2000 years. In the Bible, the books of Galatians and Colossians address this question head on. Does godly living proceed from placing yourself back under the requirements of the Mosaic Law, as the Galatian Judaizers taught? Does holiness proceed from higher life mysticism, as the Colossian heretics taught? Paul's answer in each case was an unequivocal "No!" Holiness comes from union with Christ. It comes from "Christ living in me" (Galatians 2:20). Godliness proceeds from living in Christ: "So then, just as you received Christ Jesus as Lord, continue to live in him, rooted and built up in him, strengthened in the faith as you were taught, and overflowing with thankfulness" (Colossians 2:6-7).

For the past two thousand years, the church has re-fought the battles of Galatians and Colossians. The church has produced many different teachings about the Christian life: asceticism, legalism, perfectionism, higher life and second blessing movements, etc. Other churches have emphasized discipleship, and many books have been published on the Christian disciplines. This is a critical emphasis for the church. However, many schemes of discipleship focus on methods of disciplining yourself for holiness. They hardly even mention union with Christ or the power of the gospel to produce holiness. Such schemes quickly become legalism. They leave those who attempt them frustrated, condemned, and powerless. They certainly give lip service to grace, but they do not put grace into practice to empower Christian living. It is always a message of "Grace, but…" "Yes, you are certainly saved by grace, **but** make sure you discipline yourself and live a good life if you really want to be **sure** God is happy with you…."

# Introduction

The Apostle Paul was confident that gospel grace would empower God's people to live godly lives. "For the grace of God that brings salvation has appeared to all men. It teaches us to say 'No' to ungodliness and worldly passions, and to live self-controlled, upright and godly lives in this present age, while we wait for the blessed hope—the glorious appearing of our great God and Savior, Jesus Christ, who gave himself for us to redeem us from all wickedness and to purify for himself a people that are his very own, eager to do what is good" (Titus 2:12-13).

He also said, "At one time, we too were foolish, disobedient, deceived and enslaved by all kinds of passions and pleasures. We lived in malice and envy, being hated and hating one another. But when the kindness and love of God our Savior appeared, he saved us, not because of righteous things we had done, but because of his mercy. He saved us through the washing of rebirth and renewal by the Holy Spirit, whom he poured out on us generously through Jesus Christ our Savior, so that, having been justified by his grace, we might become heirs having the hope of eternal life. This is a trustworthy saying. *And I want you to stress these things, so that those who have trusted in God may be careful to devote themselves to doing what is good.* These things are excellent and profitable for everyone" (Titus 3:3-8).

For Paul, the gospel brings a double blessing: the forgiveness of sin **and** the power for holiness. As Augustus Toplady said in his famous hymn, "Rock of Ages cleft for me…, be of sin the double-cure, cleanse me from its **guilt** and **power**." That is why Paul was so concerned that church leaders stress the grace of the gospel. *Only the gospel can empower obedience.* That is why every generation of the church must discover afresh the sufficiency of the gospel of grace, and the power of the cross of Jesus Christ both to save and to sanctify

There is currently something of a "grace awakening" in the church. Just as Martin Luther, John Calvin, John Wesley and George Whitefield discovered the truth of the gospel and were spiritually energized, so now many are rediscovering the riches of grace. However, there is also a very healthy discussion going on. Legitimate questions are also being raised about Christian growth and sanctification: What exactly **is** our part in sanctification? Does the sufficiency of grace mean we do nothing at all? What is the place of the law? Are we supposed to keep it or not? What is the role of faith in sanctification? What is the role of the Holy Spirit in sanctification? What is the place of the "spiritual disciplines" in the Christian life? In short, how do God's grace and our pursuit of Christian growth fit together?

These are all important questions. And when it comes to sanctification, people tend to fall into one of two extremes. On the one hand, people can fall into legalism – that is, they place human righteousness and human effort at the center of sanctification, and supplant the work of Christ and the Spirit. On the other had, people can fall into license – that is, they say, "since grace and forgiveness are free, it does not matter how we live; there is no need to keep the law."

Christians must of course avoid both of these extremes – for neither one is true. The Bible is clear: Christians are saved totally apart from their works, through faith in Christ alone. The Bible is also clear about this: Christians are called, and empowered, to live holy lives, by that same faith. Christian growth is not a self-help scheme, where "God helps those who help themselves." Christian growth is not like a weight loss program – it cannot be packaged into a simplistic, easy, do-it-yourself program located in the self-help section of a secular bookstore.

The issue of sanctification was obviously a hot topic during Walter Marshall's day as well. He also was flanked by the two extremes just mentioned. In the terminology of his day, he had the Neo-Nomians on the one side, and the Anti-Nomians on the other. The Anti-Nomians ("the lawless ones") said that since you are forgiven by free grace, you have no obligation to keep the law whatsoever. The Neo-Nominans grew up in reaction to the Anti-Nomians. As the word "Neo-Nomian" suggests, they brought in a "new law." They became a party of "new legalism." They did not want people to fall into the Anti-Nomian error, so they told people, "Yes, you are saved by the grace of Christ, **but** you must keep the law to guarantee your stake in Christ's grace." They had confused justification and sanctification. To try to keep people from falling into the cheap grace of Anti-Nomianism, they placed people back under the law again.

Walter Marshall addresses both of these extremes in his book. Marshall had been something of a legalistic Neo-Nomian himself, so he spoke from personal experience. In short, he says that neither of these extremes can help anyone live a holy life. Both extremes misunderstand the gospel. Both extremes snatch holiness away from the people who follow them. On the one hand, Lawlessness just flat-out tells people that they do not have to live a holy life. On the other hand, Legalism tells people that they have to live a holy life, but that they have to live a holy

# Introduction

life apart from the grace of Christ, out of their own strength. As Marshall says over and over again in his book, legalism has no power to change anyone. **Legalism** turns people into **lawless** people, because they do not have Christ living in them! They have no power to obey!

The same two extremes are still present today, in various forms. However, the gospel gives a way far above either legalism or cheap grace. The gospel says, "grace is the power for holiness." In order to bring this out, Walter Marshall emphasizes several ideas:

- ❑ If you have come to faith in Christ, you participate in two blessings: your sins have been forgiven, and you have received a new heart and a new nature through the filling of the Holy Spirit. You have become a "new creation."

- ❑ As a Christian, you do not grow in holiness by "improving your flesh" through disciplined self-effort. You grow in holiness as you live out of your new nature. You grow in obedience as you live in union with Christ, and as Christ lives in you.

- ❑ You have a responsibility to actively pursue sanctification. How? You must continually live by faith in Christ who loved you and gave himself for you.

- ❑ In order to live the life of faith in Christ, you must vigorously pursue and participate in the means of grace God has given you to live by faith (Bible reading, prayer, repentance, church membership, the sacraments, etc.).

I first began to use Walter Marshall's book when I served as a local church pastor. The key issue I faced in trying to disciple Christians for holiness was this: they constantly felt defeated and discouraged in their Christian lives because they had tried and failed to change so many times! Walter Marshall addressed this issue better than any other book that I had ever read. This is largely because Walter Marshall was a pastor himself, and he continually observed Christians all around him struggling – and failing – to grow in holiness. Because of the difficulty of the original language version, I found it necessary to rewrite the book in modern English, so that people could read it, understand it, and profit from it.

# The Gospel Mystery of Sanctification

Christians today desperately need to hear and understand the message of Walter Marshall's book. People need to understand how the life of grace truly will energize them for godliness. The main point of his book is that union with Christ by faith is necessary and sufficient for both our justification and our sanctification. The gospel of Christ is sufficient for both our forgiveness and our growth in holiness. We cannot rely on our own abilities for either one of them. As he says, the key error of the Christian life is that people *think that even though they have been justified by a righteousness produced totally by Christ, they must be sanctified by a holiness produced totally by themselves.* The message of this book will bring freedom and encouragement to many Christians who are struggling, and failing, in their Christian growth.

Who was Walter Marshall? He was born in 1628 in Wearmouth, England. He was appointed as a parish pastor in England in 1661, but he had to leave when the British Act of Uniformity was passed in 1662. He then was called to pastor a congregation at Gosport, in Hampshire, where he labored until his death. He was considered an able preacher and a faithful pastor. It was during this time at Gosport that he wrote this book consisting of fourteen "Directions" about the Christian life. The book flowed out of his own personal experience, and his struggles to live a holy life. The book was only published after his death.

It is very helpful to know what gave rise to The Gospel Mystery of Sanctification in the first place. In Direction Six in his book, he wrote:

> This doctrine of salvation by sincere obedience is one of the worst Antinomian errors there is. I hate it with a perfect hatred. I consider it my enemy, because it has been my enemy. I have discovered in my own experience the truth of what the apostle Paul says in Romans 6:14, that the only way to be freed from the slavery and dominion of sin is not to be under the law but under grace.

He is very clearly referring to his early life, when his religion was not a source of joy and consolation to him. His religion only caused him affliction and heartache. He had been very distressed about the state of his soul for many years, and he had tried to put his sins to death with many different methods. He had tried to gain peace of conscience by his own efforts, but his mental anguish only increased. He went around mourning in his soul most of the day, because his conscience felt so guilty all the time. He always thought that God was displeased and angry with him. He

# Introduction

began to consult with some of his friends to try to obtain relief from his guilt, such as the Rev. Richard Baxter, of Kidderminster, who wrote <u>The Reformed Pastor</u>.

Next, he consulted with Dr. Thomas Goodwin, a very eminent Puritan theologian. Marshall opened up his heart to Dr. Goodwin. He mentioned several of his sins that were weighing heavily upon his conscience. After he had finished describing his sins, Dr. Goodwin replied in this way: "You have forgotten to mention the greatest sin of all: the sin of unbelief. You do not believe in the Lord Jesus Christ to forgive your sins, and to sanctify your nature."

This reply was powerfully used by God to bring the issue home to Walter Marshall's heart. He came to see the mistake he had been making, without even knowing it. He had been trying to establish his own righteousness. He was not submitting himself to the righteousness of God. He was acting just like the Old Covenant Jews. He was trying to attain his righteousness by the works of the law. He was not seeking his righteousness by faith.

After his conversation with Thomas Goodwin, Marshall began his journey of becoming freed from his fears, and from the spirit of bondage that had oppressed him for so long. He saw that at the root of all of his fears lay an evil, unbelieving heart. This evil, unbelieving heart was preventing him from attaining holiness, even though he was trying to attain holiness with all of his might. Once he came to understand his unbelief, he was soon able to believe the gospel from his heart. He determined from then on to study and preach Christ in his ministry. Over time, he grew in holiness, with great peace of conscience and joy in the Holy Spirit. He also determined to put in writing the lessons he had learned from the Scriptures, which he had found so powerful in giving him peace in his soul. The result was <u>The Gospel Mystery of Sanctification.</u>

Just before his death, Marshall said to people around him who had come to watch his departure, "I am dying with the full assurance of the truth, and in the comfort of that doctrine I have preached to you." After a short pause, he uttered, with great emotion, these comprehensive words, "For the wages of sin is death, but the gift of God is eternal life through Jesus Christ our Lord." When he had spoken these words, he breathed his last, and he entered into his rest in the year 1680.[1]

11

# The Gospel Mystery of Sanctification

The Gospel Mystery of Sanctification flowed right out of Walter Marshall's own personal experience, and his vast knowledge of Scripture. The book has been used to bring countless others to the same freedom which Marshall himself experienced. One such person was the poet and hymn writer William Cowper. He said in a letter to his cousin,

> Marshall *is an old acquaintance of mine*. I have both read him and heard him read with pleasure and edification. The doctrines he maintains are, under the influence of the Divine Spirit, the very life of my soul, and the soul of all my happiness; that Jesus is a *present* Savior from the guilt of sin by his most precious blood, and from the power of it by his Spirit; that [even though we are] corrupt and wretched in ourselves, in him, and in *Him only*, we are complete.... I never met with a man who understood the plan of salvation better, or was more happy in explaining it.[2]

In his original version of The Gospel Mystery, Marshall did not use a polished, refined style of writing. James Hervey said that in Marshall's writing "we are not to expect much pathos of address, or any delicacy of composition. Here the gospel-diamond is set, not in gold, but in steel."[3] Marshall's simplicity of style is now difficult to see because of the way the English language has changed over the past 300 years. The original version is extremely difficult to read. I believe that Marshall's book is so important, it needs to be re-discovered by the church. However, if this rich resource is to be recovered, it must be put into modern language. That is what I have attempted to do in this volume. In my edition, I have not altered any of Marshall's thinking. This version is essentially a word for word translation. I have not sought to edit out his repetition or produce a more "popular" version of his book. I have simply modernized the vocabulary where it was necessary to do so, and tightened the sentence structure.

In his introduction to the 1954 publication of The Gospel Mystery of Sanctification, Percy O. Ruoff gives an excellent summary of the value of Walter Marshall's classic book:

> The Gospel Mystery of Sanctification (first published in 1692) has been submerged by an avalanche of minor and relatively unimportant literature on the subject. This classic is now rescued from regrettable obscurity, and put within the reach of modern students. Readers will look kindly upon its somewhat archaic structure, and eagerly search for the gold mines of spiritual truth

within. It has been said that the author's style is obscure, and the arrangement of his massive argument is not the best. This is correct, but the reader gets a reward for patience. One writer has said – "The beauty of Marshall's book is that he makes the doctrine of our union with Christ our starting point in the Christian course;" and, "What a new direction would be given to the spiritual struggles of thousands if they could but receive the teaching which Marshall seeks so earnestly to inculcate."[4]

One word of advice as you read Marshall's book. Do not become frustrated with the book's structure and repetition. Grasp the main idea, which he expresses over and over again, relying upon his vast knowledge of Scripture: "You are more sinful than you can imagine! The doctrine of Original Sin is true! You cannot reform your flesh! You cannot become a better person by your own strength no matter how hard you try! But cheer up! If you are a Christian, you have come into union with Christ. Through faith in Jesus Christ you are forgiven. Through faith in Jesus Christ you are sanctified and made holy. Through Christ, you are a new creation! The Holy Spirit lives in you! Therefore, pursue the life of faith in Christ with all diligence!"

---

[1]This summary of Walter Marshall's Life comes from Walter Marshall, The Gospel Mystery of Sanctification (Grand Rapids, Michigan: Zondervan Publishing House, 1954), pp. 249-252.
[2]Ibid. pp. 263-264.
[3]Ibid. p. 260.
[4]Ibid. p. v.

The Gospel Mystery of Sanctification

# Chapter One

## Principle Number One

**God in his law calls you to live a holy and righteous life. In order to do this, you first have to learn the only possible way you *can* live a holy life.**

My goal is to tell you why God has saved you. He has saved you for a purpose: to live a holy life. Therefore, I want to teach you how you can live out the way of life that the Bible calls holiness, righteousness, godliness, obedience, and true religion. This is what God requires of you in his moral law, which he has summarized in the Ten Commandments — and particularly in the two Great Commandments of love to God and love to your neighbor (Matthew 22:37-39). All the rest of the Bible more fully explains these laws.

My real purpose is to show you **how** you can actually keep these laws once you know what they require of you. It is not my purpose here to give a major explanation of what all these laws mean. Many books, catechisms and commentaries have already done this very adequately. However, I do want you to know enough so you do not miss the mark of God's law. I want you to see how grand it really is.

First of all, the holiness that God wants you to have is **spiritual** (see Romans 7:14). Real obedience does not only consist of external good works and acts of love. They are important, but they alone are not true holiness. True holiness is a matter of the heart. True holiness means that you have holy thoughts, motives, and feelings. This holiness consists chiefly in love, from which all other good works must flow. Every good thing you do must flow from this kind of inner life, or else it is not acceptable to God. God commands you to love him with your whole heart, soul, mind and strength.

Second, true holiness is not simply of matter of refraining from acting out your sinful lusts. Again, this is important, but there is also a positive side to true holiness. True holiness means that you delight in doing God's will; you long to do it more than you long to do anything else! True holiness means that you cheerfully obey God. You do not obey God grudgingly, with your heart filled with grumbling, whining, and complaining. You do not view obeying God as a terrible burden and a pain in the neck!

Third, the law you are aiming to keep is exceedingly broad. James 2:10 says that if you break one commandment, you have broken them all! The summary of this law is to love God with all your heart, spirit, and might. You are to love everything in him: his justice, his holiness, his sovereign authority, his all-seeing eye. You are to love all of his decrees, all of his commands, all of his judgments, and all of his doings. You are called to love God more than anything else, in single-minded devotion, seeing him as the fountain of all goodness. Whenever anything else stands in competition with your enjoyment of him – any kind of fleshly or worldly enjoyment – you must reject them and even hate them.

You are called to love God with all your heart. You are called to yield yourself to him completely, in constant service to him at all times. You are called to make him the absolute Lord of your life, in plenty or in want, in life or in death. In addition to all these things, God tells you that for his sake, you are to love your neighbors. Who does this include? This includes **everyone** – whether they are your friends or your enemies. You are to do them all the good you can, and treat them as you would want to be treated.

This is what I want you to aim for in your Christian life: complete spiritual obedience — total love for God from your whole heart. When you think about what a wonderful way of life this is, you will, I am sure, quickly desire to find out how you can live such a life. The angels in heaven have no more wonderful calling than this!

God first created you to live a holy life. This is what he wanted when he first made humans in his image. Now, God is re-creating this kind of holiness in your life through the new birth and through sanctification in Jesus Christ. God's image is now being restored to you, and it will be finally, perfectly complete when you are glorified with God in heaven. This obedience to the law is, by nature, holy, just and good (Romans 7:12), and it is right for you to do because of your dependence upon God as your creator. You are naturally obligated to obey God!

When you think about it, even non-Christians have some sense of their obligation before God. There are many non-Christians who have never read the Bible, and therefore they have no direct revelation from God. However, even though they do not have God's written law, the Bible says that God's law is written on their hearts (Romans 2:14-15). We might call this natural law, or the moral law; every non-Christian has some kind of natural religion. God still holds them accountable for obeying his law, and he will punish them if they do not do it. Indeed, there are many non-Christians who are quite moral, at least in a human sense.

I dare to join with these people in saying that the most moral man, the most honest man, is the greatest saint. All true religion indeed does make people more moral. There is a sense in which this is the chief test of true religion. Without this kind of real change in your life, your faith is dead, and all religious performance is just vain show and hypocrisy. However, by this kind of life change, I am not talking about the "mere morality" that any non-Christian can affirm. I am talking about the fact that God calls you to obey the two greatest, and most moral, commandments of them all: love to God, and love to neighbor. There is no other commandment greater than these, and on these two commandments hang all of the law and the prophets (Matthew 22:36-40, Mark 12:31).

Now I know that you are probably rejecting this goal of love for God and neighbor because you know it is absolutely impossible to do! What a lofty goal! Therefore, it is absolutely critical that you learn the only powerful and effective **way** you can live this kind of a godly life. This is the first thing you have to learn, before you can expect any success in attaining your goal of holy living.

I really need to emphasize this point. Many people will probably skip right over this part on **how** they can become holy. My whole book is about the **means** by which you can become holy, but many people will see this part as irrelevant and useless. Why? Because they only want to know what they have to **do.** They only want to know what the law requires of them. They think that once they know what the law requires of them, they can just go out and do it. They will blindly rush into it and immediately try to do everything they are told. However, they will run hard, but they will get nowhere! They will make many promises to obey God, just like the Israelites of old told the Lord, "All that the Lord has spoken, we will do" (Exodus 19:8). What is the problem? They never first sit down and count the cost. They never think about what will enable them and empower them to obey God.

Their basic problem is that they view holy living as a means to an end. They view holiness as a way to earn eternal life. They do not see holiness as an end in itself, an end that requires ways and means to actually do it. Most people, when they begin to have some sense about religion, say, like the rich young man who asked Jesus, "What good thing shall I do, that I may obtain eternal life?" (Matthew 19:16). They do not ask the question they **should** be asking: "How can I be empowered and enabled to do anything that is good?"

Many pastors contribute to this problem. They spend all their time telling their people what the law requires of them. They tell people all that they have to do, but they never spend any time telling their people **how** they can actually do it! They never tell people about the **means** to attain true obedience to the law. They look at righteous living as if it were manual labor, where you need no training or skill whatsoever. They consider holy living just a matter of putting your nose to the grindstone and doing it.

I do not want you to fall flat on your face right at the beginning of your Christian life by making this very common mistake. It is not enough for you to simply know what your duty is. It is not enough for you to merely know what the law calls you to do. You must certainly learn this, but you also have to learn **how** you can effectively do your duty before God. You have to learn the only powerful and effective **means** by which you can keep the law of God. In fact, you have to sit down and learn this before you can do **anything** for God!

Why is this so? There is a key reason for this. Quite simply, you are, by nature, totally powerless and unable to live the holy and righteous life God requires of you in his law. You are dead in trespasses and sins, and a child of wrath. This all goes back to the sin of your first father, Adam (Romans 5:12-21, Ephesians 2:1-3, Romans 8:7-8). This is the doctrine of original sin. This doctrine of original sin is the basis, the foundation, and the groundwork for what I am about to say, and for many of the other things that I will say in this book.

The doctrine of original sin has one major implication for your life: it means that you cannot live a holy life by your own power. You have to be empowered by God to live a holy life. When humans were first created, in the image of God, they were upright. They were able to sincerely do the will of God as soon as they knew what it was. However, after Adam fell, he quickly became afraid, because of his nakedness. He could not help himself at all, until God revealed to him the way that he could be restored (Genesis 3:10-15).   As a result of Adam's fall into sin, you are now powerless to live a holy life in your own strength.

If you tell a strong, healthy servant, "Go," he goes; if you tell him, "Come," he comes.  However, a sick, bed-ridden servant cannot do this. He first has to know how he can be **enabled** to come and go before he can do it!  There is no doubt that the fallen angels know that holiness is necessary, and they are scared to death because of the guilt of their sin. However, they do not have any idea how they can actually become holy, and so they continue in their wickedness.   It was useless for Sampson to say, after he allowed Delilah to cut off his hair, "I will go out as at other times before, and shake myself," when he had sinned away his strength (Judges 16:20).

It is hard for me to believe how many people hypocritically profess to believe in original sin by what they say in their prayers, catechisms, and confessions of faith.  Yet, by their actions they deny original sin.  How?  They tell themselves and others to keep the law, but they never even think about how they will be made alive and empowered to keep the law!  They think they can "just do it."  They think the only thing they are lacking is effort and activity.  They do not understand their real problem: they have no **ability** to do anything good!

This is certainly something that every non-Christian needs to come to know.  As I said above, non-Christians know the work of the law by the common light of natural reason and understanding (Romans 2:14), for it is written on their hearts.  However, through natural reason, no one can discover the means to keep the law.  You can only learn how to keep the law of God through the teaching that comes from God's supernatural revelation.

As a fallen person, you only have a few sparks and glimmers of what was in Adam before he fell into sin.  Even for Adam, this light was not sufficient to enable him to live a holy life, once he had fallen into sin and lost his perfection.  God had only told him that he would die if he sinned against God's commandment not to eat of the tree in the garden (Genesis 2:17).  Therefore, after Adam sinned, after he understood the shame of his nakedness, he hid himself from God.  He expected no favor from God at all.  In the same way, you are like a sheep who has gone astray.  You do not know which way to return, until you hear the Shepherd's voice.  "Can these dry bones live" to God in holiness?  "Oh Lord, you know."  You cannot know it, unless you learn it from God himself.

Sanctification is the process whereby your heart and life are conformed to the law of God. Sanctification is a grace that is imparted to you by means, just like justification is. The means, of course, is faith in Christ. Sanctification is something you can only come to understand from the word of God. There are several things pertaining to life and godliness that are given through knowledge (II Peter 1:2). There is a doctrine that God uses to make people free from sin, and to become servants of righteousness (Romans 6:17-18). There are several pieces of the whole armor of God you must know and put on, so you can stand against sin and Satan in the evil day (Ephesians 6:13). When so many books have been written about the doctrine of justification, do not overlook the doctrine of sanctification. Do not consider it unimportant for your Christian life.

God has given you plenty of instruction in his holy Word, so you may be equipped for every good work (II Timothy 3:15-16). When the Lord Jesus Christ appeared, the day-spring from on high visited us, to guide our feet in the path of peace (Luke 1:78-79). Since God has condescended so very low to teach you this way of life in the Scriptures through Christ, it is very necessary for you to sit down at his feet and learn it.

The only way you can possibly learn how to live a godly life is by reading the Holy Scriptures. The Scriptures tell you two things about living a godly life: first, they tell you what God wants you to do (the law); second, they tell you how you can actually do it (the gospel). Which of these two is easier to learn? The former. It is much easier to learn what God's law tells you to do than it is to learn how you can actually do it! After all, the law of nature written on your heart gives you a good idea of what the law requires of you. That makes it easier for you to agree with what God tells you to do in his word.

However, the way to actually keep the law is much harder to learn. Why? Because it is the way in which the dead are brought to life to live for God. It is far above the way you normally think, in your human wisdom and conjectures. It is the way of salvation, whereby God will "destroy the wisdom of the wise and bring to nothing the understanding of the intelligent," by revealing things by his Spirit, that "the natural man does not receive, for they are foolishness to him, and he cannot know them, because they are spiritually discerned" (I Corinthians 1:19,21, and

2:4). "Without any controversy, the mystery of godliness is great" (I Timothy 3:16).

When you learn the true way of godliness, you actually have to do double-the-work. On the one hand, you have to **unlearn** many of your old, deep-rooted notions of how to become godly, and become a fool that you might become wise. On the other hand, you must pray earnestly to the Lord to teach you the true way of godliness, and search his word to get this knowledge. Listen to what some of the biblical writers say: "Oh that my ways were directed to keep your statutes! Teach me, Oh Lord, the way of your statutes, and I shall keep them to the end" (Psalm 119:5, 33). "Teach me to do your will" (Psalm 143:10). "May the Lord direct your hearts into the love of God" (II Thessalonians 3:5). Surely these saints did not so much lack teaching and direction about what they had to do. They knew what God's law required of them! What they lacked was the power – the way and the means – to keep God's law.

It is absolutely essential that you learn the only powerful and effective means by which you can live a godly life. This is the only thing that will build you up in your faith, and keep you from falling into errors. The moral commands of love for God and your neighbor are absolutely essential for true religion. Do not accept anything in your faith that contradicts these holy commands that a holy God has given you. This same holy God has revealed to you everything you need to enable you to live a holy life. The Bible has the image of his holiness and righteousness engraved upon it.

Here is a litmus test you can use to test your spirits and your doctrines: they must all be in accord with true godliness (I Timothy 6:3). By this same litmus test Christ proves his doctrine is from God, because he sought the glory of God through it (John 7:17-18). Christ teaches you to discern false prophets by their fruits (Matthew 7:15-16). Specifically, you must consider what fruits their doctrines produce in people's lives. You will easily be deceived by false doctrine unless you know the means God has revealed to you by which you can live a holy life.

If you adopt some other means in your life to try to attain holiness, you will quickly fall into all kinds of errors, and you will refuse to accept the truth. However, if you get a proper understanding of the gospel's teaching on sanctification, you will be able to examine and test all the other doctrines of sanctification that will come your way – from evangelicals, legalists, lawless people, mystics, and others. You will stand firm in the midst of all of the controversies around you. You will also find that your true gospel faith does not have an ounce of Antinomianism[1] in it! People all around you think that the true gospel is defective, because they think that it cannot help anyone live an obedient life. Therefore, they change it, and turn it upside-down, with new doctrines and methods for godliness – all to no avail, of course.

Understanding the true way of sanctification is absolutely critical for living a holy life in your Christian life. You will not be able to successfully live a holy life unless you believe this: God will not help you live a holy life unless you use the means God has given you to pursue this holy life! God has chosen and ordained the means of salvation and sanctification that will give **him** all the glory! These are the only means that he will bless in your life. He will not crown any man who strives, unless he strives lawfully (II Timothy 2:5).

Experience shows how misunderstanding God's way of sanctification will completely ruin your attempt to live a holy life! Both Christians and non-Christians have found this out! Non-Christians, of course, always fall short of keeping the law of God -- even though they know the law -- because they do not know God's way of holiness through

---

[1] The word "Antinomian" is a word that will come up again and again in Marshall's book. Antinomian is a technical word that literally means "against law" (anti-nomos). Antinomian has always been used to describe the theological position of people who say that since we are saved by grace, we therefore are not required to keep the law of God. Paul often heard this accusation against the gospel, and he reflects this objection against the gospel in Romans 6:1 and 6:14 where he says, "What shall we say? Shall we go on sinning so that grace may abound?" "What then? Shall we sin because we are not under law but under grace?" In Marshall's day, as in our own, many so-called Christian groups reject the gospel of grace because they do not understand how such a gospel can motivate anyone to live a godly life; they accuse the gospel of inevitably producing Antinomianism – "people who believe the gospel of free grace will not want to keep the law of God, since salvation is already bought and paid-for." In a sense, Marshall's entire book is refutation of this accusation that the true gospel inevitably produces antinomianism. As he says, the gospel does not have an ounce of Antinomianism in it. Rather, the gospel, and only the gospel, saves us, and actually empowers us as Christians to keep the law of God; no other system of religion can enable sinful humans to keep the law of God. Throughout his book, Marshall encourages us not to be discouraged by these accusations by false religion. He continually encourages us to have confidence that the true gospel will not produce Antinomianism at all, but will in fact produce true godliness in all those who believe it and accept it.

Christ. However, Christians often fall short too. Why is this? There are several reasons.

Many Christians fail in Christian living because they are satisfied with keeping only the external requirements of the law. They are very concerned about looking good on the outside, but they never learn how they can actually do true spiritual service to God from their hearts.

Other people give up the way of holiness because they think holy living is totally unpleasant! If they knew God's way of sanctification, they would find this way of wisdom to be "ways of pleasantness, and all her paths to be peace." As a result of this wrong view, they put off repentance, because they find it so distasteful.

Still others work very hard to produce holiness, but they work in the wrong way. They run very fast, but do they not run a single step on the right path. They fail in all their attempts. Then, they are so frequently overcome by their sinful lusts, they completely give up and go back to wallowing in the mire once again. There have been many books written about how far these religious people have been willing to go before they have given up the quest for godliness. This discourages many weak Christians. They think, "If these people went so far to try to attain godliness and could not do it, what hope is there for me?" However, most of these supposedly religious people never understood the right way of godliness, and they never even set one foot upon it. For as Jesus said, "there are few that find it" (Matthew 7:14).

Some of the most zealous people actually punish their bodies with fasting and other austere measures to try to kill their lusts. When they see that their lusts are still too hard for them, they fall into despair. They are driven by the horror of their conscience to live very wicked lives – which of course brings religion into all the more disrepute.

My friends, I do not want any of this to happen to you. My prayer is that God will bless my effort to show you God's powerful way of attaining holiness. I want to keep you and others from killing yourselves through failed attempts at holiness! I hope that through my work, God will enlarge your heart, and the hearts of many, to run in the way of his commandments with great cheerfulness, joy, and thanksgiving!

The Gospel Mystery of Sanctification

# Chapter Two

### Principle Number Two

**You have to receive certain qualifications to keep the law of God. There are four qualifications for living a godly life which you must receive from God:**
1) **Your heart has to be freely willing to live a godly life,**
2) **You have to be assured that you are forgiven and reconciled to God,**
3) **You have to be sure of a happy, eternal future with the Lord, and**
4) **You have to have sufficient strength both to will and to do what God calls you to do.**

Let me now tell you how you can reach this grand goal of holy living. I am going to tell you the means by which you can live this holy life. If you want to keep God's law, he must equip you to do it. There are several things God must give you to live a holy life. You must have them all the time, or you will simply not be able to live a holy life. Very few people understand that they need these qualifications, but they are absolutely critical for Christian growth.

The first Adam was able to live a holy life, when he was first created in the image of God. The second Adam was even more qualified to live a holy life, and you know that his task of obedience was even harder. However, ever since the fall of Adam, you have a much harder task, because of the temptations you will face. Since you are called to be an imitator of Christ, you need to be empowered just as he was. You certainly need to have power that is greater than Adam first had, since your work is now much harder than his!

"What king going to make war against another king, does not sit down first, and consider whether he will be able, with ten thousand, to meet someone that comes against him with twenty-thousand?" (Luke 14:31). Will you rush into battle against all the powers of darkness, against the world and its temptations, and against your own indwelling sin and corruption, without considering whether or not you have the right spiritual equipment to stand in that evil day? As foolish as this is, many people use their own natural abilities to stand against sin. As a result, they are no better empowered for spiritual battle than non-Christians are, who are of course always defeated by the evil one. Believe me, your own natural ability will not enable you to stand against sin and evil at all! You need something much better than that!

Your bodily ability and agility is sustained by spirits, nerves, ligaments, and bones. However, your spiritual ability is much different. It is much harder to understand what makes it up, and how you receive it. However, I want to try to explain it as best I can from the Scriptures. I am going to tell you about four things God must give you if you are going to live a godly life. You must have them if you are going to continue on in holy living. Then, after I tell you what they are, I am going to tell you how you receive them. However, let me warn you about something. These gifts have a certain mystery about them – so much so, in fact, that many people think that something less than these will enable them to live a holy life. Some people also actually think that these qualifications from God will encourage you to live a licentious, sinful life, rather than a godly life, because you have to have them before you actually can obey God's law. They think that other methods that contradict the gospel would better equip you for holy living. However, this is not the case at all. God tells you that there are at least four qualifications you must receive from him if you are going to truly be able to live a godly life.

**The first qualification** is this: Your heart has to be freely motivated to obey God's law. You cannot just have a blind compulsion. You cannot act the way unreasoning animals naturally do, by instinct. You must have a total inward inclination to want to obey God and to avoid sin. This qualification has to come before any other qualification. You have to really **want** to obey God, more than you want to do anything else. You have to cheerfully obey God and hate the practice of sin.

Some people think that all you need to obey God is a free will. I agree that free will is important, but there is something deeper. They never think about the fact that no one **wants** to do good or obey God. Every human being has a heart that is totally inclined toward evil, not toward good. In your natural state, the direction of your heart is completely toward evil. Such a "free will" as this can never free you from slavery to sin and Satan, and enable you to keep God's law! Therefore, stop debating about free will, and get to the real issue: in your natural state, all you ever **want** to do is evil. So, in your natural state, that is all you will choose to do. Let me explain why understanding this is so important for your Christian growth.

# Qualifications for Living a Godly Life

You cannot possibly keep the commands of God if you hate them! You cannot be indifferent or "so-so" in your heart to what the law requires of you if you are going to keep these commandments. Remember, the greatest of all the commandments is to love the Lord with your whole heart, soul, mind, and strength. This means that you love everything that is in him, you love his will, you love his ways, and you see Him as the best thing in the world! Everything you do has to be driven by this kind of love for God. You have to delight to do the will of God. It must be sweeter than honey to you (Psalm 19:8). And, you must continually love, like, delight in, long for, thirst for, and relish God for your entire life. All of your sinful lusts must be taken over by love to God and neighbor. You must fight against your sin, and hate it (Galatians 5:17, Psalm 36:4).

This is quite different than the way people normally think of obedience. Most people think of true obedience as just a matter of pure duty. They think that obedience is like a salesman who sells his unpleasant goods in the market for money, or like a sick man loves his unpleasant medicine, or like a captive slave who works hard simply because he is afraid he will get something worse if he does not work! These are things you can do even if you do not want to do them, or even if you hate them. However, this is not true obedience to God.

True obedience means you love to obey God! You love to obey God as the salesman loves profit, as a sick man loves health, as a hungry man loves meat and drink, and as a captive slave loves liberty! You will have no willpower for real obedience unless you really love the will of God. Your heart has to be made just like his heart, and you have to hate sin with all your heart. You have to love God like nothing else in the world! Love to God must flow from a clean heart (I Timothy 1:5). Your heart has to be cleansed of its evil directions and inclinations. Your heart has to be changed and turned in the direction of holiness. You know quite well that only a heart that desires holiness of life can conquer sinful lusts.

Remember also how human beings were first created. When God created Adam, he was righteous, upright, and truly holy. It was not just that he obeyed God out of sheer willpower. Sheer willpower is neither holy nor unholy in and of itself. You can use your willpower to serve either God or Satan. You can worship either the true God or Baal. The real issue is: What do you really want to do? That is why you choose to do what you do.

# The Gospel Mystery of Sanctification

Think about the first Adam. God created him and placed in his soul a heart-direction that was totally toward good – even though he was able to act against this natural inclination if he chose to do so. Once he sinned, of course, his heart became wholly inclined toward evil, and he could no longer choose to do what is good. Think now about Jesus, the second Adam. Jesus Christ was born completely holy (Luke 1:35). His heart and soul were completely holy, so of course everything that he did was good.

There is only one way that you can rise to the life of holiness from which the first Adam fell, and become an imitator of Christ. Now that you have fallen into sin, now that it is impossible to do any good, you must be renewed in the image of God. You must be given a heart that desires to do good. You must be empowered by God to do it.

Original sin, which makes you dead to God and to godliness right from the time you are born, makes you a willing slave to sinful actions. You will continue to sin until Jesus, the Son of God, makes you free and enables your heart to move away from sin and move toward holiness. Apart from the gospel, you are filled with the poison of sin! You are filled with an adulterous spirit, which makes you refuse to return to God (Hosea 5:4). The tree is corrupt, and so is your fruit (Matthew 12:33). The mind of the flesh is at continual warfare against the law of God (Romans 8:7).

The greatest evil you have to deal with in your soul is your indwelling sin. This indwelling sin makes you naturally inclined to move toward evil. This indwelling sin produces all of your actual sins. This natural inclination has to be removed if you are going to stop sinning. In order for this natural inclination to be removed, the image of God has to be restored in you. You have to regain the inner desire to do the will of God. Without this new inclination of heart, you will go backwards; you will be totally unable to do any good work. You will have a "free will" all right, but the only freedom you will have is the "freedom" to serve sin!

In the work of the gospel, God addresses your slavery to sin. God restores you to holiness by giving you a new heart and a new spirit. He takes away your heart of stone, and gives you a heart of flesh (Ezekiel 36:26,27). He circumcises your heart to love him with your whole heart and soul. He requires that you be transformed in the renewing of your mind, that you may prove what is his acceptable will (Romans 12:2). David prayed for this same thing, that God would create in him a clean heart, and renew a right spirit within him (Psalm 51:10). In this work, God changes the direction of your inner life. You always have the free will to choose what you want to do. Through the gospel, when God cleanses and circumcises your heart, he changes your desire for evil into a desire for good. This is the root of all true obedience to God.

**The second qualification** for living a godly life is this: You have to be totally assured that you are reconciled to God and accepted by him. You have to be absolutely sure that the chasm sin has caused between you and God has been completely filled, and that you are now totally under his love and favor. This is one of the great blessings and results of being justified by faith in Christ. Your sins are forgiven, righteousness is credited to you, and you are totally reconciled to God (Romans 4:5-7). This is a great mystery to many, but it is nonetheless true: you have to be reconciled to God, and justified (which includes both the forgiveness of sins and the crediting of Christ's righteousness to your account) before you can truly obey the law of God. Once you are justified, you truly will be empowered to keep the law of God.

Many people think that the gospel's doctrine of free forgiveness and justification by grace through faith overthrows holy living. They think the gospel will turn people into lawless people. They say the only way to get people to really obey the law of God is to make their obedience a condition for their reconciliation with God. Many people completely give up the doctrine of justification by faith because they do not believe that such free grace will enable anyone to live a holy life. They think it will encourage people to live ungodly lives because people will say, "I can live any way I want to because I am totally forgiven of all of my sins." Therefore, they take the doctrine of justification by faith, they place it on their anvil, and they hammer it into another form. They think this new doctrine they have made will encourage people to live godly, rather than lawless, lives.

However, when they do this, their labor is empty and destructive. They are the ones who turn people into disobedient lawless people. Or, at best they turn people into painted hypocrites! The truth is just the opposite of what they think. You cannot truly live a holy life unless you are totally assured of your justification and reconciliation with God, totally apart from the works of the law. This is the only way you can truly obey the law! This is totally contrary, of course, to the way the world understands good works. Everyone outside of the gospel of grace thinks that good works earn you God's forgiveness. However, the gospel does not conform to worldly wisdom. The gospel says that when you are firmly assured of

God's love for you, you will respond by living a holy life. If you do not understand God's love for you, you will fall into a sinful life!

In this regard, think about the first Adam. When God first made him to live a holy life, Adam was of course under the total favor of God. Because he had been created perfectly, he was guilty of no sin, and he was counted righteous in God's sight. This righteous state, in God's plan, enabled him to live a righteous life. However, when he fell into sin, he became unrighteous and dead in his sin.

Think also about Jesus, the second Adam. He was the Father's beloved one, totally righteous before God, and guilty of no sin at all. The only relationship he had to sin was that he bore the sin of others! Your job of obedience is now much more difficulty than the first Adam's was before his fall into sin. You can only expect to become an imitator of Christ when you are first returned to a righteous state before God. You of course have no righteousness of your own you can offer to God. Your righteousness can only come through God forgiving your sins, reconciling you to himself, and crediting you with the righteousness of Christ.

You know how dead you are under the power of sin and Satan! You know that if God leaves you to do what your own heart wants to do, you can do nothing but sin. You will not be able to do any good works that please God unless God, in his great love and mercy, does them through you (John 8:36, Philippians 2:13, Romans 8:7-8). You know that if you are going to do anything holy, you must be confident that God will work his salvation in you. Now, can you really be confident that God will work in you unless you are absolutely convinced that God has loved you and reconciled you to himself? Can you really be confident that God will work in you unless you believe that your reconciliation with God had nothing to do with your works? This is the truth of the gospel: you can be confident that God will work his salvation out in you precisely **because** your reconciliation with God is what produces your good works.

You also know that your death from sin was the result of Adam's first sin, and that you are under the same sentence of death as he was (Genesis 2:17). You are still under this death sentence, and you are still under the curse of the law. You will never receive any spiritual life that can free you from this dominion of sin unless this guilt and curse of sin is removed from you. This, of course, is what happens when God justifies you – the guilt and curse of sin are removed from you (Galatians 3:13-14, Romans 6:14). You know that as long as you see yourself still under the curse and the wrath of God, you can have nothing but despair. You will never be able to live to God in holiness.

Think also about what God is calling you to do when we speak of holiness of life. The nature of true obedience to the law absolutely requires you to understand that you are reconciled to God, loved by him, and under his favor, if you really are going to obey the law. Remember, your great call is to love the Lord God with all your heart. When we speak of love, we are not talking about the kind of love that a scientist might have toward his experiments, where he is just trying to please himself by gaining more knowledge. We are talking about a practical, life-changing love.

Real love for God means that he must be the only thing that matters to you. He must be your greatest happiness. You are to love him as your absolute Lord and Master. You love everything about him, and you have no desire for him to be any better than he is. You want his will to be done in you so much, that you will do it no matter what it costs you. You want his will to be done whether it is prosperity or suffering, whether it is life or death. You rejoice in him in all things, and you love to obey him – even if it means you suffer the worst thing possible: death. In short, when you love God, you make him the greatest pleasure of your life.

When you consider what real love for God is, you can easily see that you cannot love God in this way if you think you are under the curse and wrath of God. You cannot love God if you are under the continual, secret suspicion that he is really your enemy! You cannot love God if you secretly think he condemns and hates you. This kind of slavish fear will compel you to some hypocritical obedience – such as what Pharaoh did when he let the Israelites go against his will. However, you will never truly love God if you are compelled only by fear. Your love for God must be won and drawn out by your understanding of God's love and goodness towards you – just as John testifies in I John 4:18-19: "There is no fear in love, but perfect love casts out fear, because fear consists of torment; The one who fears is not made perfect in love. We love him, because he first loved us." You simply cannot love God unless you know and understand how much he loves you.

Just look to your own experience in this matter. Can you think of any time you had true love for God without first having had an enormous sense of God's love towards you? When you love him, it is because you see that he has been so good to you! The demons have some understanding of God's excellent nature and character, as do speculative philosophers. However, this only fills them all the more with fear and trembling (James 2:19). They do not love God at all! If you think you are still under God's curse and wrath, the more you understand his excellence and perfection, the more evil he will seem to you.

In the gospel, you can come to know that God truly loves you through Christ. When you have this assurance, you can even love your enemies, because you know that you are reconciled to God. You know that God's love will make people's hatred of you work together for your good. If you believe God is your enemy, you have no basis whatsoever to love him. The only thing that can free you from the evil of hatred, and turn your heart to love, is the wonderful understanding that you are reconciled to God through Christ.

There is another reason why you must know you have been reconciled to God if you are going to do good works: your conscience must be cleansed from dead works so you can serve the living God. This happens when your sins are actually forgiven by the blood of Christ, and your conscience comes to see this. Christ died for this purpose (see Hebrews 9 and 10).

If your conscience is under the guilt of sin and the wrath of God, it is called an evil conscience in the Bible. This evil conscience comes from the evil of sin. It causes you to commit more sin, until your conscience is cleansed and received into God's favor. Love that fulfills the law must flow from a good conscience, as well as from any other cleanness of heart (I Timothy 1:5). David's mouth could not be opened to show forth the praise of God until he was delivered from blood guiltiness (Psalm 51:14-15).

When you have an evil, guilty conscience, you think God is your enemy. You think that his justice is against you, and that he will condemn you forever because of your sins. When you think this way, sin and Satan actually have greater power over you. An evil conscience will move your soul away from godliness. It can even make you hate God, and wish there were no God, no heaven, and no hell — just so you can escape the punishment you deserve. An evil conscience can so turn people off to God that they cannot even endure to think, speak, or hear of him and his law. Instead, they try to put him out of their minds by sinful pleasures and other worldly activities. This process alienates them from true spirituality. It leads them into all kinds of strange religious performance, false religion, idolatry, and inhuman superstitions.

I am convinced that this is what happened to the first Adam. When he fell into sin, he fell under the wrath of God, and he of course received an evil, guilty conscience. His guilty conscience told him that God was now against him, and that he was under God's curse for that one sin. This was enough to turn his love wholly away from God and toward creatures, and to desire to be completely hidden from the presence of God. Hence, the image of God's holiness in him was ruined. This is the origin of all sin against God and his holiness: malice, hatred, and anger flow from people whose consciences tell them that they have been alienated from God. Therefore, if you are going to serve God from a pure heart, you must be reconciled to God, and your conscience must be cleansed.

God has made it very clear in his word how he brings his people from sin to holy living — he first makes them understand that he loves them, and that their sins are totally blotted out. When he gave the ten commandments on mount Sinai, he first told the Israelites that he was their God, and that he had given them a sure pledge of his salvation — their delivery from Egypt (Exodus 20:2). During the whole time of the Old Testament, the sign of the covenant was circumcision. Circumcision was not just a sign, but also a seal of the righteousness you receive by faith — the righteousness by which God justifies all of his people. This seal was given to children when they were eight days old, before they could sincerely obey God. God was preparing and equipping them for a holy life long before they had done anything good.

In addition, in the Old Testament, God gave many washings, the blood of bulls and goats, the ashes of a heifer sprinkling the unclean, to prepare and sanctify the people for other parts of worship in the tabernacle and temple. These were all symbols of how he cleansed their consciences from dead works by the blood of Christ, that they might serve the living God (Hebrews 9:10, 13, 14, 22).

All of these things pictured sanctification. Sanctification refers to all the things that prepare you for the service of God – chiefly the forgiveness of sin (Hebrews 10:10, 14, 18). God also reminded the Old Testament people how they had to have their guilt cleansed away first, to make their service acceptable to God, by commanding them to offer the sin-offering before the burnt offering (Leviticus 5:8). Also, because the guilt of their sins polluted all of their service to God, God appointed a general atonement for all their sins one day every year, in which the scapegoat bore on himself all their sins into an uninhabited land (Leviticus 16:22,34).

In the New Testament, God motivates you to holy living in the same way — he first loves you, and washes away your sins by the blood of Christ, to make you a priest to offer the sacrifices of praise and good works to the Father. He entered you into his service by washing away your sins through Christ. He feeds and strengthens you for his service by the forgiveness of your sins, given to you in the blood of Christ at the Lord's Supper. He exhorts you to obey him, because he has already loved you, and because your sins are already pardoned. "Forgive one another, even as God for Christ's sake has forgiven you. Be followers of God as dear children, and walk in love, as Christ has loved us" (Ephesians 4:32, 5:1-2).

There are so many Biblical texts that say the same thing! God has made it abundantly clear, in both the Old Testament and the New Testament, that he first cleanses his people from guilt and reconciles them to himself, and then he equips them for holy living. Forgiveness is the horse that pulls the cart of good works. Don't put the cart before the horse! Get rid of all other "works-based" methods of attempting to live a holy life! They simply will not work!

**The third qualification** to live a holy life is this: you have to be absolutely assured that you are going to have a happy, eternal future with the Lord in the new heaven and the new earth. I am speaking about what we usually call "eternal security." This will really enable you to live a holy life!

This eternal security will be attacked on many fronts. Some people think that if you have complete assurance about a wonderful future with God – before you have "paid your way" with a life of sincere obedience -- you will think you can live a life of sin.. They think the only way to assure a life of good works is to make people work for a happy eternal future! Other people will tell you that if you keep heaven in mind, you are just being selfish and self-focused. If you are thinking about heaven, you really are not doing things because you love God. They will tell you that if you really want to serve God, you should not think about the hope of reward, or the fear of punishment. However, consider all of these things.

# Qualifications for Living a Godly Life

First, you cannot keep the law of God if you are not assured of your own happy future in heaven. Sincere obedience can only come from this conviction. Think about people like the Sadducees, from the New Testament times, who did not believe in eternal life. Can such people really love God with all their heart, soul, mind, and strength? You cannot love anyone very much if you know you will soon have to part with them at your death! If you do not believe in an afterlife, you will think loving God in this life is in vain. How could anyone lay down his life for God if he knew he would never see God again, after his death? If there is no eternal future with the Lord, why would anyone choose suffering for Christ rather than sin – when all he would get from it is a life of misery? Any reasonable person would rather never live at all, than to have such a fleeting life as that!

Second, everywhere in Scripture, since the fall of Adam, God uses the sure hope of the glory of heaven to encourage his people to obey him. Consider Jesus himself, "who for the joy that was set before him, endured the cross, despising its shame (Hebrews 12:2). Adam himself, before he fell into sin, had the assurance of a present earthly paradise he knew would last, as long as he continued to obey God. The apostles did not give up when they faced affliction, because they knew it would bring about for them "a far more exceeding and eternal weight of glory" (II Corinthians 4:16-17). The Christians in the book of Hebrews "received with the joy the taking away of their goods, knowing that they a better and lasting inheritance in heaven" (Hebrews 10:34).

The Apostle Paul said that all his sufferings were totally in vain if there were no resurrection from the dead, and that Christians would be of all men most miserable. If there is no afterlife, it would be better to live like the pagans, "Let us eat and drink, for tomorrow we shall die." However, since there is a resurrection from the dead, Paul tells you to "abound in the work of the Lord, knowing that your labor in the Lord is not in vain" (I Corinthians 15:58). The world gives people fleeting hope to keep them at work in their various vocations. God gives his people the hope of his glory to keep them serving him (Hebrews 6:11-12, I John 3:3). This is such a sure hope that you will never be ashamed (Romans 5:5). Anyone who thinks it is beneath him to serve God out of a hope of a glorious heavenly reward has placed himself above the apostles, the early Christians, and even Christ himself.

Third, this absolute assurance of eternal, heavenly happiness will not lead you to live a sinful life if you understand how it fits into your

Christian life. Holy living is part of your salvation. God has made you his own through free justification and adoption. Having been saved in this way, you now are called to walk in the way of holiness (I John 3:1-3). Just because you have eternal assurance, and serve God out of it, does not mean that you are trying to earn your salvation by your works. Your assurance cannot come through the works of the law, but only by free grace through faith (Galatians 5:5). You are not working out of selfish self-love if you are thinking about heaven! Rather, it is a holy self-love – you prefer God above the flesh and the world, as he tells you to, when he exhorts you to save yourself (Acts 2:40, I Timothy 4:16). This conviction is not in opposition to the pure love of God, but it brings you to love God more purely and more completely.

When you have this assurance of eternal life, you will desire God above the flesh and the world, as God tells you to. Why? Because the more you see how good God has been to you, the more lovely God will appear to you, and the more your heart will be inflamed for him! God would be dishonored if you loved him without understanding that he has prepared a city for you (Hebrews 11:16). God draws you with cords of love to himself, and one of the ways he does this is by laying his wonderful privileges and benefits before you. One of God's greatest gifts is that he has given you a wonderful, eternal inheritance, absolutely free! Who could not love him more, with this great inheritance lying ahead?

**The fourth qualification** to live a holy life is this: you have to be totally assured that you have sufficient strength both to **will** and to **do** what God calls you to do. You have to have both the desire and the power to do the will of God. Some people think they have it all in themselves to obey God by their own sheer willpower – but the fact is, they do not. Other people think that living a godly life is easy. They think all they have to do is change some bad habits, or just "do their best." Most people do not realize their own powerlessness. Most people do not realize that what they need most for living a holy life is sufficient strength to do so. Above all else, you have to understand your need for strength from God if you are going to live a holy life.

Consider these things. First, you are, by nature, dead in trespasses and sins, and you are totally unable to will or do anything that is spiritually good until Christ makes you alive (Ephesians 2:1, Romans 8:7-9). Those who are enlightened and humbled by Christ soon realize this about themselves. They recognize not only that they do not have any power to do anything good, but also that they do not have hearts that want to do good. They know they will not be able to do anything to please God unless God works in them both to will and to do (Philippians 2:13). They know that if God leaves them to their own sinfulness, they will get nowhere! If you think you can keep the law of God in your own strength, you have never truly been humbled and brought to understand the sinfulness of your own heart. You really do not believe in original sin, even though you may say you believe in it.

Second, if you think obeying the law of God is easy, you know neither the law nor yourself! Is it an easy thing to fight against principalities, powers, and spiritual forces of evil in heavenly places (Ephesians 6:12)? Is it easy not to lust or covet according to the tenth commandment? Paul found it so difficult to obey this commandment that his lust and coveting began to dominate him all the more, the more he understood the commandment! Remember, your real goal is not simply to change some bad habits. Your real goal is to put to death your corrupt, sinful desires which give rise to those bad habits. Also, you are called not only to stop fulfilling your sinful lusts, but also to become filled with holy love and holy desires.

Non-Christian people know they must obey God. They know they are guilty for their disobedience and that they deserve eternal punishment (see Romans 1:18-32). However, if obedience is so easy, why do so many non-Christian people make vows and promises to obey God, but never succeed? All the while, they feel all the more guilty for failing in their attempts. Obeying God is "easy" and pleasant only if God is at work in your heart, empowering you to obey! Anyone who thinks it is easy to obey God apart from God's empowering grace shows they do not understand what most Christians and non-Christians have experienced in their lives – failure! It is easier to move a mountain than it is to obey God, unless God is at work in your heart!

Third, in his wisdom, God has assured you that he will give you sufficient strength to enable you both to will and to do what you are called to do. The first Adam, before he fell into sin, obviously knew that he had the strength to obey God. When he lost that strength through his fall into sin, he could not live a holy life again until he came to know a greater strength, by which the head of Satan would be crushed (Genesis 3:15). The Lord Jesus Christ obviously knew that the infinite power of his deity would enable him to do all that he had to do and suffer when he took on human nature.

# The Gospel Mystery of Sanctification

The rest of the Bible shows how God assured his people that he would give them strength when he called them to do great things. Think of Moses, Joshua, and Gideon. Think of the Israelites, when he called them to subdue the land of Canaan. Christ cautioned the sons of Zebedee by asking them to consider if they could "drink of his cup and be baptized with the baptism that he was baptized with" (Mathew 20:22).

Paul encourages you as a Christian to a life of obedience by assuring you that sin shall not have dominion over you, because you are not under the law, but under grace (Romans 6:13-14). He tells you to be strong in the Lord, and in his mighty power, that you may be able to stand against the schemes of the devil (Ephesians 6:10-11). John encourages believers not to love the world, nor the things of the world, because they were strong, and had overcome the wicked one (I John 2:14-15). People who were called by God to work miracles were given the power to do them. No one with any sense would even attempt to do a miracle unless he knew he had the power to do it! In the same way, you who were dead in sin are called to live a holy life. When you do this, this is the greatest miracle of all! Therefore, God wants you to know that you have the power from him to live a holy life. He wants to encourage you to walk in his holiness!

# Chapter Three

## Principle Three

**You receive the qualifications to enable you to keep the law of God out of the fullness of Christ, through fellowship with him. In order to have this fellowship, you must be in union with him. You must be in Christ, and Christ himself must be in you.**

The key to living a holy life is **union with Christ**. Now, we have to acknowledge that union with Christ is a great mystery. Beyond dispute, the mystery of godliness is great! No human being ever would have thought of it. God had to make it known through supernatural revelation. Indeed, even though it is revealed in the Scriptures, non-Christians do not have eyes to see it. It is foolishness to them. Even when God expresses it plainly, they still think God is speaking in riddles and parables. Even the best of us can only partially understand this.

In order to keep the law of God, your soul must be empowered out of the fullness of Christ. The power to live a holy life is something that is produced in you by Christ, and treasured up for you in him. Sanctification is similar to justification in this sense. In justification, you are justified by a righteousness earned by Christ and credited to you. In sanctification, Christ lived a completely holy life, and he imparts to you a holy disposition as you live in him.

Think of it this way. The first Adam fell into sin, and because you were in union with him as the head of the human race, you inherited a sinful nature from him. Now that you are in union with Christ, he begins to impart his godly nature to you. In other words, you do not produce a godly nature by yourself, out of yourself. Rather, you take it to yourself by receiving it from Christ. Through fellowship with him, you begin to receive that holy frame of mind which is in Christ himself. This is such a great mystery, it is difficult to understand.

Here is where many people fall into a terrible mistake. Many devout people kill themselves trying to put to death their sinful nature and produce a holy heart. They diligently work to conquer their sinful lusts and motivate themselves to godly living – but this is like trying to squeeze oil out of a stone! This is the key error Christians fall into in their lives: *they think that even though they have been justified by a righteousness*

***produced totally by Christ, they must be sanctified by a holiness
produced totally by themselves.***

To be sure, they admit that God must give grace to help them live
a godly life. However, they think they must get this grace and help by
their own strivings — as if the saying were true that "God helps those who
help themselves." As a result, they think living a godly life is harsh and
unpleasant because they have to struggle so hard to change their hearts and
desires. What they really need to know is that trying to live a godly life in
this way is impossible. They need to understand the gospel of grace —
the only true way of putting sin to death, and living for righteousness, is to
receive a new nature out of the fullness of Christ. You simply cannot
produce this new nature in yourself on your own. If you can understand
this, you will save yourself much bitter agony, and much misspent,
burdensome labor. Put your energy into a path of holiness that will be
more pleasant and successful!

Another mysterious part of God's way of sanctification is the
glorious fellowship you have in union with Christ, as you receive a holy
attitude of heart from him. The key to holy living is the gospel's truth of
**union with Christ**. If you are a Christian, you are in Christ, and Christ
himself is in you. You are in him by a close union, so that in fact you are
one spirit with Christ. Again, this is a mystery, and it is rightly called a
mystical union. Paul himself calls it a great mystery in Ephesians 5:22,
when he speaks of Christ's relationship with the church, his bride. It is
similar to the mysteries of the Trinity with the union of three persons in
one Godhead, and the mystery of the union of the divine and human
natures in the one person, Jesus Christ.

Even though your union with Christ is a mystery, the Scriptures
are very plain when they speak of it. They affirm that Christ lives in
believers, and they in him (John 6:56, 14:20). Christ and believers are so
joined together as to become one Spirit (I Corinthians 6:17). Believers are
members of Christ's body, of his flesh and of his bones, and Christ and the
Church are one flesh (Ephesians 5:30-31).

The Bible also illustrates your union with Christ with many
different pictures and illustrations. Union with Christ resembles: the
union between God the Father and Christ (John 14:20, 17:21-23); the
union between the vine and its branches (John 15:4-5); the union between
the head and body (Ephesians 1:22-23); and the union between bread and
the eater (John 6:51-54). This union is sealed in the Lord's Supper, where

you feed on Christ by faith. Even though Christ is in heaven, and you are on earth, he has joined your soul to his own through the gospel! He lives in you through his Spirit, who is one with him. The Holy Spirit unites you to Christ, and he continually brings you into a closer, more intimate union with Christ.

Make sure you do not misunderstand this mystery. Through union with Christ, you do not become one person with Christ, any more than Christ is one person with the Father by his union with him. Also, as a Christian you are not made God – you are only the temple of God, just as Christ is in a much greater sense the temple of God. Furthermore, in this life you will never be made perfect in holiness. You will only be perfect in heaven! In this life, you will be made holy in so far as Christ lives in you.

Now, you might think that you are unworthy to have such a great gift as union with Christ. Remember, however, Christ shed his precious blood to redeem you. That precious blood will enable you to miraculously advance in holiness through your union with Christ. Union with Christ is not a privilege you earn by your sincere obedience, or by your own attempts at holiness. Your union with Christ is not a reward of your own good works. Rather, union with Christ is a privilege that God gives to every Christian when they first become a Christian! Right when you enter into the kingdom of God, you also enter into union with Christ! This union with Christ is the foundation for all of your obedience to God. All of your good works as a Christian flow out of your union with Christ. All of your sincere obedience to the law is the fruit of your union with Christ.

Although this truth of union with Christ is something of a mystery, the Bible clearly teaches it in many different ways. First, several places in the Bible plainly express your union with Christ. Some texts show that all aspects of your salvation are treasured up for you in Christ and his fullness (Colossians 1:19). It pleased the Father that in him all fullness should dwell. In Colossians 2:11-13, Paul shows that the holy nature that enables you to live to God was produced in you by Christ's death and resurrection: "In him you also were circumcised, in the putting off from the body the sins of the flesh; you were buried with him, and made alive together with him, when you were dead in your sins."

"We have been blessed with all spiritual blessings in heavenly places in Christ" (Ephesians 1:3). When God speaks of all spiritual blessings, he certainly includes in that a holy frame of mind. These blessings are given to you in Christ – they are prepared and treasured up for you in him while you are upon earth. The only place that your new nature, your holy frame of heart, can come from is from Christ himself!

Think also of I Corinthians 1:30, which shows that Christ is made for you sanctification, which enables you to walk in holiness. He is your wisdom, which makes you wise for salvation. He is your righteousness, Christ's very righteousness that is credited to your account through justification. He is your redemption, through which you are redeemed from all of your misery, and brought into the enjoyment of his glory and happiness in his heavenly kingdom!

Other Bible passages show that you receive your holiness out of Christ's fullness by fellowship with him: "Out of his fullness we have received grace upon grace" (John 1:16-17). This grace certainly includes your sanctification. "Truly our fellowship is with the Father, and with his Son Jesus Christ. God is light. If we walk in the light, as he is in the light, we have fellowship with one another" (I John 1:3-7). Your fellowship with Christ includes your having light, and walking in that light in holiness and righteousness.

Other Bible passages show directly that not only are your spiritual qualifications made ready first in Christ for you, and received from Christ, but that you receive them by union with Christ. "You have put on the new man, which is renewed after the image of him that created him; where Christ is all and in all" (Colossians 3:10-11). "He that is joined to the Lord is one spirit" (I Corinthians 6:17). "I live, yet not I, but Christ lives in me" (Galatians 2:20). "This is the record, that God has given to us eternal life, and this life is in his Son. He that has the Son has life; and he that does not have the Son does not have life" (John 5:11-12). Can God be any clearer? The fullness of the new man is in Christ! The only way you can have a new spiritual nature, and live a life of holiness, is if you are inseparably joined to him, so that he lives in you.

In the Bible, God also illustrates your sanctification through union with Christ with a variety of illustrations, to make doubly sure you understand it. Consider these different illustrations God uses to show you how your new spiritual nature, and your power for holy living, come from union and fellowship with Christ:

❑    As Christ lives in your nature by the Father (John 6:57)

# Living in Union with Christ

- ❑ As you receive original sin and death from the first Adam (Romans 5:12-21)

- ❑ As the physical body receives sense, motion, and nourishment from the head (Colossians 2:19)

- ❑ As the branch receives its sap, juice, and nourishing power from the vine (John 15:1-7)

- ❑ As a wife brings forth fruit through her marital union with her husband (Romans 7:4)

- ❑ As stones become a holy temple by being built upon the foundation and joined with the chief cornerstone (I Peter 2:4-6)

- ❑ As you receive the nourishing virtue of bread by eating it, and of wine by drinking it (John 6:51-57). This illustration is used to describe your fellowship with Christ in the Lord's Supper

All of these illustrations teach that your new life and your holy nature are first in Christ, and then in you, through union and fellowship with him. It is very much like the union of a married couple. Just as Eve, the first woman, was bone of Adam's bone, and flesh of his flesh, so is the church in union with Christ (Genesis 2:22-24, Ephesians 5:30-32). Those who are joined to the Lord are not one with him in flesh, but are one with him in spirit.

Indeed, the whole purpose of Christ's incarnation, death, and resurrection was to create a holy nature for you through himself. He imparts this holy nature to you as you live in union and fellowship with him. He did not suffer, die, and rise again to enable you to produce a new nature by your own effort! If you could do that, Christ lived, died and rose again in vain!

In his incarnation, Jesus became a man who was completely holy. No other human being has ever been like this. In Adam, you have become completely guilty and corrupt. Jesus was completely holy because his divine nature was joined to his human nature in a close, inseparable union. In his earthly life, he was in complete union with his father. The words that he spoke he spoke not by himself, by any mere human power, but because the Father lived in him and he did his Father's works (John 14:10).

# The Gospel Mystery of Sanctification

Christ became a man to make you alive as well. Just as you have borne the image of the earthly man, so also you will bear the image of the heavenly man (I Corinthians 15:45, 49) — in holiness in this life and in glory in the next life. Christ was born Immanuel, God with us, because the fullness of the Godhead, with all holiness, lived in him when he lived on earth with a human nature (Matthew 1:23, Colossians 2:9-120). He came down from heaven as living bread, so that those who eat him may live by him (John 6:52, 56).

In his death, Christ freed himself from the guilt of your sins that were placed upon him. In his death, your sins were heaped upon him, and he bore them on the cross. Through his death, he also prepared a freedom for you, so that you might live in freedom from your natural, sinful condition. The Bible describes this as your old man being crucified together with Christ, so that the body of sin might be destroyed. It is not destroyed in you by any wounds you yourself give to it. It is destroyed as you partake of your freedom from it, and death to it, produced for you by the death of Christ. This truth of dying to sin is signified by your baptism, in which you are buried with Christ by the application of his death to you (Romans 6:1-11).

Paul also says "God sent his own son in the likeness of sinful flesh, for sin, and condemned sin in the flesh, so that the righteousness of the law might be fulfilled in us, who do not walk according to the flesh but according to the Spirit" (Romans 8:3-4). Note two key truths here. First, Christ died so that you might be justified by the righteousness of God by faith, and not by your own righteousness which comes from the law (Romans 10:4-6, Philippians 3:9). Second, Christ also died so that the righteousness of the law might be fulfilled in you as you walk according to his Spirit as one who is in Christ (Romans 8:3-4). Here justification and sanctification are closely related. It is through union with Christ that you are justified by his cross, and it is through union with Christ that you are sanctified by his Spirit.

Christ is compared to the death of a kernel of wheat dying in the earth, so it might reproduce its own nature, by bringing forth much fruit (John 12:24). He is compared to the Passover that was slain, so that a feast might be kept upon it (I Corinthians 5:7-8, and 9:24). He is compared to the rock that was smitten, so that water might gush out of it for you to drink (I Corinthians 10:4). He died, that he might make out of Jews and Gentiles one new man in himself (Ephesians 2:15).

Living in Union with Christ

These Scriptures clearly say that Christ did not die to enable you to produce a holy nature by yourself. Christ died so you might receive a holy nature prepared and created in him for you, through your union and fellowship with him.

In his resurrection, Christ took possession of spiritual life for you – he earned it and procured it for you. It is now your right because of his death. Paul tells you that you have been made alive together with Christ, even when you were dead in sins. You have been raised up together with him, and made to sit with him in heavenly places, in Christ Jesus, who is your head (Ephesians 2:1-10). All of this happens in you while you live on the earth! Just as Adam's fall into spiritual death was your fall into spiritual death, so also Christ's resurrection was your resurrection to the life of holiness. You yourself do not create your new holy nature, any more than you create your original sin! Rather, both of these natures are already created — the sinful nature by Adam, and the new nature by Christ.

You automatically partake of Adam's original sin when you are born into this world. When you are **reborn** into God's kingdom, you partake of Christ's nature. Through this union with Christ, you experience the spiritual life that he gained for you through his resurrection. As a result of this union, you are empowered to bring forth the fruit of holy living. This is exactly what Paul says in Romans 7:4, when he says you "have been joined to him who is risen from the dead, so that you might bring forth fruit to God." This truth, again, is signified by your baptism. In Christ, you have died, and you have been raised again to newness of life. Because Christ "died to sin once, and lives to God, you should likewise consider yourself to be dead to sin, and alive to God through Christ Jesus our Lord" (Romans 6:4-11).

The Holy Spirit brings about your sanctification. As you live in him and by him, you live in holiness (Romans 15:16, Galatians 5:25). The Holy Spirit first rested upon Christ, so that Christ might pour out his Spirit upon you. This is what it means when Jesus was baptized, and the Holy Spirit descended upon him in the form of a dove from the opened heavens, and rested upon him (John 1:22-23). When the Holy Spirit sanctifies you, he baptizes you into Christ, and joins you to Christ, in an inseparable union (I Corinthians 12:13). In the Bible, it is the same thing to have Christ himself, and to have the Spirit of Christ, in you (Romans 8:9-10). The Holy Spirit glorifies Christ, for he receives the things that are Christ's, and he shows them to you (John 16:14-15). The Holy Spirit gives you the experiential knowledge of all of those spiritual blessings that he himself has prepared for you in the incarnation, death, and resurrection of Christ.

Remember what I have said to you thus far. The law of God calls you to love God with all your heart. The problem is, you are powerless to love God because of your sinful nature. Therefore, God must empower you to live a holy life. There are four qualifications you have to receive from God — 1) your heart must be freely willing to live a godly life, 2) you must have assurance of your forgiveness reconciliation with God, 3) you must have assurance of a happy, eternal life, and 4) you must have sufficient strength both to desire and to do what God requires of you.

I also said that all of these spiritual blessings are in the fullness of Christ, and treasured up for you in him. You receive these qualifications through union and fellowship with Christ. If you are joined to Christ, your heart will no longer be left only under the power of your sinful inclinations. You will no longer be indifferent towards good or evil. If you are in Christ, the Spirit of Christ living in you will give you both the desire and the power to live a holy life. It is Christ in you who moves you to pursue the things of the Spirit and to war against the lusts of the flesh (Romans 8:1-5, Galatians 5:17).

In Christ, God has fully reconciled you to himself. You are completely under his favor. You now have the righteousness of God, which Christ produced for you by his obedience unto death, which is credited to you for your justification. This righteousness is called "the righteousness of God" because Jesus the God-Man produces it, and because it is of sufficient value to satisfy the justice of God for all of your sins. It is completely sufficient to procure his pardon, and to bring you into his highest favor (II Corinthians 5:21, Romans 5:19).

Now, this truth of free forgiveness is very hard to believe. Therefore, so you can be totally assured of this marvelous reconciliation with God, you have received the Spirit of adoption through Christ, through whom you cry out "Abba, Father" (Romans 8:15). The Spirit assures you of your future enjoyment of everlasting happiness. The Spirit testifies to you that you will have sufficient strength both to will and to do what God wants you to do. The Spirit of adoption teaches you that, if you are indeed a child of God, then you are also an heir of God, and a co-heir with Christ. He teaches you that the law of the spirit of life that is in Christ Jesus has made you free from the law of sin and death. He teaches you that nothing shall be against you, that nothing shall separate you from the love of God in Christ.   Whatever opposition and difficulties you might face, you shall be more than a conqueror through him who loved you (Romans 8:17-39).

Contrary to popular belief, this marvelous assurance of forgiveness and everlasting life will not motivate you to ungodly living. Why?  Because these wonderful blessings are given to you only through union with Christ.  The Spirit of Christ inseparably joins these blessings with the gift of sanctification.  You cannot have justification, or any spiritual privilege in Christ, unless you receive Christ himself.  That includes receiving the holiness of Christ.

Justification and sanctification are different, in that justification deals with the guilt of your sin, and sanctification deals with the power of your sin.  However, justification and sanctification are similar, in that they both come from your union with Christ.  Paul joins them both together in this way in Romans 8:1: "Therefore, there is now no condemnation for those who are in Christ Jesus, who walk not according to the flesh, but according to the Spirit..."

You might wonder how believers who lived before the coming of Christ could possibly be in union with Christ.  How could they receive a new nature through union and fellowship with him, prepared for them, out of his fullness?  What you need to remember is that the same Christ that took on our flesh "was before Abraham" (John 8:58).  He was foreordained before the foundation of the world, to be sacrificed as a lamb without blemish, that he might redeem us from all iniquity by his precious blood (I Peter 1:18-20).  He had the same Spirit at that time, which later filled his human nature with all his fullness, and raised him from the dead. He then gave that Spirit to the church (I Peter 1:11, 3:18-19).  This same Holy Spirit was able to unite the Old Testament believers with Christ, and to give them grace to live for Christ.

David spoke of Christ's death and resurrection as his own, beforehand, in Psalm 16:9-11: "My flesh also shall rest in hope, for you will not leave my soul in hell, nor will you allow your Holy One to see corruption.  You will show me the path of life."  Even before David's time, believers "all ate of the same spiritual food, and drank of the same spiritual drink."  They had a relationship with the same Christ as you do. The Old Testament believers, therefore, were partakers of this wonderful privilege of union and fellowship with Christ (I Corinthians 10:3-4). When Christ appeared in the flesh, in the fullness of time, he came as the head of all of his people.  The church of Christ is "built upon the foundation of the apostles and prophets, with Christ Jesus himself as the chief cornerstone. In him the whole building is joined together and rises to become a holy temple in the Lord" (Ephesians 2:20-21).

Christ's incarnation, death, and resurrection are the cause of all the holiness that ever has been, or ever shall be given to anyone – from the fall of Adam to the end of the world. Any holy attitude you have, or any holy action you take, comes only through the mighty power of Christ's Spirit. The presence and power of Christ's Spirit are yours because, through the gospel, you have been brought into that one body of which Christ is the head. You are in union with Christ.

# Chapter Four

### Principle Four

**The Gospel is the way the Holy Spirit brings you into union with Christ, and into fellowship with him and his holiness. Through the gospel, Christ enters your heart and gives you faith. Faith is the way you actually receive Christ himself, and all his fullness, into your heart. Even this faith is a grace of the Holy Spirit. When you have faith, you believe the gospel with all your heart. When you have faith, you believe in Christ, as he is revealed and freely promised to you in the gospel, for all his salvation.**

Here is what I have been saying to you up to this point: If you are going to live a holy life, you must be in Christ, and Christ must be in you through a mystical union. Now, when you realize this, you might completely stop trying to live a holy life. Why? Because you cannot imagine how you could ever raise yourself out of your natural sphere into this glorious union and fellowship with Christ. This is the good news: God has told you, by supernatural revelation, how God's Spirit enables you to come into union with Christ. God has revealed the two ways his Spirit brings you into this mystical union and fellowship with Christ. What are those two ways? The gospel and faith. Through the gospel, and through faith, you will be able to live in union with Christ as his Spirit works in you.

The first way God has revealed is the gospel of the grace of God. In the gospel, God makes known to you the unsearchable riches of Christ, and Christ in you, the hope of glory (Ephesians 3:8, Colossians 1:27). God also invites you and commands you to believe in Christ for his salvation, and he encourages you by a free promise of salvation to all those who believe in him (Acts 16:31, Romans 10:9-11). The gospel is the way God sends Christ to you, and blesses you with his salvation (Acts 3:26). The gospel is the ministry of the Spirit and of righteousness (II Corinthians 3:6-9). Faith comes when you hear the gospel. Therefore, the gospel is the way you come to new birth in Christ, and Christ is formed in you (Romans 10:16-17, I Corinthians 4:15, Galatians 4:19).

There is no need for you to say in your heart, "Who shall ascend into heaven, to bring Christ down from above? Or, who shall descend into

49

the deep, to bring Christ up from the dead?" in order to be united to Christ and to have fellowship with him in his death and resurrection. "For the word is near to you," the gospel, the word of faith in which Christ himself graciously condescends to come near to you. You can come to him right there, without going anywhere else, if you desire to be joined to him (Romans 10:6-8).

The second way that God brings you into union and fellowship with Christ is faith – the faith that is produced in you by the gospel. Faith is the way you receive Christ. Faith is the way you bring about the union between Christ and yourself. Faith is the way you receive Christ himself, and all his fullness, into your heart.

Let me explain more about the nature of faith. Non-Christian philosophers talk about faith, but they speak of it only as a habit of the understanding. What they mean by faith is that you intellectually assent to some truth because the person who says it has authority. Very similarly, some people think faith in Christ is just a matter of believing that religious things are true, based upon Jesus' authority when he said these things. However, faith is much more than just the bare assent to truth – it is more than just believing that something is true. The Apostle Paul shows that the faith by which you are justified is "faith in Christ's blood" (Romans 3:24-25), not just in the fact that he has authority to testify to the truth.

If you have a faith that merely assents to authoritative truth, you will indeed gain some knowledge about that truth – just like the non-Christian philosophers have. However, the purpose of saving faith is not simply to intellectually know the truth of Christ and his salvation, testified and promised in the gospel. The purpose of saving faith is so you grasp and receive Christ and his salvation, which are given by and with the gospel promise. Therefore, true saving faith has two elements. First, it means that you believe the truth of the gospel. Second, it means that you personally believe in Christ, as he is promised freely to you in the gospel, for all your salvation.

When you believe the truth of the gospel, you receive the truth in which the knowledge of Christ is delivered to you. When you believe in Christ, you receive Christ himself, and his salvation, which are spoken of in the truth of the gospel. It is like this. It is one act when you receive a cup filled with wine, and it is another act to drink the wine in the cup. Those are two separate actions, but if you are going to drink wine, you must do both – you must receive the cup, and you must drink the wine.

# Union with Christ through the Gospel

This is what true saving faith is like. You must have both of these elements. First, you must wholeheartedly believe the truth of the gospel, and love that truth. Second, you must desire Christ and his salvation above everything else, and wholeheartedly receive him. You have to have a "spiritual appetite," which leads you to eat and drink Christ, the bread and wine of life – in the same way that a physical appetite leads you to eat real bread and drink real wine. Spiritually speaking, faith means that you feed on Christ, in the same way that you partake of a delicious meal.

True saving faith is not simply a matter of believing bare truth. Even wicked men, and the demons themselves, can do that. In their case, they wish the gospel were not true! True saving faith is also not simply a matter of believing in Christ because you are afraid of going to hell; faith is not simply a matter of avoiding punishment, where you do not have any desire to love and enjoy Christ. Rather, true saving faith means that you come to a deep, heartfelt conviction of how precious Christ is, and "account all things loss for the excellency of the knowledge of Christ Jesus our Lord, and count them but rubbish, that you may gain Christ and be found in him" (Philippians 3:8-9, II Thessalonians 2:10). You come to see Christ as all your salvation and happiness (Colossians 3:1), "in whom all fullness lives" (Colossians 1:19).

True saving faith also means that you love every part of Christ's salvation – holiness as well as the forgiveness of sins. It means that you earnestly desire God to "create in you a clean heart and a right spirit" as well as "hide his face from your sins" (Psalm 51:9-10). Do not be like those who care nothing about Christ at all, except to be delivered from hell. "Blessed are those who hunger and thirst for righteousness, for they shall be filled" (Matthew 5:6).

You can see how both parts of saving faith fit together – believing the truth of the gospel and receiving Christ personally. If you are going to receive Christ personally, you obviously have to know the truth of the gospel. It often works this way: once you know the truth of the gospel, your soul will want to receive Christ personally into your heart. If you believe the truth of the gospel with your heart, and if you consider it a precious truth, you will certainly believe on Christ for salvation from your heart. "Those who know the name of the Lord will certainly put their trust in him" (Psalm 9:10).

In Scripture, saving faith is described in both ways – it is sometimes described as believing the gospel, and it is sometimes described

51

as believing on Christ, or in Christ. "If you believe in your heart that God raised him from the dead, you shall be saved. The Scripture says that whoever believes on him shall not be ashamed" (Romans 10:9). "Whoever believes that Jesus is the Christ is born of God" (I John 5:1). "These things I have written to you who believe in the name of the Son of God, that you may know that you have eternal life, and that you may believe on the name of the Son of God" (I John 5:13).

There is something else you must know about the nature of faith: when you believe in Christ, you also believe in God the Father, the Son, and the Holy Spirit. Why? Because they are one and the same infinite God, and they all work together to accomplish your salvation in Christ – who is the only mediator between God and you, "in whom all the promises of God are yes and amen" (II Corinthians 1:20). In him, as mediator, you believe "on God, who raised him from the dead, and gave him glory, that your faith and hope might be in God" (I Peter 1:21).

All of these phrases describe what it means to trust in God, or in the Lord, which the whole Scripture so highly commends. The Old Testament spoke of Christ, just as the New Testament does. The only difference is that it spoke of Christ before his coming, as the promised Savior. The New Testament speaks of Christ as already having come in the flesh. "Believing in the Lord" and "trusting on his salvation" are equivalent terms – they explain each other.

If you trust in things that you can see and know by the light of your own reason – such as wisdom, power, riches, princes, or any arm of the flesh – you are not really "believing on them." However, when you trust in a Savior, you believe on him. This is the same thing as when Scripture speaks of resting, relying, leaning, staying yourself on the Lord, and hoping in the Lord. When you believe and trust, it is for the present as well as for the future of your salvation. The reason why the New Testament speaks of believing in Christ is because, when the New Testament was written, the writers were urging people to believe the testimony that was then newly being revealed in the gospel.

Once you understand the true nature of saving faith, you can then understand its place in your salvation. Faith is the means by which you actually receive Christ and all his fullness in your heart. The place of faith is often terribly misunderstood. For one thing, some people think that faith is too small and insignificant to accomplish anything major at all. It is just like Naaman in the Old Testament who thought that washing in the Jordan

River was too far beneath him to cure his leprosy! They condemn faith as the true way to enter in at the narrow gate of God's kingdom, because it just seems too easy! Ironically, when they think this, they make entering into God's kingdom not just difficult but impossible for themselves.

Some other people will acknowledge the true biblical, evangelical teaching that faith is the only way you can be justified before God, and that faith is the only way you receive salvation in Christ. However, they also say that faith is not enough for your sanctification – it is powerless for your growth in holiness. They say that faith will only produce an ungodly life. Therefore, they say, you must do something else in addition to faith, if you want to be able to live a holy life. To be sure, they will commend salvation through faith as a very comforting teaching for people on their deathbeds, or for people who are always terrified in their conscience because of the guilt of their sins. However, they say faith is not good "ordinary food" for "normal Christians." In fact, they even maintain that ministers should preach about faith very seldom and sparingly! When they do preach about faith, they say, ministers should make sure they offer antidotes and corrective advice to faith, in order to prevent people from going out and living ungodly lives.

The most common antidote they give to faith is this: "In order to be saved, sanctification is just as necessary as justification. Even though you are justified by faith, you are sanctified by your own law keeping." In essence they set up a system of salvation by works. They completely set aside the grace of justification. By doing so they remove its ability to comfort people by assuring them that they are acceptable to God.

However, people who do this are completely wrong. If justification by faith indeed has such a bad influence on your life, a holy God never would have given it to you in the first place! If they are right about justification by faith, it can offer your soul no comfort at all! There are people who actually try to "remodel" the gospel teaching of justification by faith. They say that if you want to be truly acceptable to God, you must believe in Christ, and also actually live a righteous life. They call this true saving faith!  However, it is a kind of "conditional faith." They say that trusting in God or Christ for salvation is really not the primary way you find acceptance with God. In their view, you first have to keep the law. If you do that, you will have the right to believe in Christ by faith.

Now, why do people "remodel" and "refine" the doctrine of

justification by faith in this way? They think that only the doctrine of salvation by works will compel people to live holy lives. They can show you many loose, wicked people who say they have trusted in God and Christ for salvation. They can show you that this supposed faith in Christ has only hardened them all the more in their wickedness because they have a false confidence.

In order to correct this situation, people have made obedience to Christ's laws the condition for salvation. They know that people cannot totally keep Christ's laws, so they say that as long as you **resolve** to keep Christ's law, that is good enough to save you. You can be saved as long as you say that Christ is your Lord, and as long as you promise to submit to his lordship in everything you do. You know the Bible's teaching has fallen into disregard when people reduce "trusting in the Lord" to a worthless, ordinary thing! People will try to scare you away from faith by saying that when you believe in Christ, since you are the one who believes, you are really saving yourself. This is not true. When you believe in Christ, you are simply receiving the salvation God gives you – and therefore, **he** gets all the glory.

If you come to understand what the Bible teaches about faith, all of these errors about faith will fade away from your mind. The Bible teaches that faith is just an "instrument" – it is the way that you actually receive Christ himself into your heart. Faith brings you into union and fellowship with Christ. Union with Christ not only brings you justification, but it brings you holiness of heart and life as well. Consider what the Bible teaches about faith.

When you have faith, you actually enjoy and possess Christ himself. This brings you both forgiveness of sins, and life and holiness as well. "Christ dwells in your heart by faith" (Ephesians 3:17). "You live to God, and yet not you, but Christ lives in you by faith in the Son of God" (Galatians 2:19-20). He who believes on the Son of God, has the Son, and the everlasting life that is in him" (I John 5:12, John 3:36). "He who hears Christ's word, and believes on him that sent Christ, has everlasting life, and has passed from death to life" (John 5:24).

These passages say exactly what I have been saying about faith. Faith does not just give you the title or the right to enjoy Christ. Faith means you **actually** enter in, and take possession of, Christ. "We have our access and entrance by faith into that grace of Christ in which we stand" (Romans 5:2).

# Union with Christ through the Gospel

The Bible also says that when you receive Christ by faith, you put him on, and you are rooted and grounded in him. When you believe, you receive the Holy Spirit, the forgiveness of sins, and an inheritance among those who are sanctified (John 1:12, Galatians 3:26-27, Colossians 2:6-7, Galatians 3:14, Acts 26:18). The Bible illustrates receiving Christ with the picture of eating and drinking. "He who believes on Christ drinks the living water of his Spirit" (John 7:37-39). "Christ is the bread of life; his flesh is meat indeed, and his blood is drink indeed." The way to eat and drink Christ is to believe in Christ. When you believe in Christ, you live in Christ, Christ lives in you, and you have everlasting life (John 6:35, 47, 48, 54, 55, 56).

How could the Bible teach it more clearly? You receive Christ himself into your soul by faith, just as you receive food into your body by eating and drinking. Christ is just as united to you as your food is united to you after you eat and drink. Faith is not simply something that gives you the "title" or the "right" to enjoy Christ at some future point in your life – any more than eating and drinking gives you the "right" to enjoy your food at some later time! Rather, faith is the way you actually receive Christ – just as you actually eat and drink food!

Here is another reason why faith is so important: Christ and all of his salvation are freely given by God's grace to everyone who believes in him. For, "you are saved by grace through faith, and this is not of yourself, it is the gift of God" (Ephesians 2:8-9). "We are justified freely by his grace, through faith in his blood" (Romans 3:24-25). The Holy Spirit – who is the bond of union between Christ and you – is a gift (Acts 2:38). Now, anything that is a gift of grace is not something that can be earned, purchased, or attained by any work you do. In other words, your works do not give you the right to have a gift of grace. Faith is not something that earns you grace. "If it is by grace, it is not longer of works. Otherwise, grace would no longer be grace" (Romans 11:6).

A free gift simply tells you this: "Take, and receive." If you pay one single penny to earn that gift, then the gift is no longer **free**. Christ **freely** offers his salvation to you. By faith, you freely receive Christ and his salvation as yours. Because you receive Christ by faith as a free gift, you can see what faith really is. Faith has no power in and of itself, it is just the way you receive Christ. Faith is the hand that receives Christ and all of his blessings.

I have already shown you from Scripture that all of your spiritual life and holiness are treasured up in the fullness of Christ, and you receive them through union with him. Therefore, coming into union with Christ must be the first work of saving grace in your heart. Faith itself is a holy grace, an essential part of your spiritual life. Faith is given to you right when you come into union with Christ. Faith is not something you have to "do" to earn the right to come into union with Christ. Faith is simply the way you actually receive and embrace Christ. Remember, when you believe, he has already come into your soul and made it his home.

True saving faith, by its very nature, is especially designed to receive Christ and his salvation, and to unite your soul to him. Faith also is designed to give your soul a new, holy nature, which results in a holy life as you live in union with Christ. God has made the parts of your body, such as your hands and feet, to fulfill specific functions. When you look at them, you can tell what they are designed to do. In the same way, God has made faith for a very specific purpose: to receive Christ, and to walk in him for sanctification. You must understand what a precious gift faith is! I want you to see with your "eyes" how faith has been given to you by God to enable you to walk in union with Christ, and thus live a holy life.

Here is why faith is specifically designed to receive Christ and his salvation. When you believe in Christ from your heart, you cast away everything else that keeps you distant from Christ. You put aside all your confidence in your own strength, endeavors, works, and privileges. You do not place any trust in any worldly pleasures, profit, or honor. You do not place any trust in any human help for happiness or salvation. Why? You understand that if you place any confidence in any of these things, you are not putting all your confidence in Christ alone for salvation.

When Paul placed his confidence in Christ, he put aside all his confidence in the flesh. He gave up glorying in his religious privileges, and in his works of righteousness. He considered everything from the world, or from religion, that he might enjoy, to be "rubbish, that he might gain Christ and be found in him" (Philippians 3:3-9). Faith says, "Assyria shall not save us, we will not ride upon horses, neither will we say any more to the work of our hands, 'You are our gods.' For in you the fatherless finds mercy" (Hosea 14:3). Faith also says, "We have no power against this great army" of our spiritual enemies, "nor do we know what to do. But, our eyes are upon you" (II Chronicles 20:12).

I could show you many places in Scripture that tell you what a self-emptying grace faith is. When you have faith, you completely stop putting confidence in anything other than Christ. You rise above all fleshly confidence, and you place your confidence in Christ alone as your only happiness and salvation. Believing in Christ, or in God, is the very way your soul comes to Christ (John 6:35). The Scripture also speaks of: "drawing near to the Lord" (Psalm 73:28), "making your refuge in the shadow of his wings" (Psalm 57:1), "staying yourself and your mind upon the Lord" (Isaiah 50:10, 26:3), "laying hold of eternal life" (I Timothy 6:12), "lifting up your soul to the Lord" (Psalm 25:1, "committing your way, or casting your burden upon the Lord" (Psalm 37:5, 55:22), and eating and drinking of Christ.

You know that you cannot see, hold, or gain Christ and his salvation by any physical act. Christ and salvation are only revealed and promised to you in the Word of God. The only way you can receive this unseen, promised salvation is by believing God's Word and by trusting in Christ. You do not earn Christ and his salvation by your works. You only receive them by faith.

In addition to being the only way you can receive Christ, faith has another important characteristic: faith is designed to give your soul a holy nature and mindset, which you receive out of the fullness of Christ. When you believe in Christ for your salvation, as he is freely promised to you, you naturally want to live a holy life. Even more than that, when you believe in Christ, you are empowered to live a holy life. Why? When you trust in Christ, you believe and begin to comprehend that "through Christ, you are dead to sin, and alive to God," "that your old man is crucified" (Romans 6:2-4), that "you live by the Spirit" (Galatians 5:25), that you "have forgiveness of sin," that "God is your God" (Psalm 68:14), that "you have in the Lord righteousness and strength" which enables you to do all things (Isaiah 45:24, Philippians 4:13), and that "you shall be gloriously happy and that you shall enjoy Christ for all eternity" (Philippians 3:20-21).

When believers in the Bible speak so highly of your glorious spiritual privileges, they show you what faith really is. Faith is trust in God and Christ. Faith is receiving every spiritual blessing out of Christ's fullness. The biblical believers really loved Christ! Their faith in Christ gave them both the desire and the power to live holy lives.

I have been telling you that faith is given to you by God to strengthen your soul for holy living. Since this is the case, you can be sure that it is completely sufficient to enable you to live a holy life. When you believe in Christ for the free gift of salvation, you will find that by that same faith, you will be enabled to love God because he has loved you first (I John 4:19). You will praise him, and pray to him, in the name of Christ (Ephesians 5:20, John 16:26-27). You will be patient with joy, and even in suffering you will give thanks to the Father who has called you to his heavenly inheritance (Colossians 1:11-12). You will love all the children of God out of love to your heavenly Father (I John 5:1). You will walk as Christ walked (I John 2:6). You will give yourself over to living for Christ in all things, compelled by his love in dying for you (II Corinthians 5:14). You have a whole cloud of witnesses before you showing the amazing works that faith brings about (Hebrews 11).

Some people think trusting in Christ is beneath them, because it is so simple. However, I do not know of any act of obedience that faith cannot produce! Look what faith can do in your life! By faith you live and act in every good work, as a person in Christ. When you live by faith, you live "beyond your capacity," so to speak. In other words, you do not live by what you are naturally able to do on your own. Rather, when you come to Christ and his salvation by faith, you do everything in his name, for his sake. Only the Christian gospel can enable you to live to God in holiness. This holiness is something of a mystery, because the gospel says that when you live, it is not you who live, but Christ who lives in you (Galatians 2:20). There is no other way you can live a holy life. Christ and all his salvation are revealed to you only in the gospel!

The Bible calls your faith a most "holy faith," because of its ability to enable you to live a holy life. When you trust in Christ, you will not move toward godless living, but toward holiness. Faith roots you and grounds you in holiness better than anything else can. Living by faith is far more powerful than simply consenting to make Christ the Lord of your life. When you live by faith, you have far more power to live a holy life than you do when you make resolutions to keep the law better in order to earn eternal life. Whenever you try to do anything that does not come from faith, you are just acting like a hypocrite. Indeed, there are many wicked people who have this kind of counterfeit, dead "faith" – which is really no faith at all. This "dead faith" will certainly lead people to live godless lives. However, do not blame true faith for that! Be very familiar with what true faith looks like, so you will not be deceived by counterfeit faith.

Some people reject living by faith because they think it is too easy and simple. So, let me say something about your faith-union with Christ.

58

Then, you will understand that the way of faith in Christ is not so "simple" and "easy" as it might first appear. What brings about faith in the first place? Who is the "author and finisher" of your faith? Who is it that brings you into union and fellowship with Christ, by faith? The infinite Spirit of God! God and Christ bring you into union with Christ by the Holy Spirit. For "by one Spirit you are all baptized into one body of Christ, and you are all made to drink by one Spirit" (I Corinthians 12:12-13). "May God grant you, according to the riches of his glory, to be strengthened with all power, by the Spirit, in the inner man, that Christ may live in your hearts through faith" (Ephesians 3:16-17). Consider what faith does! Faith raises you up to live above and beyond your natural condition. By faith, you live by Christ and his Spirit living in you. Nothing in the power of your own nature can do anything to raise you up so high!

When God sanctifies you, he does more than just give you the natural holiness that Adam first had in the Garden of Eden. When God sanctifies you, he uses his almighty power to give life to those who are dead in sin. In order to live a life of holiness, you need God's almighty power. You now live by a higher principle of life than was given to Adam at first. You live by Christ and his Spirit living and acting in you.

Natural, physical human beings produce children who are just like them. They use their own natural abilities to be fruitful and multiply, as God commanded them to do right from the beginning of creation. These children are natural and physical. Christ, the second Adam, also produces children in his image. In this case, these children are born "by the Spirit" (John 3:5). "For as many as received him, to those who believe in his name, he gave the right to become children of God – children born not of blood, nor by the will of the flesh, nor by the will of man, but born of God" (John 1:12-13).

Christ took upon himself a human nature, when he was conceived in the womb of the Virgin Mary. The Holy Spirit came upon her, and the power of the Most High overshadowed her (Luke 1:35). This is the same power that created the world. In the same way, Christ takes you into a mystical union and fellowship with himself. When he does this, he uses this same infinite, creating power. For "you are God's workmanship, created in Christ Jesus to do good works" (Ephesians 2:10. "If anyone is in Christ, he is a new creation" (II Corinthians 5:17).

In order to make you a new creation in Christ, the Spirit of God first works in your heart through the gospel. By this work, he gives you the grace of faith. You see, the gospel comes to you in word, but it does not come to you in word **only**. The gospel comes to you in power, and with the Holy Spirit. Without the power and presence of the Holy Spirit, Paul would plant, and Apollos would water, without any success. Why? Because you cannot receive the things of the Spirit of God on your own. You just consider them foolishness, until the Spirit of God enables you to understand them (I Thessalonians 1:5, I Corinthians 2:14, 3:6).

You can never come to Christ by any human teaching. You must also hear and learn from the Father. You must be drawn to Christ by his Spirit (John 6:44-45). When God gives you saving faith, the Holy Spirit enables you to hold fast to Christ by this same faith. The Father opens your mouth of faith to receive Christ, and he fills it with Christ. True faith is not like a dream, where you think you are eating and drinking – but then you wake up and find that you are still empty. The same Holy Spirit both gave faith to enable people to work miracles, and he worked miracles by that faith. In the same way, the same Holy Spirit of Christ gives saving faith to you, and he accomplishes the purpose of that faith: he brings you into union and fellowship with Christ by that faith. When he works in this way, none of the glory belongs to faith. All of the glory belongs to Christ and his Spirit.

True faith has a humble, self-denying nature. Faith does not claim any credit for itself when it receives Christ. All the credit and glory goes to the grace of God. The Bible says that "God saves you through faith" so that all the glory might be ascribed to his "free grace" (Romans 4:16). You are not able to bring yourself into union with Christ by your own natural abilities. Faith in and of itself does not have any virtue to unite you to Christ. Rather, faith unites you to Christ because the Holy Spirit works by faith and with faith.

In the work of salvation, there is a sense in which you are first passive, and then active, in this great work of mystical union with Christ. First, Christ apprehends you. Then, however, you are told to apprehend Christ. At first, Christ enters into your soul, and joins himself to you, by giving you the spirit of faith. In other words, your soul receives Christ and his Spirit by **their** power – not yours. It is like this: when it is dark, and the sun comes up, the sun first gives light to your eyes. After that, you live your life by the light of the sun in broad daylight.

Salvation by faith really reveals the glory of God's grace! When

60

you come into union with Christ and receive his Spirit, it is Christ who gives the spirit of faith to you. In and of yourself, you are not even able to produce the faith that receives Christ! When God gives you this spirit of faith by grace, your soul then wants to actively receive Christ.

I have no doubt that many infants come into union with Christ. Why? Because God gives them the Spirit of faith. These infants cannot yet act in faith like adults do, because they are not yet able to use their understanding to full capacity. However, because of the work of Christ in their hearts, they can be united to him. As they get older, those who have been passively joined to Christ by the Spirit of faith will begin to join themselves to him actively by faith. When they begin to act in faith in this way, they will know and enjoy their union with Christ. They will really come to understand how comforting saving faith is! They will also begin to live by faith more and more, and thus, they will begin more and more to live holy lives.

# Chapter Five

### Principle Five

**You cannot live a holy life, no matter how hard you try, if you still have your old nature.  In order to live a holy life, you have to receive, by faith, a new heart and a new nature, through your union and fellowship with Christ.**

I have been talking to you about how precious, and how powerful, saving faith is.  However, it is obvious that not everyone has this kind of saving faith, where Christ lives in their hearts.  Indeed, the number of people who have true saving faith is very small, compared to the "whole world that lies in wickedness" (I John 5:19-20).  There are many people who live without saving faith for a very long time in their lives, but they eventually come to saving faith (Ephesians 2:12).  There are other people who have the spirit of faith given to them in their mother's womb – such as John the Baptist (Luke 1:15, 44).  Yet, even these people have to be conceived as physical beings before they can become spiritual beings through the new birth of the Spirit (I Corinthians 15:46).

Human beings can live in two states, or two conditions, before God.  These two states are totally different from each other.  If you have received the new birth, and are a new creation in Christ through faith, you are in a blessed state.  You have been justified, and you have been credited with Christ's righteousness.  You have also received the Spirit of Christ, who lives in you.  Through him, you will live in holiness in this life, and in glory forever after.

If you are not in Christ by faith, you are in no better state than the one you received from the first Adam.  You received a sinful nature from him, because you were born and created in him, so to speak.  In your life, you can attain only what the power of your own nature enables you to do – plus any help that God might be pleased to give you.  I call this state your **natural state.**  I call it your natural state because it consists only of what you have received through your natural birth, and what you can attain by your own natural abilities.  The Bible calls this state "the natural man" (I Corinthians 2:14).

When you became a Christian, you entered into what I call a **new state**, because you can only enter into it through the new birth in Christ.  I also call it a **spiritual state**, because you received from Christ the Spirit who makes you alive. Now, the natural man and the spiritual man are totally opposed (Corinthians 2:14-15). They both have to do with the state of your soul, but they are moved by totally different principles.

Here is a very common mistake that non-Christians, natural men, make. They try to reform their lives and become better people — and even try to keep the law of God — without realizing that their nature must be changed. They do not realize that their very nature itself must be changed before their lives can be changed from sin to righteousness. Many people have tried to change their lives without being in a new state in Christ, but of course they have failed completely.

Non-Christians know they must obey the law, and they make some attempt to do it (Romans 2:14-15). The nation of Israel had zeal for God and for godliness, and they tried to keep the written law externally – even though in their hearts they were enemies to faith in Christ! The apostle Paul considered himself blameless in keeping the external requirements of the law's righteousness, even though he was a persecutor and a murderer (Philippians 3:6).

There are other people who seem to be very near to the kingdom of God. Even though they are non-Christians, they understand the depth and the spirituality of the law of God. They know that it calls them to love God with all their heart, soul, mind, and strength, and to love their neighbor as themselves. They know that they are commanded to obey God completely – both in their inward attitudes and their outward actions. They know that they are called to love their neighbor out of a total love from their heart (Mark 12:33-34).

People like this do all kinds of things to attain holiness. They try to subdue their inward thoughts; they try to avoid all known sins; they try to perform every known duty of the law with their heart and soul; they are very devout in their religious practice; they are even ready to kill their bodies with fasting, and other painful activity, to try to put to death their sinful lusts. In their hearts, they know holiness is necessary for their salvation, and they are terrified of being eternally condemned. Yet, they do not understand the truth of the gospel. They do not know they must have a new nature in Christ if they are going to live a new, obedient life. They labor in vain, trying to reform their natural state, instead of rising above their natural state through Christ. Many such people struggle for years against their lusts without any success. Eventually, they fall into despair in their conscience, and they go back to living a life of sinful indulgence.

I want to deliver you from this fruitless, tormenting labor! If you are tempted to fall into this trap, know this: if you want to be holy, you cannot attain it in your natural state, by your own natural abilities. If you want to live a holy life, you have to have a new nature that comes to you by faith in Christ. If you are in Christ, you will be able to live a new life, without such tormenting labor and anxiety! In order to be convinced that you can only attain holiness by having a new nature in Christ, consider these eight biblical truths:

First, the Bible clearly teaches that the only way you can be empowered to live a holy life is through union and fellowship with Christ by faith. You cannot live a holy life by the natural power of your own free will. You can only live a holy life by the power of Christ, who comes into your soul by his Spirit. The Holy Spirit unites you to Christ. It is completely hopeless to live a holy life, even when you try as hard as you can, as long as you are still in your natural condition.

Second, the Bible makes very clear the reason why you cannot live a holy life as long as you are still in your natural state. What is it? "You must be born of water and of the Spirit, or else you cannot enter into the kingdom of God" (John 3:3-5). You "are created in Christ Jesus for good works, which God prepared beforehand that you should walk in" (Ephesians 2:10). If you could love God and your neighbor, as the law requires, without the new birth and the new creation, then you might as well live without them! For Christ said, "Do this and you shall live" (Luke 10:28). However, you cannot keep the law without them!

In the new birth and the new creation, God does more than just merely reform and repair your natural state, your old nature. Your first birth and creation put you into a certain state, and how much more did your second birth do this. Your first birth gave you both a physical body and a spiritual state. Your second birth did not give you a new physical body, but it did give you a new spiritual state. When you were first created and born in Adam, you inherited a totally corrupt nature from Adam. When you were born again in Christ, you became a new creation, and a spiritual person. God says, "if anyone is in Christ, he is in a new state" – he is far different from the state of Adam before the fall. He is a wholly "new creation" – "old things are passed away, behold all things have become new" (II Corinthians 5:17).

Third, Paul speaks of your old nature as "the flesh." He very clearly says "those who are in the flesh cannot please God" (Romans 8:8). Many people do not consider what it means to be in the flesh. They think that being in "the flesh" means that you sin from time to time, or that you are overly addicted to pleasing your physical appetite. However, consider what the Apostle Paul means by being "in the flesh." Being in the flesh does not simply mean that you do some sinful things from time to time. Rather, being in the flesh is the cause of sinfulness, just as being in the Spirit is the cause of holiness. Sin is the property of the flesh, something that lives in the flesh (Romans 7:18). The flesh is what lusts against the Spirit (Galatians 5:17). The flesh is not simply having some bad habits.

What is the flesh? The flesh is the nature of man as it is corrupted by the fall of Adam. The flesh it is the nature you receive because you are descended from Adam. To be in the flesh is to be in a natural state. To be in the Spirit is to be in a new state, by the Spirit of Christ living in you (Romans 8:9). The corrupt nature is called the flesh, because it is what you receive when you are born as a member of the human race descended from Adam. The new nature is called Spirit, because you receive God's Spirit when you are born again, and born into God's kingdom. "That which is born of the flesh is flesh, and that which is born of the Spirit is spirit," Jesus said (John 3:6). You cannot possibly attain true holiness as long as you remain in your natural state, in the flesh.

Fourth, the Apostle Paul testifies that those who "have been taught as the truth is in Jesus," have learned to avoid their normal sinful way of life, by "putting off the old man, which is corrupt according to deceitful lusts, and by putting on the new man, created to be like God in true righteousness and holiness" (Ephesians 4:21-24). Putting off the old man, and putting on the new man, is the same as not living by the flesh, but by the Spirit. In other words, you put off your natural state, and put on your new state, by union and fellowship with Christ. Paul shows you that the new man is the blessed state where "Christ is all, and in all" (Colossians 3:11).

The old man is the natural state of man, where he has no relationship with Christ whatsoever. It is called the old man, because believers are brought into a new state through the new birth in Christ. Sanctification is far more than just "turning over a new leaf" in the way you live. Sanctification is living out of your new nature in Christ.

# Receiving a New Nature through Christ

The old man and the new man are two completely contrary conditions of life – the old man moves you toward sinful living, and the new man moves you toward holy living. The old man must be put off, as crucified with Christ, before you can be freed from the practice of sin (Romans 6:6-7). You simply cannot live a new life until you have first received a new nature through faith in Christ. This is exactly what Paul says in Romans 13:12-13, where he directs you to put on the Lord Jesus Christ. This is the only way you can cast off the deeds of darkness and walk in the daytime, not fulfilling the lusts of the flesh.

Fifth, there are reasons why your old nature is totally unable to live a holy life. By its very nature, your old nature prevents you from living a godly life. The only thing your old nature can do, as long as you are in your old nature, is to enslave you to a sinful life. The old man, your natural state, your life in the flesh, is characterized by several aspects which can only drag you away from a life of holiness. I told you earlier that if you are in Christ, you have been equipped with everything you need to live a godly life. However, if you are still in your natural state, everything about you is opposed to living a holy life. Consider what characterizes the flesh:

❑ **The guilt of sin.** This is the guilt of Adam's first sin, and also the corrupt nature that makes you live a life of sin. You are by nature a child of wrath (Ephesians 2:3), and under the curse of God. The forgiveness of sins, and freedom from the condemnation of sin, cannot happen in the flesh. It cannot happen in your natural state, but only in Christ (Romans 8:1, Ephesians 1:7). Can you possibly imagine that anyone can prevail against sin if he sees that God is against him, and that he is under God's curse?

❑ **An evil conscience**, which tells you that you are under God's wrath for your sin. This evil conscience makes you hate God as your enemy, rather than love him as your Father. Or, if you have a blind conscience, it hardens you even more in your sins.

❑ **An evil inclination**, which makes you move only toward sin. It is therefore called the sin that lives in you, and the law of sin in your members, that powerfully subdues and enslaves you to the service of sin (Romans 7:20-23). The flesh is a fixed inclination to lust against the law without a second thought. As a result, its lusting cannot be prevented by any amount of diligence or watchfulness. "The mind of the flesh is at enmity against God, for it is not

subject to the law of God, nor can it be so" (Romans 8:7).  How
foolish and futile it is for people to say they can do good whenever
they want to, when their minds and will are completely enslaved to
sin!

❑ **Subjection to the power of the devil**, who is the god of this
world, who has blinded the minds of all unbelievers (II
Corinthians 4:4).  He will certainly conquer all those who fight
against him on his own home turf – all of those who are still in
their old nature, and who are not in union with Christ.

All of these characteristics of the flesh clearly show that your old
nature simply has no ability to be good, because it is totally dead in sin
(Ephesians 2:1).  This goes right back to the sentence pronounced against
the first sin of Adam, "in the day that you eat of the fruit you shall surely
die" (Genesis 2:17).  You can no more bring your sinful, dead nature to
holiness through your own efforts than you can bring a dead person to life
by rubbing or chafing him!  You can stir up no strength or enabling grace
in the natural man, because there is no strength or grace in him to be
stirred up (Romans 6:6).  You can labor with all the strength you have
while you are in the flesh, but you can do nothing but sin.  Why?  Because
there is no good thing in you, as Paul himself says about his own
experience: "I know, that in me (that is, in my flesh), dwells no good
thing" (Romans 7:18).

Sixth, you have no reason to think that Christ will help you to will
or to do anything that is pleasing to him as long as you remain in your old
nature.  While you are in the flesh, you are not able to desire to do
anything that is godly, let alone **do** anything that is godly.  Christ, through
his incarnation, death, and resurrection, has done more than just repair the
decay and ruins of your natural state.  He has, if you are in a relationship
with him, given you a new nature, far better than your old nature.  He has
done this through union and fellowship with himself.  He has done this for
you so that you might live for God – not by the power of your own free
will but by the power of his Spirit living and acting in you.

You see, your old nature is totally irrecoverable and desperate.
Christ, the Savior, never aimed to restore it or repair it!  The flesh is
beyond repair!  The flesh is neither holy nor happy.  The flesh is totally
enslaved to sin, and to all its miseries, as long as it remains in you.  Jesus
simply did not come to "patch up" the flesh.  He came to give you a brand
new nature – a new heart indwelt by his Holy Spirit.

## Receiving a New Nature through Christ

Now, you might be asking, "If I have this wonderful new nature, why do I still struggle with sin?" You may wonder if you are even a Christian. Do not be discouraged by your continuing struggle against sin. Even though you are a new creation in Christ, and you now serve the law of God with your mind, you will still feel the pull of the flesh. Born-again believers serve the law of God with their mind, yet in their flesh serve the law of sin (Romans 7:25). As far as the flesh remains in them, the flesh lusts against the Spirit (Galatians 5:17). Your flesh "remains dead because of sin," even while "your spirit is alive because of righteousness" (Romans 8:10). The flesh will only be totally destroyed when you die. In this life, you will never become perfect in holiness and happiness in Christ.

This truth is pictured for you in Genesis 3, where God put Adam and Eve out of the Garden of Eden, and blocked the way back in with cherubim and a flaming sword. This first state of innocence was lost forever, with no hope of restoration. The happiness intended for him through the promised Redeemer was totally new. In the same way, your old natural man was not revived and reformed by the death of Christ. It was crucified together with him. It had to be abolished and destroyed by his death (Romans 6:6).

Your flesh is like the part of a garment infected with the plague of leprosy. When a garment was touched by leprosy, the infected part of the garment had to be totally torn off, because it was incurable. This is the only way the garment could become clean (Leviticus 13:56). "If Christ is not in you, you are an unbeliever" (II Corinthians 13:5). In other words, you are in a state where God has rejected you from partaking of salvation. You cannot expect God to help you become holy, as long as you still have your sinful nature. Your sinful nature must be completely "torn off." To enable you to live a holy life, God must deliver you from your old nature by the power of the gospel!

Seventh, non-Christians have no excuse for their life of sin. I have been showing you from Scripture that you can only live a holy life if you have been given a new nature through union with Christ by faith. However, this does not let unbelievers off the hook! Non-Christians are still required to live holy lives. They will still be held accountable for their sins when they stand before the tribunal of God's justice. The sinful nature you are born with does not excuse your life of sin! You cannot blame God for your sin. You alone are to blame.

# The Gospel Mystery of Sanctification

The Bible says, "God made man upright, but they sought out many inventions" (Ecclesiastes 7:29). Carefully observe the words of this text. Human beings were created upright at first. Then, however, they sought their own ways, rather than walking in uprightness before God. By man, the text means all humankind. The first Adam represented all mankind, just as Jacob and Esau represented two nations in the womb of Rebecca (Genesis 25:23). God made us all in our first parent, Adam, according to his own image. At first, he was willing and able to keep God's law. When he had a pure nature, he was commanded to obey God's law. However, he sinned willfully, and he brought upon himself the sentence of death that God warned him about.

When Adam fell into sin and guilt, you fell into sin as well. "In one man, Adam, all have sinned, and so death came upon all" (Romans 5:12). Adam was the representative for all humankind. All humankind was in Adam's loins, so to speak, when he committed the first sin. There is a similar situation of representation described in Hebrews 7:9-10. The Scripture says that Levi paid tithes in Abraham before Levi was born. Why? Because when Levi's father Abraham paid tithes to Melchizedek, Levi was still in the loins of Abraham.

In the gospel, God has promised that he will not punish children for the sins of their parents. This is a new covenant promise, confirmed by the blood of Christ. This promise is yes and amen to you only in Christ. He alone can give you a nature different than the sinful nature your natural parents gave you. You cannot claim the benefit of this gospel promise as long as you are still in your old, natural state (Jeremiah 31:29-31, II Corinthians 1:20).

You are indeed powerless to live a godly life if you are not in Christ. However, your powerlessness to obey God does not excuse you for your sinfulness, and guilt, before God. If you try to excuse yourself from your guilt, you show that you have never been truly humbled for your sins. You have never really understood the depths of the sin of which all human beings are guilty – which goes right back to when Adam willfully disobeyed God the first time.

Think of it this way. Suppose a person receives a large inheritance, but then he wastes it through wild living. Then, he becomes a debtor who is not able to pay back his debts. His **inability** to pay back his debts does not excuse him for not paying back his debts! He is still responsible to pay them! He is without excuse! In the same way, if a

70

person commits many mad and sinful acts while he is drunk, his state of drunkenness does not excuse his sinful actions. His state of drunkenness simply makes him sin all the more.

In the same way, your powerlessness to obey God does not excuse your sin before God. Remember, your powerlessness to obey God consists of two things. First, you do not have the power or ability to obey God. Second, you do not even have a willing mind to live in true holiness and righteousness. By nature, you do not **want** live a holy life. You do not love holiness. You lust against holiness (Galatians 5:17). By nature, you hate the light (John 3:20. No one can even desire to love holiness, and live in holiness, until God begins a good work in their souls. When God begins this work, he will perfect this work (Philippians 1:6). True Christians will of course fall short of holiness time and again in their lives. Nonetheless, God gives them a mind to obey (II Corinthians 8:12).

If you are still in your natural state you are justly condemned, because you "love darkness rather than light." You deserve to be a partaker with the devils in torment if you do not know Christ, because you partake with them in living in evil lusts. Your inability to do good in your natural state does not excuse your evil lusts – any more than it excuses devils. You are still accountable before God for your life. You are without excuse for your sin.

Eighth, let me make sure you understand one more thing. You might think that because non-Christians are lost in sin, and unable to obey God, it is useless to preach the gospel to them. This is not so! It is not useless to preach the gospel to non-Christians, and call them to repentance and faith in Christ. You preach the gospel to non-Christians so they will be converted to Christ and saved. The goal of preaching to non-Christians is not to enable them to come to holiness while they remain in their old nature. The goal is to raise them above their natural state, to present them "perfect in Christ" (Colossians 1:28) – not in themselves.

To be sure, they cannot live holy lives while they remain in their natural state. However, the gospel is the power of God for their conversion and salvation, by the power of the Holy Spirit. When the gospel is preached, the Holy Spirit works in people. He gives life to those who are dead in sin, and he makes them new creations in Christ. He gives people repentance unto life, and he gives them true faith in Christ. The gospel comes to those who are elect by God, not "only in word, but also in power, and in the Holy Spirit," and in such assurance that they "receive it with joy in the Holy Spirit" (II Thessalonians 1:5-6). "The gospel is the ministry of the Spirit, who gives life" (II Corinthians 3:6-8). The gospel is "mighty because of God" (II Corinthians 10:4).

The gospel does not depend at all upon the power of your own free will to successfully convert you and bring you to Christ. The gospel gives life to your soul, and it gives you the power to receive it and obey it. Christ makes those who are dead in sin to "hear his voice and live" (John 5:25). Therefore, he can speak to them through his gospel, and he can command them to repent and believe, with hope of success – just as he could speak to a dead person, *talitha Sumi*, "Little girl, I say to you, get up!" (Mark 5:41); just as he could say "Lazarus, come forth!" (John 11:43-44); and just as he could say to the paralyzed man, "Arise, take up your bed, and go to your own house" (Matthew 9:6).

Ninth, there is something else that might be bothering you at this point. You might look at non-Christians, and you might see that they are very moral people. You might look at people who have no saving knowledge of Christ – such as philosophers, Jews, or even atheists -- but you see that they are very good people. You see that they are wise, and that they have many moral achievements. You see that they are very devoted in their lives. This may cause you to think, "Do they really need the gospel? Aren't their moral achievements enough before God?"

No! Their moral achievements are not enough to earn their acceptance with God! Mere morality is not enough before God! Consider the Apostle Paul. He was a very zealous Pharisee, and he attained a very high level of morality – or so he thought. There were other Jews in his time who were just as zealous for the law as he was. Paul and his fellow-Jews came as close to true holiness as any non-Christian philosopher ever could in his natural state! However, after Paul came to a saving knowledge of Christ, how did he consider himself? He called himself the "chief of sinners" – even as he considered those high moral attainments in his pre-Christian life. Other people may have considered him blameless with respect to the righteousness of the law. However, he came to the point where he realized that his works of righteousness were not good enough before God. He realized it was necessary to begin to live to God in a whole new way by faith in Christ. As a result, he suffered the loss of all of his former moral achievements. He considered them **rubbish**, that he might gain Christ (I Timothy 1:15, Philippians 3:6-8).

Consider this also. None of the many Jews who tried to keep the law of righteousness ever actually accomplished it. Why? Because they did not seek to keep it "by faith in Christ" (Romans 9:31-32). What could be a greater achievement than for one to give all his earthly goods to the poor, and give over his body to be burned? Yet, the Scripture clearly tells you that someone can do all of this without having any love whatsoever. This means they can externally do these things without having any true holiness of heart and life whatsoever (I Corinthians 13:3).

Non-Christian people can, and sometimes do, have a strong conviction about the infinite power, wisdom, justice, and goodness of God. They know that he will one day judge them, and lead the godly into blessedness and the ungodly into torment. These convictions might indeed stir them up to make a profession of faith, and to say great things about godliness. They might earnestly try to avoid all known sin, to subdue their lusts, to obey God as best they can, and to serve him with their lives and possessions. However, they do not have a real love for God from their hearts. All they want to do is to escape the torments of hell, and earn eternal life, by their own good works.

Think about it. What kind of love do they really have? Their love for God is forced and fake. They really do not like God, and they do not like serving God. They consider God to be a hard master. They consider his commands to be a pain in the neck. Inwardly, they grumble, whine, and complain about having to keep God's commands. God's commands are just a burden to them! They are really not looking forward to enjoying God in heaven. They only thing driving them is the fear of everlasting fire in hell. In fact, they would love to have it both ways: they would love to continue to enjoy their lives of lust, but have no danger of being condemned in hell! Their operating principle is "how much sin can I get away with and still go to heaven?"

Why is it that non-Christians who try to keep the law of God cannot truly do it? It is because they are born only according to the flesh. They do not have a new heart. In Abraham's family, they are still "children of the slave woman" (Galatians 4:23). To be sure, they work harder in trying to serve God than many of God's true children! However, God does not accept their service, because even their best efforts are simply the work of slaves. They do not have any childlike love for God. In reality, their best efforts are just "glittering sins." Their actions may look righteous on the outside, but in reality they are still sinful, because they are not motivated by love for God. Their lives are just expressions of counterfeit holiness.

There is a sense in which even this counterfeit holiness comes from God. The reason why non-Christians can live moral lives is because God does not completely give them over to be as bad as they **could** be. Just think of what would happen if he allowed this! If God completely gave people over to their own natural corruption, and to the power of Satan, all the external expressions of religion and morality would quickly disappear from the world. All people would become totally hardened in their wickedness.

God does not give people over in this way. God – who can restrain the burning of a fiery furnace without quenching its fire, and who can restrain flowing water without changing its nature – restrains people's natural corruption, without removing it from them. In other words, he does not allow people to be as bad as they **could** possibly be. He restrains their wickedness by his common grace. In his wisdom and power, he "makes even his enemies yield obedience to him" (Psalm 66:3). Non-Christians can do many things that are good externally, even though they cannot do anything that is **truly** holy before God.

There are several different ways that God restrains the natural corruption of people: his law, terrors of conscience, consequences of sin, rewards in this life, human rulers, and the system of having to work for food and drink and other necessities of life.

The gospel also helps to restrain sin among non-Christians. God restrains sin to preserve his church. As a result, the gospel is preached to the world. Because of this, non-Christians are better able to receive the truth of the gospel. Those who are chosen by God will eventually be converted. Those who are not truly converted will nevertheless enjoy more of God's goodness here on earth, and they will suffer fewer torments in the life hereafter. The non-Christians world truly is vile and wicked! However, you can praise and magnify the free goodness of God that it is no worse than it is!

Do you see the point? Non-Christians may indeed have a certain kind of morality in their lives. This is certainly better than having no morality in their lives – at least in a human sense. However, their morality cannot earn any favor before God, because their righteousness is no better than filthy rags. With all of their external morality, they are not living truly holy lives, because their natures have not been changed by the power of the gospel and the Holy Spirit.

Here is the essence of what I have been saying in this chapter. You cannot possibly obey God if you still have your old nature. Your old, corrupt nature has no power to please God. If you want to obey God, you must receive a new heart and a new nature from Christ. When you receive this new nature, you will then be willing and able to obey God. Apart from union with Christ, you can do nothing!

The Gospel Mystery of Sanctification

# Chapter 6

### Principle Number 6

**If you try to obey the commands of Christ in order to earn your salvation, and to gain assurance of your salvation, you are seeking salvation by the works of the law. You are not seeking your salvation through faith in Christ, as he is revealed in the gospel. If you try to earn your salvation by your true obedience, you will never succeed.**

All religious people agree that people should live holy and righteous lives. Most of them also believe that living a holy and righteous life is what earns you God's favor and everlasting happiness. All of the world's prominent false religions hold this point of view. The heathen philosophers drive themselves to moral living in this way. They believe God will one day judge them. They believe those who violate God's commands to love God and neighbor are worthy of death. While they live on earth, their consciences accuse and excuse them, depending on how they live (Romans 1:32, 2:14-15). They know God is just. They know he requires obedience from people. They try to live good lives in order to avoid his wrath and enjoy his favor. Yet, they also know that they often fail to obey God. So, they hope that God will pardon their failures and accept them because they tried the best they could to obey him.

If you think you can earn your salvation by your obedience, you are thinking according to the corrupt wisdom of the world. You are not thinking according to "the wisdom of God in a mystery, that hidden wisdom which God ordained before the world for our glory." The doctrine of salvation by works does not come from the wisdom of the Spirit of God. The truths of the gospel of grace"are foolishness to the natural man. He cannot understand them, for they are spiritually discerned" (I Corinthians 2:6,7,9,14). Salvation by works is not from "the foolishness of preaching," by which it pleased God "to save those who believe" (I Corinthians 1:21).

The gospel of Christ is very clear: in the gospel, you have a better way of salvation than the "wisdom" the world can offer you. The gospel says that you come into God's favor through the gift of God's grace, completely apart from your works. However, as clear and simple as this is, it is very difficult to persuade people to leave the way they are naturally addicted to, the way of salvation by works. This system of works is part of their very bones – their minds are totally captivated by it. Therefore, it is very difficult for them to leave it. Many of these people hear the gospel over and over again, but they can never stop trying to earn their salvation by their works.

These people never truly come to love godliness. The only thing they do is try to live out of their old nature, and force themselves to do hypocritical obedience. They are trying to avoid hell, and get to heaven, by their works. Their own consciences tell them that the zeal they have for God, for "godliness," and for a strict, disciplined life are all just forced out of them by fear. They are merely like paid workers.

However, they never give up their attempts to earn their salvation by their works. They are afraid if they trust in Christ for salvation, by free grace without their works, the fire of their zeal and devotion will die down. They are afraid they will grow careless in their religious practice, and that they will unleash their lusts – bringing certain condemnation upon themselves. Because of this, they listen to only one kind of preacher – the preacher who refuses to preach about free grace. They will only listen to preachers who will only condemn sin and urge people to gain Christ and salvation by doing better. These preachers thunder about hell and the damnation of sinners, but they never talk about God's gracious salvation in Christ.

I will certainly admit that some people abuse the doctrine of grace. They turn grace into cheap grace. They turn the gospel into lawlessness by saying, "Since you are forgiven, you can live any way you please." This can only lead to a sinful lifestyle. This is tragic, and wrong.

However, what is even more tragic is that even some of our own people have caved in, and have retreated from the doctrine of justification by faith without works! Justification by faith has always been considered by evangelical Protestants to be the central doctrine of our faith! However, even some Protestants are moving away from the doctrine of justification by faith. They think the doctrine of justification by faith is powerless to bring about sanctification. They think it may even destroy sanctification! They have embraced the view that the only way to get people to obey God is by making their good works the absolutely necessary condition for their eternal salvation.

All of a sudden, for them, the rules have changed: God now requires people to sincerely obey him if they are going to be saved at all. The have "remodeled" this classic, central doctrine of our faith. They now reinterpret the Holy Scriptures in a way that will agree with their new, man-made doctrine of sanctification by human works. They have tried to lay a new foundation for obedience. They are telling people, "Leave off the doctrine of grace. You must obey if you want God to really accept you."

These teachers have laid a new foundation for Christian living, but it is not the foundation God has laid for Christian living. It is a foundation of soft sand. This rotten foundation will destroy the Christian faith. It cannot and will not enable anyone to live a holy life. However, many will be seduced by this error because it sounds so true. This is what makes it so detestable and abominable. It is simply Satan masquerading as an angel of light once again.

Satan is pretending that he cares about holiness. He is whispering in the ears of Christians, "Justification by faith cannot do anything to help you live a holy life. Give it up. The gospel really cannot help you become a better person." This is the same lie that inspired people in the Apostles' day to persecute the gospel for the sake of the law. This lie has also established and maintained many false, legalistic churches. During the time of the Reformation, the doctrine of justification by faith without works gave the legalistic church a deadly wound. In our day, this lie of salvation by works has returned, and it is attempting to heal this deadly wound. The real danger is that this lie is now even seeping into evangelical, protestant churches, and the gospel is being corrupted there!

There is one main problem with this doctrine: it proclaims a way of salvation through the works of the law, and not through faith in Christ and the gospel. Those who teach salvation by works would have you believe that this is the only way to be saved. However, do not doubt that the true gospel of salvation by faith alone is sufficient enough and powerful enough for your justification, your sanctification, and your whole salvation.

People have many ways of trying to make the false gospel of salvation by works look like the true gospel. They even try to use the Bible to make a false gospel look true! Listen to some of the things they say:

"We know that the law as a covenant of works requires you to obey all of its commands perfectly if you want to live. However, we are not going to make you do that. Just make sure you do the best you can. Also, you do not have to obey the Law of Moses; just obey the commands of Christ."

"We are really not telling you to try to be saved without Christ. We do believe that you have to be saved through the merit and righteousness of Christ. Yes, you have to be saved by obeying the law, but after all, Jesus by his grace enables you to keep the law! So, your salvation by works is still by his grace."

"Your salvation is really by faith, because Jesus gives you the faith that enables you to keep the law. You just have to make sure you diligently commit yourself, through a total resignation of your own will, to believe in Jesus who enables you to keep the law and so be saved."

All of this talk might sound good to you, but do not believe it! It is all just nice-sounding language that is masking what they really believe: that your salvation is by your own legal works.

Consider now why salvation by the works of the law is a false way of salvation.

First, if you seek to earn your salvation by sincerely trying to do good works, you are condemned. Paul says that if you try to do this, you are seeking righteousness by the works of the law, not by faith (Romans 9:32). You are seeking to be justified by the law, and thus you are falling from the grace of Christ (Galatians 5:4). If this one assertion is true, it will completely unmask the doctrine of salvation by works. Once people understand this, they will see the doctrine of salvation by works as a doctrine that will only condemn them. They will run from it, because they will see that it actually deprives its followers of salvation in Christ.

If you are willing to consider it, this point is not very difficult to prove. The Jews and the Judaizing Christians with whom Paul was disputing in this whole salvation controversy did not think they could be saved by perfect obedience. They knew they could not keep the law completely! Rather, they thought they could be saved by their sincere obedience. They would be saved as long as their obedience was not hypocritical. They thought they knew the difference between sincere and hypocritical obedience, and they tried to be sincere.

# Salvation is Not by Works

Remember what the Jewish religion required of everyone who professed it. If you were an Old Testament Jew, you had to acknowledge that you were a sinner. You had to keep the Day of Atonement (Leviticus 16), which required you to humble yourself. You had to keep many other rituals given to you by the word of God (Psalm 143:2, Proverbs 10:9, Ecclesiastes 7:20). You knew you were required to turn to the Lord with all your heart, in sincerity and uprightness, and that God would accept your sincere obedience. In other words, you knew you were not and could not be perfect; you just had to keep the law as sincerely as you could.

This is really what the Judaizing Christians were saying. Paul knew they did not require perfect obedience to the law to be saved, because no one could do it! They just required sincere obedience to the law in order to be saved. Paul wanted to show them that even their sincere obedience was not enough to save them.

Remember why else Paul condemned this teaching: Paul condemned it in a more general way, because people were **seeking** salvation by their own works. In other words, he was not interested in getting into a debate over "How much of the law do I have to keep in order to be saved?" Rather, he was focusing on a **mentality** – the mentality of seeking salvation by your own works because you think they can truly save you.

Paul knew that Old Testament believers did in fact have some obedience. Abraham, who lived long before the law of Moses, was not justified by any of his works – even though he did sincerely obey God some of the time. David lived under the Law of Moses, but he also was not justified by any of his works – although, again, he did render some sincere obedience to God in his life. This is just like your situation: you are not saved by any of your works (Romans 4:1-6), but you are now called to obey the law of Christ in your life.

Paul also knew that the Judaizing Christians were not completely rejecting Christ. He knew they were not saying, "You do not need Christ to save you." He understood their central teaching: "You need the grace of Christ to save you, and you participate in the grace of Christ as you sincerely try to keep the law." They did not blatantly deny Jesus. They believed in salvation by Jesus **plus** your own good works.

This is similar to many Jews of Paul's time. Many Pharisees, for instance, sincerely thought that a mixture of the grace of God and their own good works saved them. Many legalistic Pharisees thanked God for their good works that proceeded from his grace (Luke 18:11). If you asked them, they would have told you that their salvation was by God's grace. This is just like many people today who tell you that their salvation is by grace, even though they add in their own sincere obedience as a condition for their salvation.

Here is the point I am making. There are people who say that you must obey the law perfectly in order to earn your salvation. However, no one in the Bible ever thought this. The Jews who stumbled over Christ (Romans 9:32) were not trying to be perfect people; they were just trying to be sincere. However, Paul told them, this will still condemn you. The same is true for the Galatian Christians. They were not saying you had to be perfect in order to be saved. They were just saying that you had to sincerely try to keep the law. However, Paul told them that they were in danger of falling from Christ and grace (Galatians 5:2,4). They were in danger of falling under the curse that he had proclaimed against any man or angel who proclaimed any gospel other than the gospel he had preached (Galatians 1:8-9).

So, do not be fooled by people who say to you, "You do not have to keep the law perfectly in order to be saved. You just have to be sincere. It is Jesus plus your own sincere obedience that will save you." As attractive as those words might sound, do not accept them. They are a mask for a false gospel!

Second, remember the basic difference between the law and the gospel. It is not that the law requires **perfect** obedience, and the gospel just requires **sincere** obedience. Rather, the difference is this: the law requires **doing**, and the gospel requires **not doing**. The gospel requires **believing** for life and salvation. The "terms of the deal" are totally different. They are not just different in degree: "The law requires 100% obedience for your salvation whereas the gospel only requires 51% obedience for your salvation." No! The terms are different in their very nature! The law requires 100% **doing**. The gospel requires 100% **not doing!** The gospel requires **believing!**

Paul contrasts the **believing** required by the gospel to the **doing** required by the law in Galatians 3:12: "Yet the law is not of faith, but 'the man who does them shall live by them.'" He says the same thing in Romans 4:5: "But to him who does not work but believes on Him who justifies the ungodly, his faith is accounted for righteousness."

# Salvation is Not by Works

If you try to be saved by works, even the easiest and lowest standard of works, you bring yourself under the terms of the law. What are those terms? If you truly want to be saved by obedience to the law, you must obey the whole law perfectly! God requires nothing less than perfection if you if you want to be saved by your obedience to the law. Remember what the law tells you. If you are not willing to despair of your own good works and seek your salvation as a gift freely given by Jesus, the law tells you that you have to keep it perfectly in order to live! If you choose to live by the law, you will stand or fall by the law. If you try to be saved by your works of obedience to the law, in the end you will be judged by the law. What does the law of God require of you if you are going to be saved by it? Absolute perfection!

Third, if you truly want to sincerely obey all the commands of Christ given in the gospel, you are also obliged to keep the moral law given by Moses. Some people try to have it both ways. They say that you must keep Christ's commands to be saved, but that you do not have to keep the Law of Moses to be saved. They know the Law of Moses thunders a curse against everyone who tries to be saved by it (Galatians 3:10-12). However, they are missing something. Many good Christians in the past considered themselves obliged to obey both the moral and the ceremonial law. If they had tried to be justified by their works, they would have sought it by those laws (Acts 20:20-21). They never said something like, "we are only obligated to be justified by sincerely obeying the works of the gospel." If they were wrong about anything that was absolutely necessary for salvation, the Apostles would have told them so!

If you want to be saved by your own works, it is not enough to just try to sincerely obey the commands of Christ. You must also completely obey the Law of Moses. Jesus himself never accepted this new condition of having to obey his commands alone. He never abolished the authority of the Law of Moses; rather, he established it. He came not "to destroy the law and the prophets, but to fulfill them (Matthew 5:17). That is, he kept them perfectly. He also declared "those who break one of the least of these commandments, and teach men to do so, shall be called the least in the kingdom of heaven. But whoever does and teaches them shall be called great in the kingdom of heaven" (Matthew 5:17-19).

Jesus also commanded you to "do to others whatever you would want them to do to you, because this summarizes the law and the prophets (Matthew 7:12)." This sufficiently proves that Jesus wants you to consider yourself under the authority of the Law of Moses! Jesus required his disciples to keep and do whatever the Pharisees commanded them, because they "sat in Moses' seat" (Matthew 23:2-3).

During the time of his ministry, Jesus himself answered the questions of those who were guilty of the same error that we are now dealing with, that of seeking salvation by their own works. Jesus showed them that if they wanted to be saved by their own works, they had to obey the commands that were established in the Law of Moses in the Old Testament scriptures. When someone asked him, "What must I do to inherit eternal life?" Jesus replied, "What is written in the law? How do you read it? Do this, and you shall live…. If you want to enter into life, keep the commandments, which are, 'You shall not murder,' 'You shall not commit adultery,' etc." (Luke 10:26-28).

In the same way the apostles of Christ required believers to perform the moral duties of the Law of Moses. The Apostle Paul exhorts you to "love one another, because whoever loves another has fulfilled the law" (Romans 13:8). He commands you to "honor your father and mother, which is the first command with a promise" (Ephesians 6:2). The apostle John exhorts you to "love others," not as a new commandment but as an old commandment. The apostle James commands you to "fulfill the royal law found in Scripture, 'You shall love your neighbor as yourself.'" He commands you to keep all the commandments of the law, because "he who said 'Do not commit adultery,' also said, 'Do not kill'" (James 2:8-11).

Bible believing Christians have also said that denying the authority of the law of Moses is the antinomian error. Our latest opponents do not hold to this antinomian error, but they set up a worse error: they think their "sincere gospel works" can justify them. I personally think that this is where antinomianism came from in the first place. This viewpoint simply is not true. Jesus never set aside the Law of Moses!

Consider these things. Jesus himself, right from the beginning, established the authority of the Law of Moses. Jesus was the Lord God of Israel who gave the law by angels on Mount Sinai by the hand of Moses, who was the mediator for the Israelites. At that time, the Israelites were the only church. However, now, we who are believing Gentiles are joined as "fellow members of one and the same body" (Ephesians 3:6). To be sure, Jesus has abolished some of the commandments given by Moses – such as the figurative ceremonies and the judicial procedures. However, he has not abolished the authority of the moral law. He has left it in full force. The moral law given by Moses still has the authority to command obedience in moral duties.

The situation is something like this. Sometimes congress repeals laws that it has previously passed. However, the other laws congress has passed are still in force, because those laws have not been repealed. To be sure, God has "repealed" in some sense the ceremonial and the civil laws given under Moses. However, he has not by any means "repealed" the moral laws given by Moses. You are still required to keep them!

I know someone will object, saying that the Ten Commandments and the moral law are "the ministry of death, written and engraved upon stones," and that they are also abolished by Christ (II Corinthians 3:7). However, this passage is being misinterpreted. When Paul says that the law is the "ministry of death" and now done away with, he does not mean that the law no longer commands perfect obedience. Christ himself commands you to be perfect (Matthew 5:48).

This is what Paul means: the law is being abolished as the condition for gaining life and avoiding death. Remember the terms of the old covenant. The Old Covenant promised life to those who kept the law, and a curse to those who break the law (Galatians 3:10-12). Jesus abolished the covenant made with Israel on Mount Sinai, because he is the mediator of the new covenant (Hebrews 8:8, 9, 13). The Ten Commandments do not bind true Christians in this way. They only bind people in this way if they try to be justified by works. The law as a covenant will always stand in force to curse those who seek salvation by their own works (Galatians 3:10). If you want to try to be saved by keeping the Ten Commandments, you will inevitably fall under the curse of the law.

The Ten Commandments are only "abolished" for those who are in Christ by faith (Galatians 2:16, 20; Acts 3:22-25; Acts 15:10-11). What this means is that if you are in Christ, you do not have to perfectly obey the law to be saved. However, you are bound to the Law of Moses in another sense. The Ten Commandments were originally given to a people who were under the covenant of grace made with Abraham. The Ten Commandments gave the people a guideline for their lives. They showed the people what was holy, just, good, and well pleasing to God.

The same is true for you today. You are still required to practice the moral precepts commanded in the Law of Moses. (In fact, much more is expected of you, if you read what Jesus says about the law in the Sermon on the Mount in Matthew 5-7!) However, you must not try to be justified by keeping these laws. If you use them as a rule for your life, and not as the condition of justification, they will not be a "ministration of death" or a "letter that kills" you. To be sure, the perfection required by the Law of Moses makes it impossible to gain life by trying to keep them. No one can possibly succeed. However, the perfection of the law of Moses will have a very important affect upon you: it will give you a guide to the perfection for which you should be aiming. Also, it will reveal all your imperfections. You will be wise not to part with the authority of the Law of Moses. Do not sit around waiting for new teachers to give you another system of morality that is as complete, as excellent, as authentic, and as filled with the wisdom of God as the Law of Moses is!

Fourth, those who try to gain Christ's salvation by sincerely trying to obey all the commands of Christ act contrary to the true way of salvation given by Christ. They are going against the free grace and faith revealed by the gospel. Even though they say they believe in free grace, they really do not believe it.

Why? They are simply acting contrary to the way of salvation by Christ alone. They want to heal themselves, and save themselves, from the power and corruption of sin. They want to gain God's favor by their sincere obedience, before they come to Christ. They make their obedience the foundation of their salvation. They build their enjoyment of Christ on their own obedience, when they should be making Christ himself their only foundation for salvation. If only they could understand that Christ is the only Physician and Savior!

They also want to sanctify themselves, before they are even sure if they truly belong to Christ. In their quest to "establish their own righteousness, they are not submitting themselves to the righteousness of God in Christ" (Romans 10:3-4). Sometimes they call the righteousness of Christ their legal righteousness. By this, they are trying to make room for an evangelical righteousness of their own works that they can use to gain their justification by Christ. However, if you read the Bible, the only evangelical righteousness that the apostle Paul knew was the righteousness of Christ. He called this righteousness "the righteousness of faith apart from the law" (Romans 3:21-22), and a righteousness that was "not from the law" (Philippians 3:9).

# Salvation is Not by Works

Those who set up their own righteousness in this way set aside Christ's salvation even while they pretend to accept it. In reality, Christ profits them nothing. Christ has become of no value to them because they want to be "justified by the law" (Galatians 5:2-4). If you want to be saved by Christ, you must consider yourself a dead, lost sinner, who can have no righteousness for justification but Christ's. You must understand and admit that you have no life, and no ability to do good, until God brings you into union and fellowship with him.

The Bible teaches that there is a complete opposition between salvation by grace and salvation by works. They two are completely irreconcilable. "If it is by grace, then it is no longer by works. Otherwise, grace is no longer grace. But if it is by works, then it is no longer by grace. Otherwise, there is no more work" (Romans 11:6). There is a total opposition between a reward that is given by grace, and a reward that is a debt that is owed to you because you worked for it (Romans 4:6). There is a complete difference between a promise of happiness by the law, and a promise by grace (Romans 4:13,16). God is so jealous of the glory of his free grace that he will not save you by your works. He will only save you by his own working in you, "so that no one can boast" (Ephesians 2:9). God knows that if he saved you by your own works, you would give the glory to yourself. You would not give the glory to his grace and goodness.

People who try to be saved by sincerely obeying the law of Christ are simply acting contrary to the way of salvation by faith. As I have already shown, the faith that is required for salvation is totally contrary to doing good works in order to be saved. This is the only way to maintain the true difference between the law and the gospel. **Believing** is set in opposition to any **working** for salvation. **The law of works** is set in opposition to the **law of faith** (Romans 3:27, 4:5; Ephesians 2:8-9). Therefore, do not consider faith a work of righteousness that will give you the right to gain Christ. Do not think of faith as the hand by which you work to earn Christ as your wages, as you work to earn your food and drink in your vocational life. Faith is only the hand by which you **receive** Christ freely given to you. Faith is the mouth by which you eat and drink of him.

God gives you the right to receive Christ and his salvation by inviting you to freely receive the gospel. The only thing he tells you to do is to lay hold of Christ as a free gift. Then, the glory of your salvation will not be given at all to your faith or works. Rather, the glory will go only to this free grace of God in Christ. Salvation "is by faith, so that it may be by grace" (Romans 4:16).

Christ and his apostles never taught a gospel that requires works as a condition of salvation. Bible verses that are used to try to teach this are simply being misinterpreted. Let me give you a few examples. Paul speaks of "the obedience of faith" as the great design of gospel preaching in Romans 1:5. This is as contrary to the condition of sincere obedience for salvation as the law of faith is contrary to the law of works (Romans 3:27). Paul is referring to an obedience that consists in believing the report of the gospel, as the apostle himself explains in Romans 10:16: "They have not all obeyed the gospel, for Isaiah said, 'Lord, who has believed our message.'"

Faith is credited for righteousness, not because it is a work of righteousness in and of itself. Faith is all about not working. When you have faith, you renounce all confidence in any righteous works that you can do. When you have faith, you trust in him who justifies the ungodly (Romans 4:5).

Romans 2:6-7 is often twisted to teach salvation by works: "Who will render to every man according to his deeds; to those who, by patient continuance in well-doing, seek for glory and honor and immortality, eternal life." Some people say Paul is declaring the terms of the gospel for salvation. In reality, he is declaring the terms of the law, in order to prove that Jews and Gentiles alike are all under sin, and that no one can be justified by the works of the law (as Romans 3:9-10 say).

James 2:24 is also often misunderstood, "You see then, how a man is justified by works and not by faith alone." People say James is more correct than Paul, because James teaches justification by works, whereas Paul teaches justification by faith without works! Bible believing Protestants have always shown that James is speaking not of a true saving faith, but of a dead faith that the devils have. James is not speaking of being justified in terms of "how you get saved before God." Rather, he is speaking of the declaration and manifestation of your justification by the fruits that you have in your life. Authentic saving faith always produces the fruit of good works.

Another text that is often used to teach salvation by works is Revelation 22:14: "Blessed are those who do his commandments, so that they may have a right to the tree of life, and may enter in through the gates into the city." However, the Greek word that is here translated "right" actually means "power" or "privilege" (John 1:12). It means here a rightful possession of the fruit of the tree of life, and not a mere title to it. This passages teaches exactly what Bible believing Christians all generally acknowledge: the title to Christ and his glorious salvation are given totally apart from works, but that good works are the way in which we are to walk once we have received Christ's salvation.

Some people also refer to the fact that the happiness of heaven is called a "reward." They assume from this that good works must earn the happiness of heaven. The happiness of heaven is indeed called a reward, because it is given after people do good works. Also, it rewards good works better than any earthly wages can reward a laborer. However, it is a reward given by grace, not given by obligation (Romans 4:4). It is not wages paid for labor, but it is a free gift (Romans 6:23). "For the wages of sin is death, but the gift of God is eternal life through Jesus Christ our Lord."

There is another very important thing to remember in this discussion of whether salvation is by faith or by works. If you try to try obey God in order to earn the right to gain Christ and his salvation, you will never be able to truly obey God at all by these labors. You may labor earnestly, pray fervently, fast frequently, and obligate yourself to holiness by making many vows. You may urge yourself to keep your vows out of any number of motives: the infinite power, justice, and knowledge of God; the equity and goodness of his commands; the salvation of Christ; everlasting happiness or misery; or any other motive that you might come up with. Yet, you will never gain the true obedience that you are trying to obtain.

Why? Because the obedience you will be offering is not the obedience God requires and approves. You may be able to restrain some of your corruption, and you may be able to bring yourself to many kinds of hypocritical, slavish performance. You may even become very esteemed by people as an eminent saint! However, you will not be able to mortify one corruption, or perform even one duty, in the holy manner God approves.

I am not condemning the kind of life such people might live. I am only condemning the error that gives rise to it. Indeed, many people are, fortunately, inconsistent. Some people preach legalistically, but they pray out of the gospel. I am quite sure that the true frame of their hearts and lives is what they do in their prayers, not what they do in their sermons. Peter himself was inconsistent from time to time. Though Peter outwardly lived as a Jew, inwardly he lived like a Christian (Galatians 2:11-14). I am simply saying that no godly person has ever attained godliness by seeking it out of legalistic, wrong motives.

Let me summarize. There are people in the church who are trying to alter the biblical doctrine of justification by faith alone. Why? They do not think it will encourage obedience. They want to get people to obey God. To do this, they require sincere obedience to the laws of Christ in order for anyone to be saved. However, when they confuse the law and the gospel in this case, they are only making the situation worse. They are causing much division in the church. Their remedy is as bad as they disease they are trying to cure! Their doctrine of salvation by works only causes people to be lawless and disobedient. Why? When you abandon grace, you abandon the only power for godliness there is!

I could say many more things to disprove this doctrine of salvation by works. However, I will only say one thing. This alone will make the proponents of this doctrine angry at themselves that they ever taught it in the first place: salvation by works cannot produce true holiness of life. Why? Because salvation by sincere obedience is salvation according to the terms of the law, not according to the terms of the gospel. Let me now show you that you cannot possibly attain true holiness by the law of works. You cannot gain true holiness apart from the gospel of grace.

First, the way of salvation by the works of the law completely destroys what is required for true holiness of life. I have already shown you from Scripture that you cannot obey God from your heart unless you are convinced that you are reconciled to God by being justified before him. You must be convinced that you are eternally secure, and that God will give you the strength both to will and to do your duty before him. You can only receive these endowments in and through Christ, through union and fellowship with him. Christ himself, with all his fullness, is united to you when you believe in him. Faith is not a work that gains you the right to Christ, but faith is only the means by which you actually receive Christ into your heart. Faith is only the instrument by which you trust in Christ for the salvation that is freely promised you in the gospel.

All of these blessings that come to you in the gospel of Christ are the things in which all of your spiritual life and happiness consist. If you have them, you already have everlasting life. You do not live a holy life in order to gain and earn everlasting life. You already have it. The everlasting life God has given you in the gospel is what enables you to live a holy life.

The terms of the law are completely contrary to this way of living a holy life. The terms of the law place the practice of holiness before life. The terms of the law make holiness the cause of eternal life. "If you live a holy life, you will earn eternal life." Moses describes the terms this way: "The one who does these things shall live by them" (Romans 10:5). By these terms, you must do the holy duties that are commanded before you have any right to receive the life that is promised to you. Under these terms, you also have to live a holy life without any of the gospel blessings I just mentioned, because you have not yet earned the right to have these blessings.

This viewpoint turns the gospel on its head. In this view, the true means of holiness -- the principles of life implanted in you by the gospel -- are no longer the cause of holiness. Rather, they become the effect and the fruit of holiness. Under this view you cannot receive them until you work for them! You can see how under this view you will never be able to expect any true holiness. True holiness is destroyed because everything that produces true holiness has been taken away. This is why the apostle Paul says that the way of salvation by the works of the law makes faith empty, and the promises of no effect. The way of salvation by works frustrates the grace of God, as if Christ died in vain. It makes Christ to be of no value to you, as to those who have fallen from grace (Romans 4:14, Galatians 2:21, 5:2,4).

The doctrine of salvation by sincere obedience to the commands of Christ is just a chip off the old block of all the other versions of salvation by works that have come before it. It is equally destructive, since it cannot enable anyone to truly live a holy life. It destroys the power for holiness because it sets aside the grace of the gospel. It requires you to sincerely obey God before it gives you the means and the power to produce true holiness in your life. Why? Because in this view, true holiness must come before you are justified, before you have assurance of salvation, before you actually enjoy union and fellowship with Christ, and before you receive that new nature that you can only receive only through faith in Christ.

Salvation by works destroys the nature of saving faith by which you actually receive and enjoy Christ and all of his benefits. It knocks

91

salvation out of your hands, because it tells you that you still lack something – just as Christ told the legalistic worker, after all his labor, that he still lacked something (Mark 10:21). It tells you that it is presumptuous to take Christ as your own until you have earned the right to have him by your sincere obedience and by your good life. By this false, conditional faith, Satan keeps many poor souls in slavery. He makes them examine their hearts for years to see if they have performed enough to take Christ as their own. This doctrine is a strong wall that will keep anyone from coming to Christ! It can only be toppled when you come to the knowledge of salvation by grace -- that you do not have to earn Christ by your good works.

This doctrine of salvation by works must be toppled completely if you want to be saved and live a holy life. Even a small amount of works to gain your salvation is too much. Some people view salvation as paying a penny for a Beverly Hills Mansion – just a tiny amount of works for a great blessing. No! Even this penny must go! The strongest man in the world is not able to perform even a penny's worth of good works before God, because he is so sinful. Only the power of the gospel of grace can enable you to do that penny's worth of obedience.

Second, those who seek salvation by the works of the law inevitably act out of their natural state, or their old nature. They live and walk according to the flesh, or the old man. They do not walk according to the new state, where Christ lives in them. Some of them may indeed be true Christians, who have received a new nature in Christ. However, even true Christians still have the flesh, and they may act according to it. When they live by the works of the law, they act according to their fleshly, natural state. When the believing Galatians were seduced back into a legal way of salvation, Paul called them foolish. Having begun in the spirit, they now were trying to be "made perfect in the flesh" (Galatians 3:3). He compared those who desire to be under the law to Abraham's son Ishmael who was born to Hagar the slave woman, to show that those who walk in this way are those who are born according to the flesh, not according to the Spirit (Galatians 4:22,23,29).

The law was first given to Adam in his pure natural state to tell him what he had to do to preserve the happiness he then enjoyed. Ever since then, the flesh, or natural man, is married to the law. The "law has dominion over a man as long as he lives" – that is, until he is dead to his fleshly state through the body of Christ, and becomes "married to him who was raised from the dead" (Romans 7:1-4). As a Christian you are not at all under the law as a covenant of works, because of your new state in Christ. As Paul says, "You are not under the law, but under grace" (Romans 6:14). As he also says, "If you are led by the Spirit, you are not under the law" (Galatians 5:18). No one can possibly attain true godliness by acting according to legal terms. It is impossible to be godly while you are in the flesh, in your natural state.

Inasmuch as you act according to the flesh, you can do nothing but sin. The law is weak because of the flesh. The flesh can never fulfill the law's righteousness (Romans 8:3-4). The law is married to a rebellious flesh. The flesh is in hostility to the law, and the flesh can never be subject to the law (Romans 8:7). The law sues the natural man for that old debt of obedience that he has been utterly unable to pay since the fall of humankind. However, the law gets nothing. The flesh cannot perform one ounce of obedience to the law of God.

Those who say that salvation is gained by sincere obedience to Christ's commands do not take any better course than any other legalists who have gone before them. Their way is the same as that of the Galatians, who tried to become perfect in the flesh – not by perfect obedience, but by sincere obedience. Their attempts to gain Christ by their sincere obedience show they are not acting as people who are in Christ. They are acting as people who consider themselves outside of Christ. That is why they are seeking to gain him. Sincere obedience is as impossible to attain as perfect obedience if you act according to your dead natural state.

Third, just as the law shows you that you have no strength in your natural state, the law also gives you no strength to fulfill its own commands. This is exactly what Paul says in Galatians 3:21: "If there had been a law given that could have given life, truly righteousness would have been given by the law." The law does not promise you life until you totally obey all that the law requires of you. "The man who does these things shall live by them" (Romans 10:5). The law is rightly called a "voice of words" (Hebrews 12:19), because its high and lofty words are not accompanied by any life-giving power.

The doctrine of life and salvation by sincere obedience is no better. It requires you to obey the law before it allows you to have any life or salvation in Christ. Can you expect the strength to be able to obey the law sincerely if you follow a doctrine that does not promise to give you that strength? The law gives you nothing! The gospel, however, has a much more giving nature. The gospel promises that "God will pour out his

Spirit upon all flesh" (Acts 2:17). The gospel promises that God "will put his laws into your mind, and write them in your heart" (Hebrews 8:10). The gospel promises that God "will cause you to walk in his statutes, so that you will keep his judgments, and do them" (Ezekiel 36:27).

This word of God's grace does not require holiness of you as a condition to gain life. Rather, it promises holiness to you as a free gift. It is the only doctrine that "is able to build you up, and to give you an inheritance among those who are sanctified" (Acts 20:32). Since God wants to bring you to holiness by believing a doctrine, you may expect that God will work in you according to the nature of the doctrine that you believe.

Fourth, now that humans have fallen and have become totally corrupt, the way of gaining life and happiness by good works no longer makes any sense. The condition of life by good works was proper to preserve life before the fall. At that time, humans were able to keep the law. Now, however, it is different. The law that commands a man to live a holy life cannot restore a man who is dead in sin. It is just like telling a paralyzed man, "Rise and walk, and then you will be whole and able to walk." We sometimes joke with a child who has fallen to the ground, "Come here, and I will help you up," and the child can actually do it. However, if we say this to someone who is paralyzed on his bed, we would be guilty of mocking and insulting this poor, afflicted person.

Those who have been humbled and who have come to understand their original sin and natural deadness know they must first live by the Spirit before they can live a holy life (Galatians 5:25). They will ask, "How will we have strength to perform the duty the law requires?" If you tell them to trust in God and Christ, you will help them. They understand they are as unable to bring their hearts to obey God as a dead man is able to raise himself out of the grave.

Take another example. The principle of the doctrine of salvation by works is, "You must love God first, and if you do that, God will love you." What does the Scripture say? Something quite different: "We love God, because he loved us first" (I John 4:19). If God makes his love for you conditional, your love to him will not be an absolute love. Your life will be equally conditional. It may actually turn to a hatred of God because you know that you cannot keep the condition.

Fifth, the law simply does not heal your sinful corruption. The law actually stirs up sinful inclinations and actions in those who seek salvation according to the works of the law. Why does this happen? Your natural corruption is stirred up, and rages all the more, when the holy and just law of God is set in opposition to it. The fault, of course, is not in the law, but in your own heart.

If you do not find this to be true by your own experience, then believe the apostle Paul who plainly teaches this from his own experience (Romans 7:5,14). Paul says that for people who are still in the flesh, the law sets sin in motion. The commandments of the law actually give the occasion for sin. The command "You shall not covet" produced in Paul all kinds of covetousness. The law deceived him, killed him, and he became exceedingly sinful. Without the law he was alive, and sin was dead. However, when the commandment came, sin revived, and he died. He shows the reason for this irreconcilable hostility between his sinful nature and the law: "The law is spiritual, but I am fleshly, sold under sin."

The doctrine of salvation by sincere obedience to the law will have the same effect. The corrupt human nature is completely opposed to sincere obedience, let alone perfect obedience. If you make sincere obedience the condition of your salvation, sin will spring to life. Sin will become ever more exceedingly sinful – both in inclination and in action. If you place legalistic doctrines upon the natural, unredeemed man, you will get exactly what Proverbs 9:8 says: "Do not reprove a mocker, or he will hate you." If you rebuke a mocker, you will simply enrage him all the more.

This is the way it is with the natural man in spiritual things, ever since he fell out of his right mind by the sin of Adam. Experience shows that even though men are addicted to the principle of salvation by works, multitudes of them hate everyone who preaches and professes true holiness. Those who preach true holiness simply torment the consciences of those who live by salvation by works. They try to shelter themselves by being ignorant of the law. They reason that the less they know, the less they will have to answer for before God. Therefore, they do not want the true word of God prophesied or preached to them (Isaiah 30:10). Such people have so prevailed throughout the world, that most people do not know what true holiness really is. Therefore, the only way they can learn the nature of true holiness is through the divine revelation of the Scriptures.

# The Gospel Mystery of Sanctification

You will find how prone legalistic teachers are to corrupting the true sense of the law of God. They want to leave loopholes for their own sin. This is what the scribes and Pharisees did in the time of Jesus. Jesus had to "rescue" the law from these corrupt, "dumbed-down" interpretations of the law in his Sermon on the Mount (Matthew 5-7). No one tries to understand the purity and perfection of the law more than those who seek salvation and holiness through the free grace of God in Christ, apart from any legal works. Those who try to be saved by their sincere obedience will inevitably reduce the perfection actually required by the law of God. They have to reduce the requirements of the law so much that the nature of true obedience is lost altogether.

Those who live by salvation by works will reduce true obedience to something like this: a willingness to be saved according to Christ's terms, a consent that Christ should be their lord, or a resolution to obey his commandments without any real practice of holiness. Many actually think these things are enough to pass for the sincere obedience that will gain and maintain salvation. If they do these things, they think, they will never be considered breakers of the gospel covenant. All they are required to do, they think, is to do their best to obey Christ's commands – even though they cannot in fact do anything that is truly good.

Those who have more zeal for earning their salvation by their works will spend more time in superstitious practices. Superstition is more suitable to their fleshly nature than the spiritual commands of God and Christ. This is why so many pagan superstitions have arisen in the world. During the Reformation, much superstition was overthrown by the true doctrine of salvation by faith alone. However, many people continue to try to quiet their guilty consciences by these practices. They labor earnestly, and even ruin their bodies with fasting, trying to kill their lusts. However, their lusts are as strong as ever. These people show how much they hate the law of God by the way they grumble, whine, and complain at the law – as if the law of God were a vicious taskmaster. All they are doing is trying to restrain their external behavior through slavish fear. There is no real obedience here.

Once these people come to see the spiritual nature of the law, they will understand that God will not accept their slavish service as sincere obedience. Then, they will fall into despair for their salvation. They will see they have failed in their best attempts to keep the law and earn God's favor. They will see how much their hearts swell up in anger and hatred of the law, and even against God who has made it so hard for them to be saved by their works. They will know they will be eternally condemned for their failures to live up to God's law. This will fill them with blasphemous thoughts against God and Christ, and they can hardly refrain from blaspheming them with their tongues. When they are brought to this horrible state of mind, if God does not graciously reveal to them the way of salvation by free grace through faith alone, they will try to sear their consciences so they no longer feel the horror of their sin. They will abandon any religion that continues to torment their consciences as the gospel does. Or, if they cannot sear their consciences, some will be convinced by Satan to kill themselves rather than to live any longer in hatred and blasphemy of God, and in the continual horror of their consciences.

This is the awful effect of legalistic doctrine upon fleshly hearts. The doctrine of salvation by works stirs up and enrages the sleeping lion of your sinful corruption. It does not kill off your corruption in any way. This is the sad experience of everyone who has tried to be saved by their works. The doctrine of salvation by sincere obedience may well be ranked among the worst Antinomian errors. It will not help anyone live a holy life. I have also found by my own experience the truth that the way to be freed from the mastery and dominion of sin is "not to be under the law, but under grace" (Romans 6:14).

Sixth, the way of salvation by works was totally ruined by the curse that was announced against the first Adam's sin. The doctrine of salvation by works cannot give you any life; it will only put you to death. The law that requires both sincere and perfect obedience to God in all things was made known to Adam when he was first created. This is the way he could have kept the happy life God had given him. The law would have continued to be the means of blessing if Adam had not sinned against God by eating the forbidden fruit. When Adam brought himself and his descendants under the terrible sentence, "You shall surely die" (Genesis 2:17), the blessing was turned into a curse.

Previously, the knowledge of God and his law produced continuing life, as long as Adam obeyed. However, once he had sinned, the knowledge of God and his law was turned a different way: it now produced death – both the death of the soul in sin, and the death of the body. Therefore, it quickly moved Adam to hide himself from God as if from an enemy. It was as if God was now saying, "All the light and knowledge that you have will not be able to continue your life, or restore it. It will rather end in your death."

97

# The Gospel Mystery of Sanctification

As long as you continue in your natural state, under the first Adam's guilt and curse, the knowledge of God, his character, and his law will be a curse to you. Human beings no longer rightly use their knowledge of God and his law; they abuse it by trying to earn salvation by their own works. God has now provided salvation to you in a way that is completely contrary to the way of this first covenant of life, which said, "Obey and be blessed, disobey and be cursed." God now gives salvation to you in a way that seems totally foolish to the natural man.

God wants to abolish the way of living by your own works, or by any wisdom or knowledge that you or any other natural man can attain to. "For it is written, 'I will destroy the wisdom of the wise, and will bring to nothing the understanding of the intelligent.' Has not God made foolish the wisdom of this world? For, since in the wisdom of God, the world in its wisdom did not know God, it pleased God, by the foolishness of preaching to save those who believe" (I Corinthians 1:19-21). No truth you can know by the light of nature alone can be powerful enough to produce holiness in you. The power of the gospel is abused when you give it up for the way of a legalistic salvation by works.

Seventh, God never gave the Law to Moses for anyone to gain salvation or holiness by sincerely or perfectly obeying it. If, hypothetically, God ever did give a way of salvation through the works of the law, it would have consisted in having to obey the Law of Moses.

Remember the context in which the Law of Moses was given. God gave the Law of Moses to the church at that time to be a rule of living as well as a covenant. However, there was another covenant given before that time, to Abraham, Isaac, and Jacob. It was a covenant of grace, which promised blessing freely through Christ, the promised seed. This was the only way they could be saved, the covenant of grace declared. It was only later that the covenant of law was added, so they would see their sinfulness and their subjection to death and wrath. God wanted them to see that could not gain life or holiness by their own works. The purpose of this covenant of works was to force them to trust only in the free promise of grace for their salvation. The covenant of works was also given so that the spirit of bondage might restrain sin, until the coming of the promised seed, Jesus Christ, and the more plentiful outpouring of the sanctifying Spirit by Christ. This is what the apostle Paul teaches in Galatians 3:15-24, Romans 5:20-21, and Romans 10:3-4.

# Salvation is Not by Works

No Israelite in the Old Testament was ever saved by the Sinai Covenant. None of them ever attained true holiness by it. Some of them sincerely obeyed the law from time to time, although never perfectly. However, those who did were first justified by faith. They had become partakers of life and holiness by virtue of the better covenant made with Abraham, Isaac, and Jacob. That covenant was the same in essence as the new covenant established by the blood of Christ. If it were not for that better covenant of grace, the old Sinai covenant would have led them to sin, misery, despair, and destruction. It would have given them no happiness at all! In itself, the old Sinai Covenant was a "letter that kills, a ministry of death and condemnation." Therefore, it is now abolished by God (II Corinthians 3:6-11).

Praise God for delivering his church from this yoke of bondage by the blood of Christ! Condemn the actions of those who wish to lay upon you a more grievous and terrible yoke, by turning the new covenant of grace into a covenant of sincere works. Those who do this leave you no better covenant than the Israelites had. Such a covenant of works cannot relieve you at all!

The Gospel Mystery of Sanctification

# Chapter 7

**Principle Number 7**

**Do not think that your heart and life have to be changed from sin to holiness in any measure before you are allowed to trust in Christ for salvation.**

You are so naturally prone to base your salvation on your own works! Even if you do not try to earn your salvation by your works, you will at least try to make your works the things that prepare you to receive Christ and his salvation by faith. People can easily be deceived into thinking that this viewpoint is compatible with the doctrine of salvation by free grace. Here is a summary of what they say:

> "The only things your works do is put you in a right posture to receive the gift of God. If you were to go to meet with the President to receive a free gift, you would have good manners and proper respect. You would clean up and put on good clothes – just as Joseph did when he came out of the dungeon to visit Pharoah. How disrespectful it would be to the justice and holiness of God and Christ – what an indignity it would be – if you presumed to approach his presence covered with the awful filth of your sins. How dare you approach the majestic presence of God covered with wounds that are not bound up and cleaned! How could you even attempt to receive the Most Holy One into the abominably filthy chamber of your sinful heart before it is cleaned up and reformed. This is certainly what is being taught by the parable of the man who was bound hand and foot, and cast into the utter darkness, for coming to the royal wedding without a wedding garment (Matthew 22:11-13). This is a warning against all such presumption before God."

Do you see what they are saying? Your works do not save you, but your works make you fit and worthy to receive Christ. This view has terrible results: many will clearly see, with horror, the abominable filth of their own hearts. However, they will not come immediately to Christ because they will think they are not worthy to come to Christ. The only way they will come to Christ is if God teaches them to by the powerful illumination of his Spirit. Many do not believe the gospel for salvation because they think they are not yet prepared and qualified for it. For the same reason, many weak believers delay coming to the Lord's Supper for many years – some of them for as long as they live in this world. They would be as likely to delay their baptism for that long, if they had not been baptized as infants!

Against all of these ideas, consider the following.

First, this error ruins salvation and holy living in the same way that I discussed in chapter six. It can be overthrown with the same reasons that I gave in that chapter. Whether you think that holiness is the condition you need to gain salvation through Christ, or whether holiness is only a condition that qualifies you to receive Christ, it is the same thing: you are still brought under the legal terms of first having to keep the law in order to live. As a result, you are equally powerless to live a holy life. Why? Because you will try to live a holy life without having union and fellowship with Christ.

Remember, only union with Christ can empower you to live a holy life. You must have a relationship with him if you want to be sanctified. If you are not in union with Christ, you will still be just as accursed under your natural state. Your sinful corruption will be stirred up rather than put to death. If you are left in this state, you will never be prepared to receive Christ! If you try to prepare your way to Christ by living a holy life, you will simply be filling your life with stumbling blocks and deep pits, which will forever hinder your soul from attaining salvation. You will never be able to make yourself good enough to properly receive Christ.

Second, the word of God and the gospel never require you to change your heart from sin to holiness before you are allowed to receive Christ and his salvation by faith. Christ wants the vilest, most wretched sinners to come to him for salvation immediately. Christ never tells sinners to delay by preparing themselves for him. When the wicked jailer inquired, "What must I do to be saved?" Paul told him to immediately believe in Christ, with the promise that if he did so "you will be saved." He did, and right away, he and his whole house were baptized (Acts 16:30-33). Paul did not tell him that he must reform his heart and life first – even though he was in a very nasty pickle at the time, having just recently fastened Paul and Silas in stocks, and having attempted to kill himself!

There are other examples in the Bible. The three thousand Jews who were converted to Christ by Peter's preaching and added that same day to the church by baptism (Acts 2:41) had just recently defiled themselves with the murder of Christ himself! Yet, they were not told to take time to prepare themselves to receive Christ, they were told to receive Christ! Christ commands his servants to go out quickly into the streets and lanes of the city, and to bring into his feast the poor, the hurting, the crippled, and the blind. Indeed, they are to go out to the highways and compel them to come in. He does not tell them to wait until they had cleaned up their sores, taken off their filthy rags, and purified themselves from their swarms of lice.

Christ wants you to believe in him who justifies the ungodly; he does not require you to be godly before you believe (Romans 4:5). Jesus came as a Physician for the sick. He does not expect them to recover their health before they come to him (Matthew 9:12). The vilest sinners are properly qualified and prepared for the gospel's design, which is to show forth the exceeding riches of grace when God pardons their sins and saves them freely (Ephesians 2:5-7). This is the reason the Law of Moses was given, that the "transgression might abound; that where sin abounded, grace might abound all the more" (Romans 5:20).

Jesus loved you in your most disgusting, sinful corruption, and he died for you. He will receive you when you come to him for the salvation that he has purchased for you. Jesus has given full satisfaction to the justice of God for sinners, so that they might have salvation, righteousness, and holiness through fellowship with him by faith. It is no insult to Christ, it is no slighting of God's justice and holiness, to come to Christ while you are a corrupt sinner. The real insult to Christ is when you condemn the fullness of his grace and merit by trying to make yourself righteous and holy before you receive him! You condemn the justice and holiness of God when you try to improve yourself before you receive the righteousness and holiness that can only come through faith in Christ. Jesus did not hesitate to touch a leprous man, and he condescended to wash the feet of his disciples. Jesus did not expect the leper to heal himself before he touched him. Jesus did not expect the disciples to be washed and perfumed before he washed their feet!

Third, if you receive Christ with a sincere faith, you will never lack a wedding garment to adorn you in the sight of God. Faith itself is very precious in the sight of God, and it is most holy (II Peter 1:1, Jude 20). God loves faith, because faith gives the glory of your salvation only to the free grace of God in Christ. When you have faith, you renounce all dependence upon anything you can do to gain Christ or to make yourself acceptable to him. When you have faith, you love Christ as a Savior. You hunger and thirst for his salvation. Faith is the mouth by which your soul feeds hungrily on Jesus. What better wedding garment can sinners bring to God than their faith! God's whole purpose is to show forth the abundant riches of his glorious grace in his great wedding feast!

The father himself loves his people, because they love Christ, and they believe that he came from God (John 16:27). Here is why faith is so important: when you have faith, you understand that there is no work you can do to make you acceptable in the sight of God. Faith is not your wedding garment itself. Faith "buys" Christ, "the white garment, so you may be clothed, and so the shame of your nakedness might not appear" (Revelation 3:18). When you have faith, you love and desire holiness. However, when you have faith, you also abandon any thought of trying to practice holiness before you come to Christ for a new, holy nature. When you have faith, you put on Christ himself, and in him everything that pertains to life and godliness. Every true believer is clothed with the sun (Revelation 12:1), indeed with the "sun of righteousness," the Lord Jesus. Jesus is pleased to be both your wedding garment and your feast, and all your spiritual and eternal happiness.

What happens if you understand your own sinfulness, but you still feel that you have no right to trust in Christ until you clean up your life? What if you still think you have to change your life from sin to holiness, before you can come to Christ? If you do, I want you to consider some things. There are several things you may think you need to have in order to believe in and receive Christ. However, I want to show you that all of these things are fruits and results of faith. In reality, you cannot possibly have them before you trust in Christ for salvation, by faith.

First, you might think that it is necessary for you to repent before you believe on Christ for your salvation, because repentance is absolutely necessary for salvation. "Unless you repent you shall all likewise perish" (Luke 13:3). Christ also placed the duty of repentance before faith when he said "Repent and believe the gospel" (Mark 1:15).

There is something you must understand. Christ requires repentance first as the goal to be aimed at, and then faith next because faith is the only way you can attain true repentance. Yes, you must have repentance and faith. However, it is absolutely impossible to have repentance unless you have faith! After all, what is repentance? Repentance is turning in your heart from sin to God and to his service. And what way is there to turn to God except through Christ, who is "the way, the truth and the life, without whom no one can come to the father?" (John 14:6). What way is there of coming to Christ, except by faith?

If you want to turn to God in the right way, you must first come to Christ by faith, and faith must come before repentance. Faith is the instrument given by God so you can have repentance in the first place. Repentance is indeed a duty that sinners naturally owe to God. However, the great question is, How will sinners be able to repent? This question is resolved only by the gospel of Christ, "Repent and believe." The way to repent is to begin by believing the Gospel. Therefore the great doctrine of John, in his baptism of repentance, was that they "should believe on him that should come after him," that is, on Christ Jesus (Acts 19:4).

Second, you know that regeneration is necessary for salvation (John 3:3). Therefore you may try to produce regeneration in yourself before you trust in Christ for your salvation. However, consider what regeneration is. Regeneration occurs when you receive the new birth, and you become a new creation in Christ (I Corinthians 4:15, Ephesians 2:10). In Christ you are a partaker of a divine nature, far different than the nature you received from the first Adam. Faith is the grace that unites you to Christ, so that Christ lives in you, and you in him. Therefore, faith is the first grace regeneration produces in you, and faith is what produces all the rest. When you truly believe, you are regenerated, and not until then. Those who receive Christ by believing, and those only, are "the sons of God, which are born not of blood, nor of the will of the flesh, nor of the will of man, but of God" (John 1:12-13).

Third, you may think that it is necessary for you to receive Christ as your Lord and Lawgiver, by sincerely submitting to his lordship and resolving to obey his law, before you can receive Christ as your Savior. This is one of major tenets of many new teachers: they say that saving faith consists in receiving Christ as Lord. If you do not do this, your faith is just gross presumption. They teach that Christ will not give his salvation to you unless you first yield yourself to his kingly authority. Jesus calls people his enemies, because they did not want him to reign over them, and he requires that they be brought before him and killed (Luke 19:27). I certainly agree that Christ will only save those who resign themselves to obeying his royal position and his laws. However, they are not brought to this holy resignation, or to any sincere purpose or resolution of obedience, before they receive his salvation. They are brought to this place by receiving salvation.

# The Gospel Mystery of Sanctification

There are many people who during their earthly lives never considered themselves dead in sin. However, when they are in danger, or on their deathbeds, or when they want to take the Lord's Supper, they resolve universal obedience to God! At those times they want to make their peace with God and receive Christ and his salvation! However, all resolutions like this are empty and hypocritical. They are broken sooner than they are made!

Those who truly know the evil of their own hearts find that their mind is hostile to the law of God and Christ, and it cannot be subject to it (Romans 8:7). They know it would be easier for them to move a mountain than it would be for them to obey Christ without having a new heart. They know a new heart alone can enable them both to will and to do anything that is acceptable to God. Obviously, you are still obligated to obey Christ's laws, even if Christ had never come into the world to save you. However, Christ knew that you could never do anything good until he first saved you. He knew you would never obey him as a Lawgiver until you receive him as a Savior.

Jesus is a saving Lord. Trust in him first to save you from the guilt and power of sin. Trust in him to save you from the dominion of Satan. Trust in him to give you a new spiritual frame of mind. Then, and not until then, the love of Christ will compel you to give yourself "to live for him who died for you" (II Corinthians 5:14). Then, you will truly be able to say, with a sincere resolution, "Oh Lord, I truly am your servant. I am your servant, and the son of your maidservant. You have loosed my chains" (Psalm 116:16).

Fourth, you may think that some good works are necessary before you can safely trust in Christ for the forgiveness of your sins. After all, Jesus teaches that if you do not forgive others their sins, neither will your heavenly Father forgive your sins. He directs you to pray, "Forgive us our sins, as we forgive those who sin against us" (Matthew 6:12, 15). Also, restitution was also to be made when you wrongfully got something from someone else, before the sacramental atonement could be made by the sin-offering (Leviticus 6:5-7).

I will answer this objection this way. To be sure, forgiving others and making restitution according to your means are very closely joined with the forgiveness of your sins. They are very necessary to prepare you for prayer, and for sacramental applications of pardoning grace to yourself. When you have true faith, you will have these fruits. You cannot pray, or partake of the sacraments, in faith, without them. However, if you try to do either of these before you trust in Christ for your forgiveness and salvation, you will do them slavishly and hypocritically. You will not do them in a manner that is holy and acceptable to God. Your forgiving others will not be accompanied by any hearty love for them as for yourself, for the sake of God. Your restitution will only be a forced act – like Pharaoh when he let the Israelites go, or like Judas when he gave back the thirty pieces of silver compelled by a spirit of terror. When you no longer feel the terror that moved you to act in the first place, you will take back your forgiveness, and you will wrong others again – just as Pharaoh tried to bring the Israelites back into bondage after he had let them go (Exodus 14:5).

If you want to forgive others from your heart, you must first, by faith in Christ, understand the love and mercy of God towards you yourself. Only then will you be able to "be kind, tender-hearted, forgiving one another, just as God for Christ's sake forgave you" (Ephesians 4:32). Zaccheus was ready to make restitution because he came to understand and experience Christ's love for him. When he joyfully received Christ into his house, he was showing that he already had true faith in his heart.

Fifth, I will mention several other supposed qualifications you may think you must have in order to be properly prepared for Christ and for his salvation. Many people labor anxiously for a long time trying to prepare themselves with these things. However, they can never get there, and they lie down in sorrow and depression. They do not dare apply the consolation of the grace of God in Christ to their wounded consciences. "Oh you afflicted, tossed with tempests, and not comforted," what good qualifications do you want to have, so you will lay hold of Christ for his salvation?

You will likely answer, in bitterness of soul, "Oh, let me first have some love to God, and some godliness, in my heart. Let me have some freedom from the way my heart so often rebels against God and his service. Let me have some good thoughts of God, his justice, mercy, holiness, that I may be able to defend him even though he condemns me. Let me not be filled any longer with my grumbling against him. Let my raging lust be quieted, and let the filthy chamber of my heart be cleaned up. Let me have some holy reverence and fear of God, not simply a tormenting horror of God. Let me be more impressed with the wrath of God, let me not be so heedless of him. I want to be more humbled for sin. I want to loathe sin, be ashamed of it, and be sorry for it with a godly sorrow – not merely because of the punishment of sin, but because it grieves the Holy Spirit of God. I want to be able to willingly confess my sins. I want to pour out my soul to the Lord in passionate prayer for forgiveness. I want to praise and glorify him from my heart. I do not want to be just a lifeless stone in the duty of prayer."

Oh, you poor distressed soul, are these the things you desire? The best thing I can tell you to comfort you in your pain is that these things are good, but your desires are not well-timed! You will never be able to bring your heart and life to these things while you are still in your natural state – under the guilt of sin, and under the apprehension of God's wrath. You cannot receive them before you have received the atonement of Christ. You cannot have them without the new spiritual life that comes through Christ, through faith in his name. You are only stirring up your corruption, and hardening your heart. You are making your wounds hurt even more, because of your foolishness. These good qualifications and actions can only come into your life once you have faith in Christ. You cannot possibly have any of them before you trust in Christ for your salvation.

Consider the order in which you have to have these things. You have to have faith in order to love the salvation of God. Have faith first, and your apprehension of God's love for your soul will sweetly draw and compel you to love God and his service. "We love him because he first loved us" (I John 4:19). You cannot love God before you understand his love for you. You must perceive his love if you are going to love him. If you look upon God as someone who is against you, who hates you, and who condemns you, your own innate self-love will breed hatred and rebellion against him. The love that is the end of the law must flow from an unhypocritical faith (I Timothy 1:5).

If you have more hatred in you than you have love, how can you expect to think good thoughts of God? You will only be able to grumble against him and blaspheme him. Ill-will never thinks or speaks well. The first right and holy thoughts you can have of God are thoughts of his grace and mercy to your soul in Christ. And, these thoughts can only come by the grace of faith. Get these thoughts first by believing in Christ, and they will produce in you love to God. You will think all kinds of good thoughts about him! You will also be freed from the grumbling and blasphemy, "for love thinks no evil" (I Corinthians 13:5). You will see God as just and merciful, and you will extend his grace to others. You will be able to think well of his holiness, and of his decrees, which many cannot endure to hear of.

# Do Not Wait to Believe in Christ

The way to get rid of raging lusts is by faith, which purifies the heart and works powerfully through love (Acts 15:9, Galatians 5:6). Your soul must come to take pleasure in God and Christ by faith, or else it will just go after fleshly and worldly pleasures. The more you strive against your lusts without faith, the more your lusts will be stirred up – even though you might be able to work hard enough to restrain yourself from fulfilling your lusts. Beg God to give you a holy fear of him, with the fear of coming short of the promised rest through unbelief (Hebrews 4:1). Such a fear is an ingredient of faith, and it will produce in you a reverential and a childlike fear of God and his goodness (Hebrews 12:28, Hosea 3:5).

If you want to be free from carelessness, and from slighting the wrath of God, you must first believe and not despair. People grow careless by despairing. For their own peace of mind, they minimize the evil they have no hope of preventing in their lives. It is just as the proverb says, "Let us eat and drink, for tomorrow we die" (I Corinthians 15:32).

True humility for sin is either a part of faith or a fruit of faith. When you believe, "you remember your own evil ways and doings, that were not good, and you loathe yourself in your own sight for all your abominations" (Ezekiel 36:31). You will also then willingly renounce your own righteousness, and "consider it rubbish, that you may gain Christ by faith" (Philippians 3:7-8). Beggars will make the most of all their filthy rags until they are given better clothes. Cripples will not cast away their crutches until they have a better support to lean on.

Godly sorrow for sin is produced in you by believing the forgiving grace of God. Experience shows that a stubborn criminal will come to tears sooner from a pardon than from fear of prison. In this way the sinful woman was brought to wash Christ's feet with her tears (Luke 7:37-38). You are not likely to be sorry for grieving God with your sins while you consider him an enemy. You will never grieve over your sin if you only see God as one who takes great pleasure in your everlasting destruction.

You have to believe in God's forgiving and accepting grace if you are ever going to sincerely confess your sins. The people freely confessed their sins when they were baptized by John in the Jordan, for the forgiveness of sin (Mark 1:4-5). The confession of people in despair is forced, like the forced confessions and outcries of criminals who are being tortured on the rack. A pardon will much sooner open your mouth to a real confession of sin than the words, "Confess or be hanged," or "Confess or be condemned." If you want to freely confess your sins, first believe the gospel!  Believe that "God is faithful and just to forgive your sins" through Christ (I John 1:9).

If you want to pray to God, or praise him from your heart, you must first believe that God will hear you, and give you what is best for you for Christ's sake (John 16:23-24).  Otherwise, your praying will be only from the teeth outward.  For, "how shall they call upon him in whom they have not believed?" (Romans 10:14).  You must first come to Christ, the altar, by faith, that "by him, you may offer the sacrifice of praise to God continually" (Hebrews 13:10,15).

Finally, to pass from these specific instances to the general principle laid down in this chapter.  If you ask, "What shall we do that we may do the works of God," or get any saving qualifications?  I must direct you to faith, the work of works.  And, I must point you to Jesus, who is the one who saves you before you have any good qualifications at all.  "This is the work of God, that you believe on the one he has sent" (John 6:28-29).

# Chapter 8

### Principle Number 8

**Make sure that you seek holiness of heart and life in its proper time. You can only live a holy life after you have come into union with Christ, have been justified, and have received the Holy Spirit. Once you have received these blessings, seek holiness by faith with all your might. It is a crucial part of your salvation.**

I have been telling you that God calls you to live a holy life, now that you have come to faith in Christ. What do I mean by holiness? By holiness I mean that your whole life is conformed to all of God's moral law. Indeed, even if the gospel of salvation through Christ never existed, you would still be obligated to obey God's law. Now, if you are going to live a holy life, there are three things you must know and consider:

First, you must know where God has placed holy living in the mystery of your salvation. If you are a wise Christian, you will seek holiness of life only in the order God has given. God is certainly a God of order. You can observe that in the world, where all of his creatures must follow his order of things for their worldly needs. So it is the case in spiritual things: "God has made an everlasting covenant, ordered in all things, and sure" (II Samuel 23:5). Several of the benefits of our salvation are given to us all at the same time. However, each one of them depends upon another in order – just as the links of a golden chain depend upon one another in order.

I have already said a great deal about how God enables you to keep his moral law. In short, he unites you to Christ by faith, as a branch on the vine, that you might bring forth much fruit (John 15:4-5). He first cleanses your conscience from dead works by justification, that you may serve the living God (Hebrews 9:14). He makes you to live in the Spirit, and then to walk in the Spirit (Galatians 5:25). This is the gospel's order. The gospel is the power of God for salvation. In the gospel, God first makes you alive, and then he enables you to obey him. The Gospel says, "You live. Now do this."

The law, of course, gives you quite another method to attain holiness in your life. The law says, "Do this and you will live." The law tells you that you must first keep its commands. If you do, you will be justified and live. However, since you cannot keep the law's commands, the law becomes a letter that kills you.

The gospel gives you a much better order of things if you want to live a holy life! You have many more advantages and blessings from the gospel. You know all the things God has done for you in Christ – he has loved you, has forgiven your sins, has received you into his favor, and has given you the Spirit of adoption. God has given you the hope of his glory, freely, through Christ, to draw you to love God, because he has so dearly loved you. He also draws you to love others for his sake, and to obey all his commands out of joyful love for him from your heart. You also have the help of the Spirit of God, who gives you the desire to obey, and who enables you to obey – in the face of your own sinfulness and the temptations of Satan. Through the gospel, you have both the wind and the tide pushing you forward in your attempt to live a holy life.

However, if you rush out and try to keep the law, without having Christ's righteousness and Christ's Spirit in you, you will have both the wind and the tide against you! Your guilty conscience, and your dead corrupt nature, will frustrate and defeat all your attempts to love and serve God. The only thing you will do in this case is stir up your sinful lusts. You will not stir yourself up to true obedience. At best, you will attain the hypocritical performance of a slave.

Oh how I wish that people would see the place that holy living fits into the mystery of salvation! How I wish people would seek holiness only after they have already found the grace of the gospel! Many people fail in their eager attempts to attain godliness. Then, after they have labored for a long time in vain, God separates them from himself to their everlasting destruction – just he separated Uzzah from himself for temporal destruction – because "they did not seek him after the due order" (I Chronicles 13:10).

Second, you must understand that holiness is an absolutely necessary part of the salvation that you have received through faith in Christ. Some people are so steeped in a legalistic covenant of works, they accuse us of saying that good works have no place in salvation. They accuse us of this because we do not make good works the condition that earns us a relationship with Christ, and we do not make good works the actions that prepare us to receive Christ by faith.

Seek Holiness through Union with Christ

Other people abuse the doctrine of salvation by grace through faith. When they are taught from the Scriptures that salvation is by faith, without works, they disregard obedience to the law. They seem to think that obedience to the law is not necessary! They reason that if they totally neglect obedience, God will still save them. Indeed, some people fall so deeply into the Antinomian error, they think that their freedom from the law through Christ's blood means they can disobey the law whenever they want to.

Why do people continually fall into these two extremes, into the dual errors of legalism and lawlessness? Why do some people think they must obey the law to earn heaven? And why do other people think that since they are saved by grace, they do not have to keep the law at all? One of the reasons for this is that people misunderstand the word "salvation." People often think that salvation refers only to being delivered from hell, and being given eternal happiness and glory in heaven. In other words, salvation does not refer to anything that happens to you in this life. As a result, people conclude that good works have no place in the whole scheme of salvation.

The problem with this view is that this is too limited an understanding of "salvation." Salvation certainly does include your state of heavenly glory. However, it means much more than that. "Salvation" refers to all the freedom you have from your corrupt natural state, and all of those holy, blessed gifts that you receive from Christ your Savior – in both this world and the next.

When you understand "salvation" in this way, you can see how much of your salvation consists of benefits that you experience in this life. Justification, the gift of the Spirit to live in you, the privilege of adoption – these are all parts of your salvation that you enjoy now. Holiness – having your heart and life conformed to the law of God – is also a very necessary part of your salvation in this life. Holiness is the "fruit of righteousness with which you are filled by Jesus Christ."

Christ saved you from your sinful uncleanness in this life, through "the washing of regeneration, and renewing by the Holy Spirit" (Ezekiel 36:29, Titus 3:5), as well as from hell in the life hereafter. Christ was called Jesus, that is, a Savior, because "he saved his people from their sins" (Matthew 1:21). Being delivered from your sins is a part of your salvation. This deliverance is begun in this life through justification and sanctification, and it is perfected in the life to come through glorification.

113

# The Gospel Mystery of Sanctification

Look at the other things God has done for you in Christ. They also are part of your salvation. God has made you alive, to live to God, when you were by nature dead in trespasses and sins. He has restored his image of holiness and righteousness in you – which you lost at the fall. He has freed you from evil slavery to Satan and your own lusts, and made you a servant of God. God has given you his Spirit, and now he is enabling you to walk by the Spirit. He is empowering you to bring forth the fruits of the Spirit. What God has done for you is what empowers you to be holy in your heart and life.

You can see from all these things that holiness in this life is an absolutely necessary part of your salvation. Now, make sure you do not misunderstand this. Holiness is not a means to an end – your good works do not save you. Rather, holiness is part of the end itself – you were saved in order to do good works, "which God prepared in advance that you should walk in them" (Ephesians 2:10). Good works do not achieve salvation. Good works are the fruits and results of saving faith.

To be sure, one part of salvation is being delivered by Christ from the bondage of the covenant of works. By this I mean that in Christ, you do not have to keep the law in order to be saved. However, Christ has not delivered you from this bondage in order to give you the liberty to sin all you want to! Christ delivered you from this bondage in order for you to be able to fulfill the royal law of liberty, and that you might serve in the newness of the Spirit and not in the oldness of the letter (Galatians 5:13, Romans 7:6).

Holiness in this life is a necessary part of your salvation because it makes you fit to be "partakers of the inheritance of the saints in heavenly light" and glory. And "without holiness you can never see God" (Hebrews 12:14). Without holiness, you will never be fit for God's glorious presence – just as swine can never be fit to enter into the throne room of an earthly king.

I readily admit that many people will be converted to Christ so near the point of their death that they will have very little time to practice holiness of life in this world. However, the grace of the Spirit is active like fire (Mathew 13:11). As soon as it is given, it immediately enables people to love God and his people from their hearts. This working will be sufficient for when they stand before God on the great Day of Judgment, and he judges every man according to his work. Of course, there are always those few cases of people who have so little time on earth that their

114

inward grace will never produce outward works – such as the thief on the cross (Luke 23:40-43). Nonetheless, most people will produce some fruit before they die!

Third, you must seek holiness of heart and life by faith. Multitudes of people, who live under the preaching of the gospel, harden their hearts and ruin their souls forever. How do they do this? Because they have the wrong understanding of salvation. They do not believe that salvation consists of holiness of life. They think that salvation only consists of the forgiveness of sin and the deliverance from eternal punishment. They want to escape the punishment of sin. However, they love their sinful lusts so much, they hate holiness. They do not want to be saved from slavery to sin.

How do we counteract this false idea? We do not counteract it by denying salvation by grace through faith! Rather, we counteract it by saying that no one can trust in Christ for true salvation without trusting in him for holiness! You cannot truly trust in Christ for true salvation if you do not want to be made holy and righteous in your life! When God gives you salvation through Christ, holiness will be one part of that salvation. If Christ "does not wash you" from the filth of your sins, "you have no part of him" (John 13:8).

What a strange salvation it is, if people who are saved do not care about holiness! In this case, people want to be saved, but they want to stay dead in sin, alien from the life of God, without the image of God, deformed by the image of Satan, and in slavery to Satan and to their own filthy lusts. They seem to prefer to stay totally unfit to enjoy God in glory. Christ never purchased such a salvation as this by his own blood. Those who think they have received a salvation such as this abuse the grace of God in Christ, and turn it into license for sin. They want to be saved by Christ, but apart from Christ, so to speak. They want to be saved, but they also want to remain in a fleshly state, with a fleshly lifestyle.

This is simply not how salvation works! The only people Christ frees from condemnation are those who are "in Christ, who do not walk according to the flesh but according to the Spirit" (Romans 8:1-4). If this were not the case, people would divide Christ. They would take one part of his salvation, and leave out the rest. However, "Christ is not divided" (I Corinthians 1:13). You cannot have half a Christ!

Some people want to have their sins forgiven so that they can continue to live in enmity against him, without having any fear of punishment. They do not want to be forgiven so they can walk with God in love. However, "let them not be deceived, God cannot be mocked" (Galatians 6:7). They simply do not understand true salvation. They have never come to see their lost estate, and how evil they really are in their sin. Their trusting in Christ is a terrible presumption. They trust in Christ for something imaginary, which they have made up out of their own heads.

True gospel faith makes you come to Christ with a great thirst, that you might "drink of living water" – by which Christ means his sanctifying Spirit (John 7:37-38). True gospel faith makes you cry out earnestly for God to save you – not only from hell but from sin as well. "Create in me a clean heart, Oh God, and renew a right spirit within me" (Psalm 51:10). When you seek salvation by faith in Christ, holiness is a major part of the salvation that Christ freely gives you. You cannot divide salvation. You cannot have the forgiveness of Christ without the holiness of Christ!

# Chapter 9

### Principle Number 9

### In order to sincerely keep the law of God, you must first receive the comfort of the Gospel.

When God first created human beings in their blessed state in Paradise, they were perfectly able to obey God. However, when they fell into disobedience, God was not obligated to give them any comfort to encourage them to obey. The sentence of death hung over them for their sin. In addition, the way to holiness was walled off against them with the thorns and briars of fear, grief, and despair. God's justice was revealed to them in a legal covenant. This legal covenant declares that God promises you no life, comfort, or happiness until you have completely kept his law. This covenant was especially revealed in the command given at Mount Sinai, and further explained throughout the Old Testament.

By nature, you are completely addicted to this legal method of salvation. Even after you become a Christian by believing the gospel, your heart is still addicted to salvation by works. In your heart you still want to make the duties of the law come before the comforts of the gospel. Even if you have become assured that your salvation does not depend upon your own works, you will still tend to make all of the comforts and blessings of the gospel depend upon your own works. You will find it hard to believe that you should get any blessing before you work for it. You will think this is as unreasonable as an employee getting a paycheck before he works, or a farmer getting crops before he plants and reaps!

This is the mindset you will tend to fall into: You sincerely do want to obey the law of God. Therefore, to make sure you obey the law of God, you will make all of God's blessings depend upon how well you keep his law. You will think that if you receive God's blessings first, before you obey, that will open the floodgates to all kinds of sin in your life. Some preachers even tell you that you had better not enjoy the blessings of the gospel! They tell you to obey the law first, and if you do, you will be safe and happy before God. Just keep in mind, however, that if you go this route, you will never enjoy your salvation for as long as you live in this world!

The Bible does not teach this. You should not think this way. Notice what the Bible says. The comfort of the gospel does not only come to you before you keep the law, but God also comforts you on every side, both before and after you keep his law. He comforts you after you obey him, once you have become a Christian. And, he also comforts you before you obey him – a "payment in advance," so to speak – to enable you to obey him.

In no way do I want to give anyone false assurance. I am not speaking to people who continue to live the way they did before they professed the Christian faith. I do not want to give any false confidence to people who harden themselves in sin. The only way you can live a holy life is by the Holy Spirit, who makes you a good tree so that you can bear good fruit.

You must receive the blessings of the gospel before you can ever keep the law. However, the blessings of the gospel do not come to you in your corrupt, sinful nature. They come to you when you receive a new, holy nature. They come when you are born anew by the Holy Spirit. This new holy nature immediately enables you to live a holy life. It is the gospel coming to you, of course, that gives you this new nature in the first place. The blessings of redemption – such as justification, adoption, the gifts of the Holy Spirit, etc. – are what enable you to live a holy life. These blessings take away the fear, grief, and despair that you naturally tend to have. They give you the joy you need to truly obey God.

Consider the following reasons why you need to have these comforts of the gospel if you are truly going to keep the law of God.

First, this truth is an implication of everything that I have been saying to you about holiness thus far. I have already shown you that you need to be totally assured of your reconciliation with God, your blessed eternal future, and your ability to will and do what God requires, if you are going to live a holy life. I have also shown you that you receive these qualifications by receiving Christ himself, with his Spirit, and all his fullness. You receive Christ when you trust in him for salvation as he is promised to you in the gospel. When you believe, you really do receive Christ, just as you really receive food when you eat and drink.

Now, consider this: Can you be totally assured of God's love, of your everlasting happiness, and of your ability to serve God, and not be comforted by that assurance? Can fear, grief, and despair remain in your heart after you have believed the good news of the gospel of peace, and received Christ and his Spirit into your heart? Does the salvation of Christ bring you no comfort? Does not Christ, the bread and water of life, taste delicious when you feed on him with spiritual hunger and thirst? God gives these blessings to those who hunger and thirst for them! When you receive these blessings, you are encouraged and strengthened to live a holy life.

Second, the Bible tells you that peace, joy, and hope are the fountain from which your obedience flows. Fear and oppressing grief actually hinder your obedience. "The peace of God keeps your heart and mind in Christ Jesus" (Philippians 4:7). "Do not be sorrowful, for the joy of the Lord is your strength" (Nehemiah 8:10). "Everyone who has this hope in him purifies himself, just as he is pure" (I John 3:3). "Fear has to do with punishment; he who fears is not made perfect in love" (I John 4:18). This is the reason why Paul tells you to "rejoice in the Lord always" (Philippians 4:4). You have to have peace, joy, and hope right at the beginning of your Christian life, where the work is most difficult. That is when you need the most encouragement. You must have spiritual comfort if you are going to obey God's commandments.

Third, the usual way the Scriptures proclaim the truth of the Gospel is this: God first comforts your heart, in order to "establish you in every good work" (II Thessalonians 2:17). The apostles do this in several letters. They first proclaim to the churches God's rich grace to them in Christ, and then they show them the great spiritual blessings they have received in Christ. The apostles proclaim the gospel of grace to comfort believers. Then, the apostles exhort them to live holy lives, because of the great gospel-privileges they have.

God always encourages his people to live holy lives because of the grace he has given to them. This means you must first receive and believe the gospel in your own heart. If you do not do this, you will never be able to obey God. There are many Scripture passages that teach this, but here are a few that make God's grace your motive for obedience. You obey because…

- ❑ "you are dead to sin and alive to God through Jesus Christ your Lord" (Romans 6:11)

- ❑ "sin shall not be your master, for you are not under law but under grace" (Romans 6:14)

119

- ❑ "you are not in the flesh, but in the Spirit..., and God will make your mortal body live by his Spirit dwelling in you" (Romans 8:9,11)

- ❑ "your bodies are the members of Christ, and the temples of the Holy Spirit" (I Corinthians 6:15,19)

- ❑ "God made him who knew no sin to be sin for us, so that in him we might become the righteousness of God" (II Corinthians 5:21)

- ❑ God has promised that he "will dwell with us, an walk in us, and be to us a father, and we shall be to him sons and daughters" (II Corinthians 6:18, 7:1)

- ❑ "God has forgiven us for Christ's sake" and considers us "his dear children." "Christ has loved us, and given himself for us." "We who were once in darkness are not light in the Lord" (Ephesians 4:32, and 5:1,2,8)

- ❑ "we have been raised with Christ, and when Christ, who is our life appears, then we also shall appear with him in glory" (Colossians 3:1,4)

- ❑ "God has said, 'I will never leave you nor forsake you'" (Hebrews 13:5)

- ❑ there are "many promises made to us" (II Corinthians 7:1)

Read through the Scriptures, and you will see, with delight, that this theme runs completely through them: the gospel is what encourages you to obey God. The same theme runs through the prophetical books in the Old Testament.

Now, some people might object to this and say, "Look, the apostles said this when they wrote to Christians who already were obeying God. The apostles said this only to them, to help them obey God even more." My answer is this: if more mature Christians need this kind of encouragement, how much more do new Christians need this kind of encouragement! New Christians find the work of obedience even **more** difficult, and they need even **more** encouragement to obey! I want people to lay hold of the comfort of God's grace right at the beginning of their Christian lives.

# Receive the Comfort of the Gospel

Consider this also: the gospel freely promises peace and comfort to people who are not yet living holy lives at all. Those who receive the gospel will be transformed from sin to righteousness. When the apostles entered into a house, they were to say first, "Peace be upon this house" (Luke 10:5). When they preached to sinners, they told them of the good news of salvation in Christ, for everyone who receives it as a free gift by faith (Acts 3:26, 13:26, 32, 38, and 16:30-31). They assured people that if they would trust in Christ for salvation, they would receive it – even if they were at the present time the chief of sinners. The whole purpose of the gospel is to proclaim the riches of God's grace, for your spiritual benefit! God gives you gospel blessings both before and after you do good works, so that "you may know that he gives us everlasting comfort, and good hope through grace" (II Thessalonians 2:16) – not through our works.

Fourth, the very nature of obedience to God's law means that your soul must be comforted by the gospel if you are going to obey God. I have already told you that you have to be assured of your reconciliation with God, of your future happiness, and of your sufficient strength, if you are going to obey God. Joshua had to be strong and courageous in order to do what Moses, the servant of the Lord, commanded him to do (Joshua 1:7). You cannot possibly obey God if you have not received the comfort of the gospel.

Think about it. Can you love God and delight in him more than anything else if you consider him your everlasting enemy? Can you love God if you do not believe that he has shown you love and mercy? Can you delight in God if you do not think God is altogether lovely?

Your heart will be miserable when you try to praise God if you think that God's perfections are going to make you miserable, and not make you happy. What a heartless work it will be to pray to him, and offer yourself to serve him, if you do not have any assurance that he will accept you. Can you possibly free yourself from troublesome cares by casting your care upon the Lord, if you do not believe that he cares for you? Can you be patient in affliction, and cheerful during persecution, if you do not have "peace with God and rejoice in the hope of the glory of God?" (Romans 5:1-3). Can you obey God unto death, if you have no assurance that you have escaped the fear of horrible punishment in hell forever?

Fifth, people who are not yet Christians need to be given a rich supply of gospel assurance to encourage their souls to obey God. Remember where these non-Christians are! They are dead in sin, they are subject to the wrath of God, and they have placed their hopes in all kinds of false gospels to save them! Be a good "physician of the soul." Consider the condition of your unconverted "patients." They have no strength or life in them to do anything for God!

Think of a man who is lying on a bed, totally paralyzed. Would you tell him to get up and start exercising? If you did, you would not be considered a good physician. You would be considered a merciless, insulting torturer! It is the same thing spiritually. How can you tell non-Christians to get out there and love God? They only thing they understand is that they are under God's wrath and enmity in their current spiritual state. Can you tell a person who has no strength to work – promising that when his work is done, he will receive strength? Assurance and joy is what strengthens people to work (Nehemiah 8:10).

It is true that the law commands people to obey it. That is why it is called the "ministry of condemnation." People are condemned because they cannot obey it! Our merciful God understands that poor, miserable, powerless sinners cannot keep his law to gain salvation. God knows that he must first deliver them from the fear and despair that hold them captive under the law of sin and death. You can require a strong, healthy person to work first in order to earn his food, drink and wages after he works. However, you cannot do this with a weak person. A weak, famished person must first receive food to strengthen him, so that he **can** work.

Sixth, both Scripture and experience show you that God encourages people to live holy lives by first assuring them of the grace he has given them in the gospel. Some people will indeed be terrified by their sins for a while. For these people, Christ's salvation becomes all the more precious. Then, when they are comforted and assured by the hope of the gospel, they begin to live holy lives.

On the whole, the assurance of the gospel establishes and maintains holy living. Right at the beginning, God gave Adam the comfort of his love and favor, and the happiness of Paradise, to encourage him to obedience. When he sinned and lost these blessings, he was no longer able to obey God at all. God then restored his assurance through the promise of the gospel – the promised seed that God would send. Christ, the second Adam, set "God always before his face," and he knew that, because "God was at his right hand, he should not be moved. Therefore, his heart was glad, and his tongue rejoiced" (Psalm 16:8-9). This made Christ "obedient to death, even the death on the cross" (Philippians 2:8).

God drew the Israelites to obey him with "the cords of a man, with the bands of love," by "taking off the yoke on their jaws, and laying meat before them" (Hosea 10:4). David tells you what compelled him to live a holy life: "Your loving kindness is before my eyes, and I have walked in your truth" (Psalm 26:3). "Lord, I have hoped for your salvation, and have kept your commandments" (Psalm 119:166).

There are several examples in the New Testament of the joy sinners had when they first received Christ (see Acts 2:41). When the gospel first came to the Thessalonians, "they received the word in much affliction, with joy in the Holy Spirit" (I Thessalonians 1:4-6). "When the Gentiles heard the word of God, they were glad; and as many as were ordained to eternal life, believed" (Acts 13:48). The apostle Paul was compelled by "the love of Christ" to give himself up to "live for Christ" (II Corinthians 5:14-15).

Examine your own experience. Whenever you love God from your heart, do you ever give yourself to serve God in love without any blessed understanding of the love of God for you? I dare say that in the realm of the new birth, this cannot happen!

Seventh, look at people who do not believe they must receive the assurance of the gospel before they obey. Look at the kind of religion they have! It is a drab and depressing religion! Their pastors tell them to do things that are totally opposed to their natural inclinations. Their pastors tell people to obey God, even though those people are fearful, depressed, and totally corrupt. By doing this, they hope that people will be able to do well enough so that they can get some comfort and assurance by their attempts to obey God.

If assurance depends upon your ability to do good works, then all true spiritual assurance will totally disappear from the earth. No salvation will be possible for anyone. This is what the law requires of people – work to gain your assurance of acceptance with God. The law brings about no comfort, but only wrath (Romans 4:14-15). This is why people who try to be saved by the law come to hate godliness. They think they will never enjoy one pleasant hour in the world when they live by the law. Then, they run headlong into a life of sinful pleasures. They would rather comfort themselves with the pleasures of sin than to have no comfort at all!

People who live in this kind of depressing religion begin to inwardly grumble at its bondage. They grow more and more weary of it. Eventually, they give it up altogether, because they do not know of any religion any better. Those who preach this kind of religion say, "Please do not blame me for this – I am just preaching the gospel of Christ." However, this is not the case at all. They are preaching a gospel of their own making. It is totally opposed to the nature of the gospel of Christ, which is "good news of great joy for all people" (Luke 2:10). A depressing, uncomforting gospel cannot come from the God the Father, who is the "Father of mercies, and the God of all comfort" (II Corinthians 1:3). An uncomforting gospel cannot come from Christ, who is the "consolation of Israel" (Luke 2:25). An uncomforting gospel cannot come from the Spirit, who is "the comforter" (John 14:16-17).

God "comes to the help of those who gladly do right" (Isaiah 64:5). God wants to be served with gladness and singing. In the Old Testament, God filled the temple with music and musicians – as well as now in the church. This is to show how Christ speaks in the gospel, that "his joy may abide in you, and that your joy may be full" (John 15:11). The only kind of sorrow that God approves of is "godly sorrow." You can never have this godly sorrow unless you have received some "comfort of the love of God" towards you.

If you find that you are offended by the idea that religion is comforting and assuring, you have never known the way of true religion. If you had known it, you would have found that "the ways of wisdom are the ways of pleasantness, and all her paths are peace" Proverbs 3:17).

# Chapter 10

### Principle Number 10:

**If you are going to obey the law out of the comfort of the Gospel, you must have complete assurance of your salvation. You obtain this assurance by believing and receiving Christ into your heart. Therefore, confidently believe in Christ without delay. Be assured that when you believe in Christ, God will freely give you a personal relationship with Christ, just as he has promised.**

I have previously stated that if you are going to live a holy life, you first have to receive the comfort of the gospel. If you are going to receive the comfort of the gospel, you have to be completely assured that you indeed have a personal relationship with Christ. You have to know that you truly have received his salvation. I have already told you what some of these comforts are: you know that you are reconciled with God, you know that you will have eternal happiness in heaven, and you know that God will give you the strength both to will and to do what God wants you to do. Having assurance of these things is absolutely necessary if you are going to keep the law of God and live a holy life. I now want to tell you more about this assurance that is so very necessary to your holiness. You can only receive this assurance by faith – the very same faith by which you were justified, and by which you receive Christ himself into your heart.

Now, not everyone believes that you can have this complete assurance of your salvation. Even many professing Christians do not believe you can have it. The Reformers certainly taught assurance of faith! They commonly taught, "Faith is being totally confident of your own salvation by Christ. Be sure to believe the gospel and apply Christ and his salvation to your own life." This doctrine was one of the great forces that helped to overthrow much of the superstition that existed in the church during the time of the Reformation. One of the chief pillars of those teachers who did not believe the gospel was the "doubtfulness of salvation." In other words, they did not teach their people they could ever have complete assurance of their salvation! How destructive to true faith that doctrine of the "doubtfulness of salvation" was! The assurance of salvation is indeed one of the chief pillars of our faith, going right back to the Reformation.

# The Gospel Mystery of Sanctification

Now, however, many of our own number have abandoned the doctrine of the assurance of salvation. Many teachers of our own day think they are standing on the shoulders of their Reformation forefathers – but in fact they are not. They have been blinded by many of their own speculations. There are many reasons why many teachers today do not teach that you can be sure of your salvation.

One reason they give is that salvation is never promised to you absolutely. Salvation is always promised on the condition of believing in Christ for it. Therefore, they say, you must first believe in Christ for salvation. After that, you must continually reflect and examine yourself, to make sure you have true saving faith. You have to make sure that you have all the right signs and fruits of saving faith. In particular, you have to make sure you have the fruit of sincere obedience. Once you make absolutely sure that you have this true saving faith, then and only then can you rest in the assurance of your salvation.

One of the implications of this viewpoint is that many people will ultimately be saved who never came to any assurance of salvation while they lived on the earth. This viewpoint sets people to endless introspection, where they always are wondering, "Do I have enough fruit? Am I obeying enough? Do I really have the right to be sure of my salvation?" The fact is, you will never be able to obey enough to make yourself absolutely sure that you truly are saved!

These teachers also look to both the Bible and their own experience, and they find that many saints of God are frequently filled with doubts about whether or not they will be saved. There are many Christians who never come to assurance. Therefore, these teachers conclude that assurance of faith is not something that is absolutely necessary. You might truly be a justified Christian, but you do not have to be **sure** you are a justified, forgiven Christian. After all, look at what we will do to all these doubting Christians if we tell them they can have true assurance of faith – we will sadden their hearts and drive them to despair! Surely we do not want to do that to them!

Many present day teachers think that the protestant Reformers were crazy when they said, "assurance of faith is part of the very nature of saving faith." Why? Because there are many people who truly are saved, yet they never come to that absolute assurance that they truly are saved. What are we saying, that such people are not truly saved? Because of that potential problem, many people have abandoned the doctrine of eternal

126

security and assurance. They now say "saving faith is when you trust or rest on Christ as the only way you can be saved, but without having any assurance. Or, saving faith is when you desire or try to trust and rely upon Christ, but you remain in a state of suspense and uncertainty about your salvation. The best you can do is **hope** that you have eternal salvation in Christ."

Another objection that people raise against our doctrine of assurance of faith is this: "If you give people assurance of their salvation, you will destroy their self-examination. Assurance of faith will produce the evil fruits of pride and arrogance. People will act like they know they have a place in heaven already, before the Day of Judgment occurs. This will make people careless in their duty before God. They will be filled with false security, and they will give themselves over to all kinds of licentiousness." In other words, in order to keep people humble, we should teach them to be doubtful of their salvation. Keeping people doubtful about their eternal state is the only way to encourage them to examine themselves and remain diligent in good works and devotion to God.

I want to show you that all of these ideas are wrong and destructive to people's Christian growth. I want to defend the classic doctrine of the assurance of faith against all of these objections. Consider these things.

First, this does not apply if you are not a Christian. The assurance that I am commending to you does not apply to you if you have not received Christ and his salvation. I am not saying that anyone has in fact received Christ and his salvation, or that they have already been brought into a state of grace. I am pointing you to God's firm promise. The promise is that God is pleased to give Christ and his salvation to you, and to bring you into a state of grace, even though you have been in a state of sin and death until the present time. The doctrine of assurance of faith is not meant to breed presumption in wicked and unregenerate people, by telling them that their state is already good. We are not saying to non-Christians, "Don't worry, you are just fine, you can have assurance that you are saved by Christ." Not at all! We are telling non-Christians that they can, and must, come to Christ confidently in order to be accepted by God.

I absolutely agree that we must teach many people to doubt whether their state is good – for in fact their state is not good if they have no relationship with Christ. I also agree that we must examine ourselves to make sure our faith is sincere. We do need to look to see if our faith has any fruits of obedience if we wish to have assurance of faith. Many people who think they are saved may discover that they are just fooling themselves, and that their faith is not real. I am not commending a false, delusional faith.

I also agree that assurance of faith is not of the essence of that faith by which we are justified and saved. In other words, you can truly have saving faith, but not be absolutely **sure** that you have true saving faith. There are many precious Christians who do not have assurance of faith. They doubt all the time whether they are saved or not. They really do not know what will happen to them on the Day of Judgment. I also know that you can lose your assurance of faith once you have it. However, I still maintain that assurance of faith is something you can actually have. I also maintain that assurance is very important for you to have if you want to grow in your faith and grow in holiness.

True assurance of faith is not destructive to the good fruit you are supposed to bear in your Christian life. The doctrine of assurance of faith is often charged with all kinds of evils, but these charges are false. The kind of assurance I am talking about does not answer the questions, "Am I already in a state of grace and salvation?" I am talking about another great question that every soul must answer: "Will God be pleased to give Christ and his salvation to me, even though I have been a very wicked person in my life up to this point?"

You must be sure to resolve this question by believing, with all assurance, that God is ready to graciously receive you into his merciful arms through Jesus Christ. Even though you have been a very wicked person, God graciously promises, "I will call them my people who were not my people. And I will call her my beloved who was not beloved. And it shall come to pass in the place where it was said about them, 'You are not my people,' that they shall be called the children of the living God" (Romans 9:25-26).

Second, the assurance of salvation that I am commending to you is not an assurance that you are saved no matter what you do, or no matter how you live or walk. I indeed acknowledge that many foolish people give themselves a false assurance of salvation. They supposedly "believe in Christ," but then they go and live as they please! You can be sure that it will not go well for them on the Day of Judgment. They are truly not saved!

The assurance I am talking about is given in a limited way, to those who truly come to Christ. When you come to the free grace of Christ, you not only come to the forgiveness of your sins, but to holiness of life. You are called to walk in the way of holiness to the glory of God. In order to have this kind of assurance of salvation, you first have to realize your own sin and misery. You have to despair of your own righteousness and strength. You have to hunger and thirst for both justifying grace in Christ, and sanctifying grace in Christ. Why? So that you can walk in the ways of holiness, for the glory of God. It is simply not possibly for you to receive justification without receiving sanctification!

The faith that receives Christ is not only an assured faith but also a most holy faith. A faith like this will not make you proud, it will make you humble – unless, of course, you think it is pride to "rejoice and glory in Christ, and have no confidence in the flesh" (Philippians 3:3). This assurance of faith will not destroy a proper fear of God, or breed any kind of carnal security of salvation. Rather, this kind of assurance will make you fear moving away from Christ as your only refuge and security, and going back to walking after the flesh. Noah entered the ark and stayed there, with the full assurance that he would be saved from the flood. He did well to be afraid of going outside of the ark. He knew that staying in the ark was the only way he could be saved from the flood!

How can such an assurance of salvation in the way of holiness produce spiritual laziness, carelessness, or licentiousness in you? Such assurance encourages and stirs you up to "always abound in the work of the Lord, because you know that your labor in the Lord is not in vain" (I Corinthians 15:58). Those who are truly assured of the free grace of God to them in Jesus Christ are not concerned about trying to earn salvation by their own legal works. Satan will always be suggesting to them that this assurance will only lead them to sinful carelessness and licentiousness, but they do not listen to these suggestions! Those who believe these lies of Satan show they do not yet know what it means to serve God out of love. They are still held, in all their obedience, by the bit and bridle of slavish fear – "as the horse and the mule, which have no understanding" (Psalm 32:9).

Third, do not think that having assurance of faith is inconsistent with having doubts within your soul. Many people have abandoned this classic doctrine of assurance of faith because they have misunderstood it. They think that if you are ever troubled with doubting, then you must not be truly saved! They mistakenly think that having assurance of faith means you will never doubt again! Therefore, because they see that many true Christians indeed do doubt, they have given up the doctrine of assurance of faith. It just does not seem to fit into their experience. They do not want to deny that these doubters are true Christians!

To be sure, if you could have a perfect assurance of their salvation, you would never doubt. However, who can have such perfect assurance? Remember even the best saints on the earth still face the conflict between the flesh and the spirit (Galatians 5:17). Is there not "a law in their members warring against the law of their minds?" (Romans 7:23). May not one who truly believes say, "Lord, help my unbelief?" (Mark 9:24). Can anyone on earth say that they have received any grace from God in the highest degree possible, and that they are totally free from any corruption that is contrary to the grace of God? Absolutely not! Why, then, do you think that your assurance cannot possibly be true unless it is perfect, totally free from all doubting in your soul? Can you not have assurance of faith, yet be filled with doubts in your soul from time to time? Of course you can – and you will!

Paul considered it a great blessing that the Thessalonians had much assurance. He intimated by this that some people might have true assurance in a lesser degree (I Thessalonians 1:5). Peter certainly had a firm assurance of Christ's help when he walked on the water at Christ's command. Yet, at the same time, he had some doubt, since his fear came out when the winds picked up. He had some faith that was contrary to doubting, even though he had but little faith, as Jesus words to him show: "Oh you of little faith, why did you doubt?" (Matthew 14:29-31).

It would truly be strange if the flesh and the devil never tried to attack your assurance in Christ and fill you with doubt! That is one of the devil's main jobs – to accuse you! The fact is that true Christians will sometimes be overwhelmed with doubts. Sometimes they will feel no assurance of salvation at all. They will not feel like they have any place in heaven at all.

This is how a true believer will handle his doubts: He says to himself, with the psalmist, "Why are you cast down, oh my soul, and why are you so disquieted within me? Hope in God, for I will yet praise him" (Psalm 42:11). He condemns his doubts as sinful, and he says to himself,

## The Gospel gives you Assurance of Salvation

"This is my infirmity" (Psalm 77:10), and "these doubts come from the flesh and from the devil." He still tries to call God "Father" – even though he complains to God and doubts that God really is his Father.

Nonetheless, he asks God to give him some assurance of his fatherly love, which he does not feel at the moment. He asks God to drive away his fears and doubts. I tell you, a person who is in this state has some true assurance, even though he should try to grow to a higher degree of assurance. For, if he did not have some assurance of God's love for him, he would not condemn his fears and doubts as sinful. In the same way, he could never pray to God as his father if he did not have any assurance. He could never pray and ask God to assure him of his love if he did not have some idea that God really does love him!

Do you see what I am saying? True Christians will certainly struggle with doubts about their salvation! However, I am also saying that it is in the very nature of saving faith to resist and struggle against doubt. If you truly are a Christian, you will fight against the slavish fear that you are still under God's wrath. If you truly are saved, you will indeed have some assurance, and you will resist your doubts. If people would only understand what we really mean when we talk about assurance of salvation, they would not reject this doctrine. We do not mean that you will never have doubts. We do mean that true saving faith will resist doubts and always try to gain assurance.

Fourth, the truth of the gospel is that God freely gives Christ and salvation to you personally if you receive him. The reason you can be sure of this is not because this is true **before** you believe the gospel. Rather, it only becomes true **when** you believe the gospel. This will never be true of you unless you **do** believe the gospel! If you are not a Christian, you are currently in a state of sin and misery, and you are under the curse and wrath of God. If you are in this situation, the Bible tells you to assure yourself by believing the gospel.

When you believe the gospel, you do not believe something that is untrue, but something that is true. In your earthly life, you have to believe many things based on the evidence you have that they are true – and those things remain true whether you believe them or not. You rebel against your reason and your conscience when you deny that they are true. That will often be the case with your salvation. If you are in Christ, you are in fact saved, but you will sometimes have trouble believing this truth.

When it comes to attaining assurance of faith, you have more than just external evidence to give you assurance. You have something internal: you also have the Spirit of God living in you. The Holy Spirit is within you, working to give you the assurance that you indeed are a child of God. God is the one who "calls things that are not as though they were" (Romans 4:17). In other words, God brings things into existence that did not exist before. God works this way in your life regarding assurance of salvation: he gives it to you, even though you cannot produce it in yourself by your own efforts. He can fulfill the promise, "Whatever you desire when you pray, believe that you will receive them, and you shall have them" (Mark 11:24). If you lack assurance of your salvation, pray for it! God wants to give it to you!

Now that I have explained what we mean by assurance of faith, let me give you several reasons why you should have assurance when you truly have saving faith.

First, the assurance of salvation is built right into the very nature of saving faith. What is saving faith? Saving faith is a grace of the Holy Spirit whereby you believe the gospel, and believe in Christ as he is promised in the gospel, and receive salvation. Believing in Christ is the same as resting, relying, leaning, and staying yourself on Christ for your salvation. All of these terms describing faith include assurance. When you believe on Christ for salvation, and depend upon him, you have to be somewhat persuaded that salvation will indeed be given to you because God freely promises it. If you believe the gospel, but then wait in suspense to find out if you truly have received Christ, that can hardly be called faith! In other words, if you believe the gospel, you have to believe that it is true to a certain extent! If you did not think it were true, you would not believe it.

Believing, by its very nature, is the opposite of staggering (Romans 4:20), wavering (Hebrews 10:23), doubting (Matthew 14:31), and fear (Mark 5:36). These words that describe the opposite of faith shed light on what faith really is. They show that believing has confidence in it, and not doubt.

The other terms that we sometimes use for faith – trusting and resting on Christ – also contain assurance. Your soul trusts, rests, and finds support in Christ, so that it will have strength against fear, trouble, care, and despair. You truly trust and hope in the Lord when you assure yourself, in the face of all fears and doubts that the Lord is your God, and that he has become your salvation. "I trusted in you, O Lord. I have said, 'You are my God'" (Psalm 31:14). "The Lord is my rock and my fortress and my deliverer; my God, my strength, in whom I trust (Psalm 18:2). "Behold, God is my salvation; I will trust and not be afraid" (Isaiah 12:2). "Oh my soul, hope in God, who is the health of my countenance, and my God" (Psalm 42:11).

True hope is grounded in God only. You believe that he will bless you, that he is the "anchor for your soul, sure and steadfast" (Hebrews 6:17-19). If you trust, rely, and stay yourself on Christ, but have no assurance that you are saved by him, you are treating him as if he were a broken reed. You do not believe he has any power at all. If you want to stay yourself upon the Lord, you must look to him as your God, as Isaiah teaches: "Let him trust in the name of the Lord, and stay upon his God" (Isaiah 1:10). If you want to rest in the Lord, you have to believe that he "deals graciously with you" (Psalm 116:7).

Many people find it easy to trust in God when things are going well for them. However, during a time of trouble, their trust vanishes. What appeared to be faith just turns to shame. If you live in this kind of wavering and doubting about your salvation, you are not resting in Christ at all. You are like "a wave of the sea, driven by the wind, and tossed. You are a double-minded man, unstable in all your ways" (James 1:6,8).

You do not have to doubt in this way! You can be assured of your salvation. Why? Because God is powerful enough to save you completely when you believe in Christ. Not only that, God is kind and merciful toward you. He will in no way cast you out if you believe.

Second, many places in the Bible command you to be assured of your salvation when you believe. You are exhorted to "draw near to God with full assurance of faith" (Hebrews 10:22). This is the same faith by which "the righteous live" (Hebrews 10:38). This very same faith is also described as the "assurance of things hoped for, the evidence of things not seen" (Hebrews 11:1). Do these descriptions of faith not contain assurance in them? Faith makes the matters of your salvation clear to the eyes of your mind, just as if they were already present to you. The faith that gives you a relationship with Christ is called a "confidence:" "We are his house, if we hold fast the confidence, and rejoicing of the hope firm to the end" (Hebrews 3:6,14). What does it mean to have confidence in something? It means that you are firmly persuaded that something is true. If you only have a strong opinion about something, but are not absolutely sure, you are not confident about it.

The faith by which you are justified is like the faith Abraham had. "Abraham, against hope, believed in hope, that his seed should certainly be multiplied according to the promise of God – even though his own body and Sarah's womb were dead." Abraham had no hope from his own strength or qualifications. All appearances were to the contrary (Romans 4:18-25). As absolute as the promise was to Abraham, Abraham had assurance of faith when he believed it. So it is with you. When you believe the free promise of salvation through Jesus Christ, you have to have confidence that it is true.

James commands you to ask for good things from God in faith, without doubting. This obviously includes assurance. James tells you that without it, no one should think they will receive anything form the Lord. Without assurance, you will not receive the salvation of Christ (James 1:6-7). James is telling you not to doubt the things for which you ask the Lord.

These Scripture passages are enough to show you that when you believe, you automatically have some assurance. If you do not have it, you will never enjoy your salvation. It is not humility to live in a state of doubt about your salvation. It is proud disobedience, because you will not submit to the sufficiency of Christ and his promise. You think the assurance of your salvation really depends upon you – not upon Christ.

Third, God tells you to come to Christ with confident faith right at the very beginning. No matter how wretched and sinful you have been thus far, you can be absolutely sure that Christ and his salvation will be given to you without delay. The Bible speaks to the worst sinners in a way that gives them the assurance of salvation immediately. God does not put new Christians on probation – he does not make them "prove themselves" before he allows them to have assurance of salvation. See Acts 2:39 and 3:26. The promise is universal, that "whoever believes in Christ will not be ashamed," and it does not make any distinction between Jew or Greek (Romans 10:11-12). This promise is confirmed by the blood of Christ, who was given for the world, and lifted up on the cross, so that "whoever believes in him should not perish but have eternal life" (John 3:16). His invitation is free to everyone: "If anyone is thirsty, let him come to me and drink" (John 7:37-39). This drink is promised to everyone who believes.

# The Gospel gives you Assurance of Salvation

The promise of salvation is given personally, and it comes to people who have previously been in a state of sin and wrath – such as the wicked, persecuting, suicidal jailor (Acts 16:31). Paul told him: "Believe on the Lord Jesus, and you will be saved, along with your house." God told people who had completely walked in sin to call him their own Father, just as soon as they returned to him (Jeremiah 3:4). God says that he will say about his people, "You are my people. And they shall say, 'You are my God'" (Hosea 2:23).

God has inseparably joined **salvation** and **confidence** together. "In returning and rest you shall be saved. In quietness and confidence shall be your strength" (Isaiah 30:15). There are so many poor Christians who diminish the grace of God! They say that you can only be confident that Christ is your own if you fulfill the proper condition of believing. In other words, you have to do something if you want to have any confidence in Christ at all. They do not realize that you can be completely confident in him without having to fulfill any conditions. All you have to do is receive him as your own – eat and drink of him – and he is yours immediately.

Suppose there is an upright rich man. He comes to a poor woman and says, "I promise to be your husband, if you will have me. Just say the word, and I am yours." Can she not answer right away, with total confidence, "You are my husband, and I claim you for my husband"? Should she not say this, rather than saying, "I do not believe what you are saying"? Or, suppose an honest man should tell you, "'Take this gift, and it is yours. Just eat and drink, and you are freely welcome." Can you not take the gift, and eat and drink, without any further ado? Can you take it with the complete assurance that is freely yours? If you take the gift with doubts, your discredit the honesty of the giver. You treat him as if he were not a man of his word.

In the same way, God has freely promised Christ to you in the gospel. If you are afraid to come to Christ with too much confidence, are you not discrediting the faithfulness of God? Think about all the free invitations God has given you to come to him for salvation. If you think God is not being honest with you when he makes these invitations, are you not guilty of making God a liar? This is what the apostle John teaches about people who will not believe what God has said about his Son: "And this is the testimony, that God has given us eternal life, and this life is promised in his Son" (I John 5:10-11).

It is true, not everyone who hears the gospel believes it. Nonetheless, God promises that everyone who believes the gospel will receive the gospel. No one who comes to Christ will find that the gospel is a lie. God has joined "believing" and "salvation" inseparably together. That is why God commands everyone to believe in him with assurance. If they do, they will give him the glory for his truth. If they do not, he will reject them and punish them for dishonoring him by their unbelief.

When it comes to assurance of salvation, do not look to the secret decrees of God. Look to God's revealed commands and promises. God promised the Israelites in the wilderness that he would give them the land of Canaan. He promised that he would fight for them against their enemies. He commanded them not to fear or be discouraged, so that he could fulfill his promise. However, God never decreed that those Israelites would enter into the land of Canaan. They did not believe his promise, and so God did not let them into the land of Canaan. He made them wander forty years in the wilderness until they all died (Deuteronomy 1:20-30). However, were they still not commanded to trust in God? Were they not required to be confident that God would defeat their enemies and give the land over to them? Did they not have sufficient grounds for this kind of faith? And, was it not just for God to let them fall in the wilderness because of their unbelief? "Therefore let us fear, lest a promise being made of entering into this everlasting rest through Christ, we should come short of it, and fall after the same example of unbelief" (Hebrews 4:1,11).

Fourth, those who were truly godly in the Bible had assurance of their salvation and of their relationship with Christ. Their assurance was not based on their own good qualifications. Their assurance was based upon the promises of God, which they believed. Consider the profession of the church when it first came out of Egypt. At that time, it was very corrupt. Very few of its members could assure themselves by their own qualifications that they were in a state of grace. Even in that very corrupt time, the children of Israel sang the triumphant song of Moses: "The Lord is my strength and my song, and he has become my salvation. He is my God," etc. (Exodus 15:2). Moses taught them this song to assure them that they were truly saved by God. The people at that time did not find fault with Moses for having them sing a song filled with such confidence. Even though they had no good qualifications in their lives, they sang the song because they believed God's promises of salvation.

# The Gospel gives you Assurance of Salvation

Several other psalms and songs God gave the Old Testament people are filled with assurance of faith, such as: Psalm 23, 27, 44, and 46. The assurance expressed by these songs does not come from the sincerity of the writer. The assurance comes from the love of God.

There is a great cloud of witnesses gathered out of the whole history of the Old Testament (Hebrews 11). These people acted, suffered, and obtained great things by faith. God has given them to you as examples, so that you can follow them with faith, for the saving of your soul (Hebrews 10:39). If you look at each of these individual people, you will find that most of them guide you to a saving faith that has great assurance. Yes, you will often read about the fears and doubts of the Old Testament saints. However, you will also read how they condemned fear and doubt as the opposite of faith (Psalm 42:11, 31:22, 78:7, 10). The most sorrowful Psalm in Scripture begins with an expression of assurance (Psalm 88:1).

In addition, remember that the doubts you see in the Old Testament saints were usually brought on because of some extraordinary suffering, or some awful sin they committed. Their doubts did not come from their common failures, or from the original sinfulness of their nature. They came during times of extraordinary affliction.

During the time of the Apostles, you may well expect the level of assurance of faith to grow higher, since the salvation of Christ had been revealed. God had plentifully poured out the Spirit of adoption, and freed the church from its bondage under the old covenant's terrifying legal covenant. Paul told the early Christians that they were the "children and heirs of God, because they had not received the spirit of slavery again to fear, but the Spirit of adoption, the spirit who calls out, 'Abba, Father'" (Galatians 4:6). "The Spirit himself bears witness with our spirits that we are the children of God" (Romans 8:15-17). Paul told the Ephesians that, after they had believed, "they were sealed with the Holy Spirit, who was the down payment of their inheritance" (Ephesians 1:13-14). They were sealed right at the time they believed the gospel.

Now, why does the Spirit testify that you are a child of God? Why does the Spirit enable you to cry "Abba, Father?" Is it because you are so qualified in yourself? No! The Holy Spirit places this assurance in you. He gives you saving faith. He enables you to trust in Christ with confident assurance. He enables you to understand that you are God's adopted child. He enables you to call God Father, without looking to you own

137

qualifications (for indeed, you have none!). The Holy Spirit is the spirit of comfort and adoption to all who receive him. Your assurance of faith does not depend upon your own sincerity. It depends upon the testimony of the Holy Spirit in your heart.

In the face of all that I have said, someone will come along and set forth the examples of many Christians in our current day who do not have any assurance of their salvation. They do this to try to prove that assurance is not necessary for salvation. They ignore the many examples of believers in the Old and New Testament who doubted from time to time. I agree, very few Christians today have assurance of salvation – much fewer than in former times. We can thank certain "Bible" teachers for this situation. They have abandoned the doctrine of assurance that our spiritual forefathers taught. How do they try to disprove the doctrine of assurance? They point out doubting Christians, to prove that true Christians do not have assurance. I still maintain, however, that true saving faith always has some assurance built into it. Even though true Christians will have doubts, they resist and condemn their doubts. They pray against their doubts. They try to trust with assurance. They call God "Father."

Do not trust how people evaluate themselves. Many will falsely judge themselves. Some of them will think that because they have some doubts, they cannot have assurance of salvation. Once they become better informed, they will come to see that they have some assurance of faith.

This might go without saying, but be careful of thinking other people are Christians when in fact they are not. There are many people who are close to the kingdom, but who are not yet true, born-again believers. Some people try to assure these non-Christians by telling them that they are safe, and that God accepts them – even though these non-Christians do not believe the gospel or trust in Christ. Thus, with a kind of blind love, they give these non-Christians a false sense of security. They do not encourage these non-Christians to seek comfort through saving faith in Christ. This could end up ruining their souls forever!

Fifth, the primary purpose of faith is to receive Christ and his salvation into your heart. You cannot really have faith unless you have some assurance in your heart that you really will receive Christ. Just as your body receives things through your hands and mouth, so your soul receives and embraces Jesus Christ. Faith is the way you receive Jesus Christ. If you are unsure that God has given Christ to you, you will certainly not enjoy him. Can you really enjoy Christ if you do not believe Christ wants to have a relationship with you? Can a woman receive a man as her husband if she is unsure about whether he really wants to be her husband?

This is the way it is with salvation. You cannot live with a clear conscience unless you really believe that God has forgiven all your sins. You will not receive salvation into your heart until you are absolutely assured that God is pleased to be your Father, and that he takes you to be his child and his heir. You will never be strengthened to live a holy life in the midst of your difficulties unless you believe that God is with you, and that he will never forsake you. If you seek to be saved by faith, but do not seek to have any assurance, you deceive yourself. You are trying to be saved in your corrupt natural state. You are really not receiving and laying hold of the Lord Jesus Christ and his salvation.

Sixth, faith purifies your heart, and enables you to live and walk in holiness, as Christ lives in you. Your faith will never do this for you unless you have some assurance of your relationship with Christ. If you want to live for God, and not for yourself, through Christ living in you, you must be able to assure yourself as Paul did, "Christ loved me and gave himself for me" (Galatians 2:20). You are taught, "since you live in the Spirit, you should walk in the Spirit" (Galatians 5:25). It would be presumptuous of you to try to live beyond your natural strength and live by the Spirit if you are not sure that you really **do** live by the Spirit!

You cannot use the grace of God to enable you to live a holy life if you are not sure you have truly received the grace of God. You cannot live a holy life if you do not believe that you are dead to sin and alive to God through Christ. You cannot live a holy life if you do not believe that you are not under law but under grace. You cannot live a holy life if you do not believe that you are a member of Christ, the temple of his Spirit, and his dear child.

Now, you may try to do this. You might tell a preacher, "Encourage me to live a holy life, but do not do it with the doctrine of the assurance of salvation. That doctrine will not help me a bit. I cannot live on the basis of assurance of salvation, because I have no assurance of salvation. Preach to me about the wrath and justice of God. Preach to me about God's mercy to me if just obey and do the right things. These doctrines will make me work harder than that impractical doctrine of assurance."

# The Gospel Mystery of Sanctification

What a miserable faith you have if you believe that! You would rather base your life on legal principles than upon the gospel of grace. If you live that way, you will never be able to serve God acceptably from a heart of love. You will fail to obey God because you are not trying to obey God out of gospel principles. In order to truly obey God, you must have the assurance of God's love for you.

Think about all of the things you are called to do in your Christian life that absolutely must be based upon God's love for you, and not upon legalism:

- [ ] rejoicing in the Lord always

- [ ] having a hope that does not make you ashamed

- [ ] acknowledging the Lord as your God and Savior

- [ ] praying to the Lord as your Father in heaven

- [ ] offering up your body and soul as an acceptable sacrifice to the Lord

- [ ] casting all your cares, both body and soul, upon the Lord

- [ ] having contentment and thanksgiving in every circumstance

- [ ] boasting only in the Lord

- [ ] triumphing in his praise

- [ ] rejoicing in tribulation

- [ ] putting on Christ in your baptism

- [ ] receiving Christ's body as broken for you, and his blood shed for you in the Lord's Supper

- [ ] committing your soul willingly to God as your redeemer, whenever he will be pleased to call for you

- [ ] loving Christ's second coming, and looking for it as the blessed hope

When you fall into doubt about whether or not you are a Christian, relieve yourself of your doubts by trusting confidently in Christ for your salvation. If you do not trust in him, you will do not do what you are being called to do. For instance, when you come to the Lord's Table, if you do not have assurance of your salvation, you will refrain from coming and partaking. The Lord's Table requires assurance. There are many other Christian duties that require assurance as well. If you do not have assurance, you simply will not do them.

Give me a saving faith that will produce these fruits! No other kind of faith will work through love (Galatians 5:6). James tells you to demonstrate your faith by your works (James 2:18). When God called his people to work miracles by faith, all things were possible for them when they believed. Faith frequently produces other works of righteousness, which could also be called spiritual miracles. All of God's people throughout history have obeyed God, and suffered for him, by faith. If you are ever called to the fiery trial our spiritual forefathers suffered, you will find that their doctrine of assurance will encourage you when you must suffer for the sake of Christ.

Seventh, the contrary doctrine, which says that saving faith cannot give you any assurance, produces many evil fruits in peoples' lives. It will strip your soul of all the comfort that assurance of salvation brings. The only assurance you will have is if you obey God all the time – which of course you cannot do. You will never be able to gain assurance by your obedience. You will continually be subject to doubts about your salvation, and to the tormenting fears that you are under the wrath of God. You will have no true love for God. At best, you will be able to offer him the hypocritical obedience of a slave. You will be just like the adherents of legalistic religions, with all their penance, bodily mutilations, whippings, pilgrimages, and indulgences. Once people give up the assurance of their salvation, the will grasp at any straw to try to avoid drowning in the gulf of despair.

People who have no assurance of salvation are wounded souls indeed. There is no way to give them any solid comfort. They see themselves without holiness, under the wrath and curse of God, dead in sin, and not even able to do so much as think a good thought. You will only make them more distraught if you tell them, "Just obey God. Do the best you can. If you do all the right things, God will give you grace and favor." You will not be helping them a bit. They know they cannot believe or obey God unless God helps them. You must have a better way to comfort them than this! Tell them about the free promise of salvation to the worst of sinners, if they will only believe in Christ. Encourage them to apply those promises to themselves. Urge them to boldly trust in Christ for the forgiveness of their sins, for holiness, and for eternal glory. Assure them that God will help them to sincerely believe in Christ, if they desire it with all their heart. Also tell them that it is their duty to believe, because God commands it.

There are many other evils that the doctrine of the lack of assurance brings. People will not admit the depths of their sin. They will tend to think of themselves as better than they are, so they will be able to avoid falling into despair. Others will remain content without ever knowing whether or not they have a relationship with Christ. They do not think it is necessary for their salvation. It is only the few "elite" Christians who ever actually attain assurance of salvation. By resting in such complacency, they show little love for Christ, or for their own souls. Others think that doubting their salvation is a sign of humility – even though they will hypocritically complain about their doubts. Many spend their time looking inward to see if they can find any evidence that they have a relationship with Christ. They do this, when they should be spending their time receiving Christ, enjoying Christ, and walking in him by faith.

Some people are troubled with doubt as to whether or not they should call God "Father." They do not think they have the right to speak to him this way in their prayers. They are offended when ministers call God "Father" in their public prayers. They are not comfortable calling God "Father" or Christ "my Savior." They are also offended by many of the Psalms. They even avoid partaking of the Lord's Supper, because they simply are not sure if they have a personal relationship with Christ.

True believers have assurance of faith when they believe. However, the assurance of many true believers is being weakened by the doctrine that is being taught – that they have no right to have assurance of their salvation. Many of them are assaulted with many doubts. Many walk with bitterness in their souls. Many are filled with fears and doubts for their whole lives. This is the reason they have so little courage and passion for God! This is the reason they spend so much time focused on earthly things, and why they are so afraid of suffering and death.

The way to avoid all of these evils is to have a solid assurance of salvation. Maintain and renew your assurance continually, simply by boldly trusting in the name of the Lord, and staying yourself upon your God. Believe the gospel again and again, especially when you walk in darkness and do not see any light of your own (Isaiah 50:10). Mature Christians will testify to you that this is true.

The Gospel Mystery of Sanctification

# Chapter 11

### Principle Number 11

**Believe in Christ without delay! Then, continue to build up your faith. When you do this, you will build your relationship with Christ more and more. You will also be empowered to live a holy life.**

Thus far I have been telling you about the only effective way you can live a holy life. For the rest of the time, I want to tell you how to put these principles to work in your life. I think it has become clear to you that faith in Christ must be the basis for living a holy life. Faith in Christ is the rock bottom foundation for all your obedience to God.

I have been explaining to you from Scripture how you receive Christ into your heart by faith. When you believe in Christ, he gives you the power to live a holy life. Faith is the grace that unites you to Christ. Faith brings you into a mystical marriage with Christ. Faith makes you a branch on the vine of Christ. Faith makes you a member of his body, joined to the head, Christ. Faith makes you a living stone in his spiritual temple, built upon the precious cornerstone and sure foundation of Christ. By faith you eat and drink of the living bread and drink that came down from heaven and give life to the world. Faith is the grace by which you pass from your corrupt natural state into your new holy state in Christ, and from death in sin to life in righteousness. Faith is the grace that comforts you, so that you might be established in every good word and work.

If you ask the question, "What must we do to do the works of God?" Christ answers by telling you to "believe in him he has sent" (John 6:28-29). Jesus tells you first about the work of believing. Faith is the work of works, because all other good works proceed from faith. Let me now tell you four things about living by faith.

First, diligently labor to believe in Christ. Many people look down upon faith. They do not understand it from the light of reason, as they can understand many other moral duties. You can only understand what faith is through the supernatural revelation of the gospel. Faith is foolishness to the natural man. Some people will sometimes be terrified because of their sins, and they will examine themselves intensely. They might even write them down on lists. However, they seldom think of the greatest sin of all: not believing in Christ. They rarely ever put that sin down in their catalogue of sins!

Even people who understand they must believe in Christ do not strive to actually do it – either because they think faith is so easy to do, or because they do not see how they can possibly do it without the Spirit's help. Some people think believing is so hard, it is foolish for them to try until they feel the working of the Spirit in their hearts. Or, they think it would be presumptuous of them to believe in Christ until they know they are one of God's elect. Let me encourage you to have faith by saying this: Believing is worth striving for because it is so precious, and so necessary for your Christian life.

Nature cannot reveal God's plan of salvation to you. Do not look down upon the way God has revealed his way of salvation to you in the Holy Scriptures. The reason why the gospel is preached is so that all people will come to embrace "the obedience that comes from faith" (Romans 1:5). God wants to see people come to Christ, and thus to all obedience to him. Indeed, the reason why Scripture was given was to "make you wise for salvation by faith in Jesus Christ" (II Timothy 3:15). The "purpose of the law of Moses" was to bring about "righteousness for everyone who believes" (Romans 10:4). Christ was the way that righteousness came. God's moral law was also revealed to show you your need for salvation in Christ. The moral law does no good for fallen human beings in and of itself, because they have no ability to keep it.

If you look down upon believing, and consider it foolish, you despise the whole counsel of God revealed in the Scriptures. The law and the gospel, and Christ himself, will be of no benefit to you. The only fruit you will produce without faith are some hypocritical moral actions, and slavish performance – all of which will be filthy rags in the sight of God on Judgment Day.

Do not fall into the trap so many people fall into: do not think that the sin of unbelief is an insignificant sin. In fact, unbelief is the most destructive sin of all! Unbelief is the root of all your other sins. Unbelief is the one sin that makes it impossible for you to please God in any other duty (Hebrews 11:6). If you will not pay attention to the sin of unbelief now, God will make you pay attention to it at the end. For "he who does not believe in the Son shall not have life. The wrath of God remains on him" (John 3:36). "The Lord Jesus will be revealed from heaven in blazing fire, taking vengeance on those who do not obey the gospel of our Lord Jesus Christ" (II Thessalonians 1:7-8).

Second, believing in Christ requires diligent concentration and effort on your part. You must labor "to enter into that rest, lest any man fall by unbelief" (Hebrews 4:11). "You must show diligence to the full assurance of hope to the end, so that you may be followers of those who by faith and patience inherit the promises" (Hebrews 6:11-12). Faith requires you to exercise might and power. Thus, you have to be "strengthened with power by the Spirit in your inward man, so that Christ may dwell in your heart by faith" (Ephesians 3:16-17). Faith is easy and pleasant by nature, because it is a motion of the heart. It does not require any physically exhausting bodily labor. Faith is the way you take Christ and his salvation to be your own. This is a very comforting and delightful thing to do. This delight can make even hard work easy and pleasant. The reason why obedience is difficult for you is because of your own inner corruption, and because of Satan's temptations.

It is not easy to confidently receive Christ for your salvation, when you are burdened by the guilt of sin and the wrath of God. It will be especially difficult to receive Christ if for a long time you have been trying to earn your salvation by your own works. It will be very hard to believe in Christ if you think that salvation by free grace is foolish and worthless. It will also be difficult to believe if your heart is filled with the pleasures of the world and the flesh. Satan will do everything he can to keep you from believing in Christ.

Many works that seem easy to do will actually be very difficult for you in your particular circumstances. You are called to forgive your enemies and love them as yourself. That is easy to do in theory, but it is very hard to do from your heart. You are called to cast your care upon God for all of your earthly concerns. Rich men find this easy to do, while poor people find it very hard to do. Remember what Moses called the Israelites to do when Pharaoh and his chariots overtook them at the edge of the Red Sea: "Do not fear. Stand still, and see the salvation of the Lord, which he will show you today" (Exodus 14:13). This was not easy for them to do!

Some things are very hard to do simply because they are so easy! Naaman the Syrian found it hard to simply "wash and be cleansed" when he wanted to be healed of his leprosy. He thought that God's remedy was just too insignificant and easy. In the same way, people are offended by having to believe in Christ. They think believing is too easy and insignificant to do to cure the leprosy of their soul. They would rather have something much harder required of them, so they could say they earned their salvation by their work. They want to be able to boast about what they have done.

Faith is such an easy thing to do! However, people would rather do the most burdensome and unreasonable works to try to earn the favor of God. The Jews and the Galatian Christians took the yoke of Moses' law upon their backs, even though none of them were able to carry it (Acts 15:10). The pagan people burned their sons and daughters in the fire to earn the favor of their gods (Deuteronomy 12:31). Legalists would rather take vows of poverty, chastity and obedience. They would rather torture their bodies with fasting, whipping, and pilgrimages. They would rather perform burdensome superstitions and excessive religious rituals. All of these people would rather do all of these crushing works, rather than simply believe in Christ. Why? So they can boast before God in their accomplishments.

If you look down upon the work of faith because you think it is too simple, you have never really come to know the depths of your many sins. You really do not understand the curse of the law and the wrath of God under which you now lie. You do not understand the darkness of your mind, the corruption and hardness of your heart, and your bondage to the power of sin and Satan. You have never truly been humbled. That is why you cannot believe in Christ. Many Christians have found it a struggle to believe in Christ. Faith involves a struggle against your own corruption and against the temptations of Satan. Faith is indeed so difficult to do, you cannot do it without the mighty working of God's Spirit in your heart. Only the Holy Spirit can make faith an easy thing for you.

Even though you cannot have faith without the work of the Holy Spirit in your heart, you must still strive to believe in Christ. It is true that only the Holy Spirit can give you faith. However, this does not excuse you from believing in Christ. You must still believe in Christ, whether you feel the Spirit working in you or not. Again, you cannot do anything that is acceptable to God unless the Spirit of God enables you to do it. However, this does not absolve you from believing. On the contrary, you must have greater diligence: "Work out your salvation with fear and trembling, for it is God who works in you both to will and to do of his good pleasure" (Philippians 2:12-13).

# Believe in Christ without Delay!

The way the Spirit gives you faith is by stirring you up to believe. He uses the exhortations, commands, and invitations of the gospel. These invitations would have no value to you if you already had all the faith you need within yourself. You know the Spirit has given you faith when you see it acting. All inward graces are known by their fruits – just as seed in the ground is known when it comes up through the earth. You cannot see love for God or others unless you act it out. Children do not know whether or not they can stand on their own two feet until they have tried to walk. You do not know your spiritual strength until you have put it into practice.

Do not sit around doing nothing, just waiting for the Spirit to give you faith! Do not sit around wondering if the Spirit will give you strength to act. Step out in faith and believe! You are called to trust in Christ for salvation. When you do that, the Spirit gives you the strength you need. All the duties of obedience flow out of faith. However, the Spirit gives you faith as you hear, know, and understand the word of God. "Faith comes by hearing, and hearing by the word of God" (Romans 10:17). Do not wait to see if the Spirit will give you faith. Rather, hear the word of God and believe it. If you do, you have faith! Do not speculate as to whom God will give faith, or to whom he will not give faith. You are simply commanded to believe the gospel. When you believe the gospel, you will find that the Spirit of Christ has strengthened you to believe. Just take him at his word – do not wonder beforehand whether or not he will give you faith. Stop doubting and believe!

Do not try to figure out the mysterious work of the Holy Spirit. The Spirit gives faith to his people quite indiscernibly. It is like the wind that blows where it wants to, where no one knows where it comes from or where it goes. You can only hear its sound, when it is no longer there (John 3:8). You must simply believe the gospel, even before you know whether or not the Spirit will give you salvation. God calls you to have faith. He tells you that you have the right and the responsibility to come to Christ for salvation. Do not speculate about the secret work of the Holy Spirit. "Do not be afraid, for I am commanding you. Be strong and courageous" (Joshua 1:6). "Arise, and work, for the Lord will be with you" (I Chronicles 22:16). If you receive the gospel as the word of God, you are being taught by the Spirit. You will certainly come to Christ in faith (John 6:45). If you do not receive the Gospel, you despise God and make him a liar. You deserve to perish because of your unbelief.

Fourth, you are commanded to believe the gospel, even before you know whether or not you are one of God's elect people. The Holy Spirit only gives saving faith to God's elect people. Other people do not believe the gospel because they do not belong to Christ's sheep (John 10:26). That is why faith is called "the faith of God's elect" (Titus 1:1). However, everyone who hears the gospel is obligated to believe it. They are also obliged to keep God's moral law. They are also responsible for their own unbelief if they do not believe the gospel. They have only themselves to blame for their condemnation. "He who does not believe is condemned already, because he has not believed in the name of God's one and only Son" (John 3:18). Paul shows that the elect Israelites received salvation, but the others, who were not elect, were blinded. However, even these ones "were broken off from the good olive tree" because of their unbelief (Romans 11:7, 20). In other words, they were responsible for their condemnation before God.

You cannot know whether or not you are elect until you believe the gospel. That is something that is hidden in the unsearchable counsel of God. You only know you are elect when God calls you, and you believe in Christ. Your election is something you know after the fact. Paul knew that the Thessalonians were elect because of their faith. "The gospel came to them, not in word only, but also in power, and with the Holy Spirit, and with great assurance. They received the word with much suffering, and with great joy in the Holy Spirit" (I Thessalonians 1:4-6). If you want to know whether or not God has chosen you, look to your calling when you first became a Christian (I Corinthians 1:26-27). Do you want to know whether or not you are one of the elect? Believe in Christ. If you do not, you will never know that you are elect!

It is not presumptuous of you to trust in Christ for eternal life before you know whether or not you are elect. Remember, God, who cannot lie, has made this promise: "Whoever believes in him shall not be ashamed" (Romans 10:11-12). God does not discriminate among those who believe this promise. The promise will be fulfilled. It is as certain as any of God's other decrees and purposes. God's promise is a sure and sufficient ground for your confidence. It is absolutely certain that all whom the Father has given to Christ in election will come to Christ. At the same time, it is absolutely certain that "Christ will in no way cast out any who come to him," no matter who they are (John 6:37). Do not use your human reason to try to figure out this mysterious truth.

Do not be afraid that you will ruin God's plan for election when you believe in Christ for salvation! Do not think, "I had better not believe the Gospel. What if I am not one of God's elect people?" If you believe

the gospel, you will know that you are indeed one of God's elect people.
If you do not believe the gospel, you will place yourself among those who
are not elect, among those who "stumble at the word because of their
disobedience. For this they were appointed" (I Peter 2:18).

Do not look for evidence of your election before you believe the
gospel. Just boldly trust in Christ. He will give you his salvation,
something that belongs only to his elect people. God will give all of his
spiritual blessings to those whom "God has chosen in Christ before the
foundation of the world" (Ephesians 1:3-4). However, you must trust in
Christ to receive all of these spiritual blessings. If you do not trust in
Christ, you will not receive them at all. Pray in faith, without any doubts,
that God will "remember you with the favor that he gives to his people,
that you may see the good of his chosen ones, and that you might exult
with his inheritance" (Psalm 106:4-5). Trust boldly in God, and he will
treat you as one of his chosen, elect people.

It is not presumptuous for you to believe the gospel before you
know whether or not you are one of God's elect people. It is your duty to
do the great work of believing in Christ for salvation. Do not question
beforehand whether or not you are elect. Remember, the "secret things
belong to God, but the things revealed belong to you, so that you may do
them" (Deuteronomy 29:29).

The second main thing I want to discuss with you is this: you are
commanded to believe the gospel for salvation, as I have just been saying.
However, you must believe the gospel in the right way. There are
different kinds of faith. There is a false faith, and there is a true faith.
Make sure you have true faith.

Love, which is the fulfillment of the law, and which is the main
fruit of sanctification, must flow from an unhypocritical faith (I Timothy
1:5). You can have a false faith that does not really receive Christ into
your heart. This kind of faith will not produce any love or any true
obedience. Simon the Magician had this kind of faith. Even though he
believed in some way, he was still filled with the "gall of bitterness, and he
was in the chains of iniquity" (Acts 8:13, 23). The Jews had this kind of
faith. Jesus would not commit himself to them, because they did not
confess him out of fear of being put out of the synagogue (John 2:23 and
12:42). James speaks of people who have this kind of false faith: "What
does it profit, my brothers, if a man says he has faith, but does not have
works? Can such faith save him? The demons also believe, and tremble"

(James 2:14, 19). Be very careful that you do not deceive your soul with counterfeit faith. Make sure you have the real thing, the precious faith of God's elect.

How can you tell the difference between counterfeit faith and real faith? It all comes down to believing in the right way, in the way God has directed you in his word. One of the reasons why people miss salvation is that they never believe in the right way. I have already told you what true saving faith is. It has two parts. First, you believe the truth of the gospel. Second, you believe in Christ who is freely promised to you in the gospel, for your salvation. You have to make sure you do both of these things in the right way.

You have to believe the truth of the gospel in the right way, if you are going to personally receive Christ. If you understand how wonderful Christ is, you would never fail to receive him personally. You will often be tempted to doubt the truths of the gospel. If you give in to these lies, you will never be able to trust Christ personally. Let me tell you how you can make sure you will always have full confidence in the truth of the Gospel.

First, you must believe how bad you really are apart from Christ. This is obviously a hard pill to swallow, but if you are going to understand how wonderful the gospel is, you have to know how awful you are! What are you apart from Christ? You are a child of wrath by nature. You have fallen from God because of the sin of the first Adam. You are dead in sins and trespasses. You are under the curse of the law of God. You are under the power of Satan. You will face misery for all eternity. You cannot possibly gain the favor of God by any of your good works. You cannot receive any spiritual life by trying to earn it through keeping a legal covenant of works. And, you will never be able to get out of this awful situation by any plan of your own making. You can only be freed from it by God himself – the one who raises the dead.

Very few people want to believe these truths. However, do not be afraid to understand the depth of your own sinfulness. Do not think you are better than you really are! Be glad when you come to know the worst about yourself. Be willing to believe that your heart is "deceitful, and desperately wicked" (Jeremiah 17:9). When you realize this, you will come to true humility and self-despair. Once you realize this, you will earnestly seek Christ's salvation. You will see that as the only thing you have to do. Once you grow weary of your sin, and see your need for the

# Believe in Christ without Delay!

Great Physician, you will follow his prescription not matter what it costs. You will no longer look to your own wisdom regarding how to get right with God (Matthew 9:12). It was because of lack of humility that the scribes and Pharisees did not enter into the kingdom of heaven – unlike the tax collectors and sinners, who did enter the kingdom (Matthew 21:31).

Second, believe that there is no way to be saved in a partial way. In other words, when you believe in Christ, you receive all of the blessings of his salvation. You receive his Holy Spirit as well as his forgiveness, you receive sanctification as well as justification.

Why is this so important to understand? Many people believe in Christ in order to be forgiven for their sins, but they have no desire to start living a holy life. They want to be forgiven of their sins, but they do not want to give up their sins. However, it is not possible to trust in Christ in this partial way. You cannot receive half a Christ. Justification and sanctification are inseparably joined in Christ. You cannot have one without the other. The only ones who are freed from condemnation by Christ are those who are empowered to live in holiness -- not according to the flesh but according to the Spirit (Romans 8:1). Many people ruin their souls because they try to have forgiveness without holiness.

Many other people ruin their souls because they seek to have their sins forgiven through faith in Christ, but then they try to produce holiness in their lives by their own efforts. They set up a system of laws to try to become godly people by their own endeavors. You can never live to God in holiness unless you become dead to the law. You can only live a godly life when Christ lives in you by faith. The faith that does not seek both forgiveness and holiness from Christ will never sanctify you. That kind of faith will never bring you to the glory of heaven.

Third, make sure you believe that Jesus Christ is completely sufficient to save you. Trust that his work is totally sufficient. His blood cleanses you from all your sin (I John 1:7), no matter how bad you have been.

This is the wonderful truth of the Gospel: No matter how sinful you have been in your life, Jesus is able to deliver you. Even if you have lived in slavery to sin and corruption for your whole life, he is able to free you from this slavery – not matter how strong it might be. The Bible tells you that Jesus has saved abominably wicked persons: idolaters, adulterers, homosexuals, coveters, drunkards, greedy people, etc. (I Corinthians 6:9-

10). Who else? The pagans, who sinned against the light of nature, and the Jews, who sinned against the light of Scripture. And also, Peter, who denied Jesus, and Paul, who persecuted and blasphemed Jesus.

Many people who have fallen into great sins ruin themselves forever because they do not think the grace of God is sufficient to forgive them and to sanctify them. They move into hopelessness, beyond all hope of recovery. Many people fall into this kind of despair. Ironically, they become careless about their souls. They get even worse, because they think, "It is too late. I am so bad, Christ will never save me. I might as well continue to indulge in my sins." They need to hear the word of the gospel, that "all kinds of sin and blasphemy will be forgiven, except the blasphemy of the Holy Spirit" (Matthew 12:31).

Some people also fall into tremendous guilt and despair because they think they have committed the "unforgivable sin" of blaspheming the Holy Spirit. This is not true, however. The reason why they are never forgiven is not because Christ's blood is not sufficient to save them, or because that God is not merciful enough to save them. The reason they are not forgiven is not because they never repent of that sin of blaspheming the Holy Spirit. The reason they are not forgiven is because they never seek God to have mercy on them through Christ. They are not forgiven because they continue obstinate right until their death. The Scripture says that it is "impossible to renew them to repentance" (Hebrews 6:5-6). The merits of Christ's work are totally sufficient for everyone who comes to him for mercy by believing the gospel.

Some people have no hope that they will ever be able to gain any victory over their sinful lusts. They have formerly made many vows and resolutions to try to gain victory over their lusts, but all of these rigorous efforts have failed. If this has happened to you, believe that the grace of Christ is sufficient for you, even when all other means have failed. It is just like the woman who had the flow of blood that no doctor could heal. Her condition only grew worse when the doctors tried to help. What did she do? She was absolutely sure that if she could just touch the garments of Christ, she would be healed (Mark 5:25-28). She touched him, and she was healed.

If you think your sin and guilt is too great for God to forgive, you are dishonoring the grace of God. You are undervaluing God's infinite mercy, the infinite merits of Christ's blood, and the power of the Holy Spirit. You deserve to perish with Cain and Judas! Many people who give themselves over to all kinds of sinful living actually live in this secret despair. They do not believe God will forgive them. This is what makes them pursue blaspheming, adultery, drunkenness, and all other kinds of wickedness.

This is the truth of the gospel: no matter how sordid your life has been, no matter how many your sins have been, they are small compared to the grace of Christ. Jesus, the eternal Son of God, became a man, and he offered himself on the cross, through the eternal Spirit, to be a sacrifice of infinite value for your salvation. He can make you a new person just as easily as he brought the entire universe into existence by speaking.

Fourth, make sure you believe that the general promise of the gospel applies personally to you when you believe it. God offers the gospel to everyone: "whoever believes in him shall not perish but have eternal life" (John 3:16). Make sure you always remember that this general promise applies to you when you believe it and receive Christ. If you believe, you will receive eternal life. You do not have to do any work to have a relationship with Christ. You receive him by faith. The universal promise is for you to personally claim: "Whoever believes in him will not be ashamed" (Romans 9:33). This promise applies to you. If God does not exclude you from his promise, you must not exclude yourself. You must believe that no matter how wicked and unworthy you might be, if you come to Christ, you will be completely accepted by God.

Believe what you regularly say in the Apostles' Creed: "I believe in…the forgiveness of sins." Believe that this is true for you! It will not have any value for you if you believe that others are forgiven, but that you are not forgiven. This is why many wounded souls do not come to Christ as their Great Physician, once they understand how wicked their hearts really are. They think that it will be vain for them, as filthy as they are, to trust in Christ for salvation. They think, "I am so bad, the promise of the gospel cannot apply to me. Christ will never save a person like me." They see themselves as so lost that they forget about the simple truth of the gospel: "Christ came to seek those who are lost." If people who are dead in sin cannot be saved, then there is no hope for anyone. Everyone would perish! Why? Because no one has any spiritual life until they receive it by believing in Christ.

Some people think they are worse than anyone else. They think no one else has as wicked a heart as they do. Yet, they think others will be accepted by God, but they will not. If you fall into this kind of thinking, understand that "Christ came to save the worst of sinners" (I Timothy 1:15). The purpose of God in salvation is to "show the exceeding riches of his grace" through your salvation (Ephesians 2:7). God's grace is most glorified when he pardons the worst sinners! Do not consider yourself worse than anyone else. Everyone else, like you, is "dead in trespasses and sins." Their "mind is hostile to God, and is not subject to his law, and indeed it cannot be" (Romans 8:7). "Every imagination of the thoughts of their hearts are only evil all the time" (Genesis 6:5). Everyone has the same corrupt fountain of sin in their hearts. Even though you may have outwardly sinned more than they have, their hearts are no better than yours – no matter how good they might look on the outside.

Some people think they have delayed too long to believe in Christ. They think that now they will "find no place for repentance, even though they seek it carefully with tears" (Hebrews 12:17). They must understand the truth of the gospel: "Now is the accepted time, now is the day of salvation" (II Corinthians 6:2). If you have fallen into this way of thinking, remember that for as long as you live, God is calling you to come to the gospel. Yes, Esau was rejected, because he sought earthly blessings. He did not seek to have the spiritual blessings from God that his birthright represented. If you come to Christ to receive his salvation as your only happiness, you will not be rejected. If you come into Christ's vineyard at the eleventh hour of the day, you will receive your penny, just as those who came to the vineyard early in the morning. Why? Because the reward comes by grace, and not by human merit (Matthew 20:9-10).

Believe that Christ and his salvation will be given to you as a free gift if you do not try to work to gain it. Do not work for the right to have Christ. Do not think you are worthy to receive him. Simply "believe in him who justifies the ungodly" (Romans 4:5). If you say you must be a good enough person to deserve Christ, you will never receive Christ. If you say you must be a good person to have a relationship with Christ, you are setting up a wall you will never be able to climb over.

Fifth, confidently believe that it is God's will for you to believe in Christ, and receive eternal life through him. God wants you to believe in Jesus! When you do, he is pleased! God will help you to believe in Jesus, just as he will help you do anything else he has commanded you to do. What he commands you to do he enables you to do. If you understand this, you will joyfully believe. It is just like when Jesus spoke to the blind man: "Be of good comfort. Get up, he is calling you" (Mark 10:49). Jesus made Peter walk on the water (Matthew 14:29).

# Believe in Christ without Delay!

Do not start to meddle with God's secret counsel of predestination, the purpose of his will to give the grace of faith to some rather than to others. Focus only on his revealed will, that he invites, and indeed commands, you to believe in Christ. This will of God is confirmed by an oath: "As I live, says the Lord God, I have no pleasure in the death of the wicked, but that the wicked person turns from his ways and lives. Turn, turn from your evil ways. Why will you die, oh house of Israel?" (Ezekiel 33:11). Jesus said that he "wanted to gather the children of Jerusalem, even as a hen gathers her chickens under her wings, but you were not willing"(Matthew 23:37). Paul says that God "wants all men to be saved and come to a knowledge of the truth" (I Timothy 2:4).

Reject every thought that says "God really does not want me to be saved." What if only a few people are saved? Your salvation will not make the number too great, because only a few people will follow you and believe. What if the wrath of God is revealed from heaven against you in many terrible judgments? What if the word of God, and your own conscience, condemn you? Interpret these things in a good light. Their purpose is to drive you to Christ. This was the purpose of the law, with all of its curses and judgments – it was meant to drive God's people to himself (Romans 10:4).

If a prophet or an angel from heaven appears to you, and tells you that you are under the sentence of eternal condemnation, then you would be called to believe that God sent them to give you a timely warning. Why? So that you might believe the gospel, and turn to God in faith and repentance before it is too late. Jeremiah prophesied against the Jews that God would "pluck them up, and pull them down, and destroy them for their sins." Yet, he also taught them "if they turned from their evil ways, God would relent from sending evil upon them" (Jeremiah 17:7, 8, 11). Jonah preached the certain destruction of Nineveh. He told them they would be destroyed in forty days (Jonah 3:4). However, the intent of that awful message was that the sinful people of Nineveh might escape destruction by turning to God in repentance – which they did!

You have to understand why God warns people. Even his most severe warnings of wrath are always meant to lead you to faith and repentance, so you receive salvation while you still have the chance. God gives you so many stern warnings because he wants you to escape his judgment by running for refuge to his free mercy in Christ.

Do not think God has already determined not to show any saving mercy to you. Do not think you have already committed the unforgivable sin. Do not think it will be in vain for you to believe the gospel, because you think God will not help you do it. If you have these kinds of thoughts in your heart, they will harm you more than the most blasphemous thoughts you could ever think. They will destroy you more than the most abominable sin you have ever committed. Why? Because these thoughts prevent you from believing in Christ for salvation. "The Spirit and the Bride say 'Come.'" Jesus says, "Whoever wills, let him take the water of life freely" (Revelation 22:17).

Why do you have such unbelieving thoughts? Has God taken you into his secret counsel? Do you know that God has also decreed that you will be condemned forever? Are you so special that he has shared this knowledge with you? Do you know these things for sure, even before the one thing that proves them to be true happens – dying in unbelief and impenitence? The only one thing that will send you to hell forever is if you die in unbelief and without repentance.

If you think you have committed the unforgivable sin, you have misunderstood what the unforgivable sin is. You commit the unforgivable sin when you reject the way of salvation through Christ with your whole heart, even after you come to understand the truth of the gospel. Those who commit the unforgivable sin are those who reject the gospel for their whole lives. Then, they die in that hardened unbelief. It is the sin that the Hebrew Christians would have been guilty of if they had rejected Christianity in favor of the religion of the unbelieving Jews – those who considered Christ an imposter, and who vigorously persecuted Christ and all his ways (Hebrews 6:4-5). Those who have committed the unforgivable sin continue to be unrepentant, malicious enemies of Christ right to their dying day.

If you find that you desire to have a personal relationship with Christ, and to be a better person than you are, you have no reason to think you have committed the unforgivable sin. If you are troubled and grieved that your life is so wicked, and that you have no faith, love, or obedience, you can be sure you have not committed the unforgivable sin. If you are not a persecutor of the gospel, and if you do not prefer atheism or false religion to the gospel, you may be sure that you have not committed the unpardonable sin!

# Believe in Christ without Delay!

Sixth, when you believe, make sure you see the incomparable glory of Jesus Christ and his salvation above everything else.

You are called to enjoy Christ and his salvation more than you enjoy anything else. Christ must be your true happiness. He must make your cup run over with abundant peace, joy, and glory to all eternity. You must consider "all things loss compared to the excellence of knowing Christ Jesus your Lord" (Philippians 3:8). This kind of assurance will move your heart to choose and embrace Christ as the most precious treasure in the world. You will never rest satisfied unless you enjoy him alone. You will reject everything that stands in competition with enjoying Jesus. Christ is precious in the hearts of all true believers (I Peter 2:7). Their passion for Christ moves them to sell everything, so that they might have this pearl of great price (Matthew 13:46). They say, "Lord, give us this bread that comes down from heaven and gives life to the world." "Lord, to whom shall we go? Only you have the words of eternal life." (John 6:33, 34, 68). In their eyes, he is "the best among ten thousand" (Song of Songs 5:10).

In the Old Testament, the glory of God appeared in the wonderful beauty of the temple, and it drew worshippers from the utmost parts of the earth. In the same way, the unparalleled excellence of Christ, prefigured by the glory of the temple, even more powerfully draws believers now that gospel has fully come. The devil – the god of this world – knows how necessary it is for people to see the glory of the cross of Christ. Therefore, wherever the gospel is proclaimed, he does his best to eclipse the glory of Christ. He tries to blind the minds of people, "lest the light of the glorious gospel of Christ shine in them" (II Corinthians 4:4). It is possible for you to be intellectually convinced that the gospel is true, yet not believe it personally. Why? Because you do not yet see the glory of the gospel. In order to personally receive the truth of the gospel, you have to be convinced that Christ is completely lovely and sufficient.

I come now to the second principal aspect of faith. As I have been saying, the first aspect of faith is believing the truth of the gospel. The second aspect of faith is receiving Christ, his Spirit, and all his saving blessings, into your heart. It is not enough to be intellectually convinced that the gospel is true. You have to personally receive the promise of the gospel into your heart. The Holy Spirit enables you to do this. He first convinces you that the gospel is true. You receive the pattern of teaching (Romans 6:17), which God gives you. You believe it and obey it with all your heart.

159

# The Gospel Mystery of Sanctification

Once you accept that the gospel is true, you must believe that Christ is alone sufficient and all sufficient for your joy and for your salvation. You do not need anything else. You must recognize that you cannot get any happiness by your own wisdom, your own strength, your own works of righteousness, or by anything else in which you might place your confidence. You must consider anything other than Christ rubbish, and consider them a "loss for the sake of Christ" (Philippians 3:3-8). Do not be grieved that you have nothing to trust in other than Christ for your salvation. Rather, rejoice that you need nothing else! Rejoice that you have a sure foundation to stand on, one much better than any other you can build. Resolve to cast the burden of your soul totally on Christ. Do not seek your salvation in any other place, not matter what happens to you.

If a disabled man leans on a rotten staff rather than on a strong staff, he will fall. If a swimmer does not trust his body completely to the water to lift him up – if he grasps for weeds – he will sink to the bottom. Christ must be your Savior completely, or not at all. If you try to be saved any other way, as the Galatians did by circumcision, "Christ will be of no value to you at all" (Galatians 5:2).

You must receive Christ as a completely free gift – a gift that is given to the worst of sinners. Resolve that you will not try to do anything to earn his love. Do not try to do anything that will give you the right to have Christ. Resolve that you will come to him as a lost sinner, as an ungodly person, believing in "him who justifies the ungodly" (Romans 4:5). Resolve that you will buy him without money, without any price whatsoever (Isaiah 55:2). Do not look to your faith, to your love, or to any of your other good characteristics. Do not make them the basis of your trust in Christ. Trust only the free grace and the loving kindness of God in Christ! "How excellent is your loving kindness, oh God! Therefore the children of men put their trust under the shadow of your wings" (Psalm 36:7). If you make your own faith, love or good works the foundation of your life, you will turn the gospel on its head. If you build your relationship with Christ upon your good works, "Christ will be of no value to you" (Galatians 5:2).

In addition to coming to Christ for forgiveness, you must also come to Christ for a new holy heart and life. To be sure, Christ forgives all your sins when you believe in him. He saves you from the wrath of God and the curse of hell. However, when you come to him, come to him to receive a whole new way of thinking and living. Have a passionate love for Christ. Value him better than a thousand worlds. Make him the most excellent thing you have. See absolutely nothing good in yourself. Consider everything else rubbish in comparison to his wonderful grace, so that you can say from the bottom of your heart: "Who have I in heaven but you? And on earth there is no one that I desire besides you" (Psalm 73:25).

Draw near to God with "full assurance of faith" (Hebrews 10:22). Trust confidently in Christ for your salvation, based upon God's promise that "whoever believes in Christ will not be ashamed" (Romans 9:33). Examine yourself to see if you are filled with doubts and fears concerning your salvation in Christ. If you find any, ask yourself, with the Psalmist, "Why are you so cast down, oh my soul? Why are you so dispirited within me?" (Psalm 42:11).

The third main thing I want to tell you is this: avoid any delay in believing in Christ. Do not wait! Until you believe in Christ, you are under the power of sin and Satan, and under the wrath of God. There is nothing between you and hell besides the breath of your nostrils. It was a dangerous thing for Lot to linger in Sodom, just before the fire and brimstone came down upon that city. The man who killed another had to run quickly to the city of refuge, lest "the avenger of blood pursue him, and slay him while his heart is hot" (Deuteronomy 19:5-6). You must "make haste, and not delay, to keep God's commandments" (Psalm 119:60). "Flee for refuge to the hope set before you" (Hebrews 6:18). God commands you to flee in this way by faith, without which it is impossible to please God in anything else you are called to do.

You can have faith as soon as you hear the gospel. You do not have to wait to believe. "As soon as they hear about me, they will obey me" (Psalm 18:44). There are many examples of people who received the word of God by faith as soon as they heard it. Three thousand people were added to the church on the very day Peter first preached the gospel in Jerusalem (Acts 2:41). Many Jews and Gentiles were converted when they first heard the apostle Paul preaching the gospel in Antioch (Acts 13:48). The Philippians jailer and his entire house believed, and were baptized, the very same night that Paul first preached to them (Acts 16:33-34). The gospel came the first time to the Thessalonians, not only with words, but also with power, and with the Holy Spirit (I Thessalonians 1:5-6). When God opens someone's heart, they can come to know Christ after hearing only one sermon. Whenever you know your duty, God commands you to do it immediately. He does not allow you to take any respite in the state of unbelief.

When Satan cannot stop people from believing the gospel, he next tries to ruin their souls by getting them to delay in believing the gospel. He fills their minds with many false reasons why they should wait to believe in Christ. The most sensual people give in to his lies, and they decide to wait to believe in Christ. They decide they will take their fill of other pleasures, profits, and honors of this world. They only stop delaying when they feel the next world calling them, through sickness or old age. When that happens, they pray and hope for a long enough time to be able to repent before they die. These people are playing with fire. In addition, they show that they really do not want to repent and believe until they are forced to do so by necessity. They show that they prefer the pleasures, profits, and honors of this world more than they prefer God, Christ, and their own souls. The more time they spend walking in sin, wasting their precious time of health and strength, the more dangerous it becomes for them. God may never give them time or grace to repent.

Other people delay in believing because they have intellectual questions about the gospel. They think God will allow them to remain in disbelief for a while, while they have time to examine the truth of other competing doctrines. Or, they demand that God give them some proof that the gospel is really true. They are not willing to take the gospel at face value. Seekers like this fritter away the day of grace. They are "always learning, but never coming to the knowledge of the truth" (I Timothy 6:3). The gospel is so clearly true by its own light, people should clearly see that it is the truth of God! However, many of them shut their eyes to it, or blind themselves with their own pride. Others love their own life of sin more than the gospel. The gospel is the obvious truth of God because the gospel is covered with God's grace, mercy, power, justice, and holiness. You cannot miss it if you look at it!

If people to do not submit to this "doctrine which is in accord with godliness" (I Timothy 6:3), it is because they are too proud to do so. If they were truly humble, and if they sincerely wanted to do the will of God, they would "find out whether the doctrine comes from God, or not" (John 7:17). If they examined the gospel, they would quickly be persuaded of its truth, as they read Moses and the Prophets, Christ and his Apostles, in the Scriptures. However, if they will not listen to them in Scripture, they will not listen and be persuaded "even if someone rose from the dead" (Luke 16:31), or if someone performed some other miracle for them.

Other people delay in believing in Christ, and ruin their souls, because they rely on performing the outward means of grace. They perform religious rituals, which are fine in and of themselves. However, they then trust in their performance rather than in Christ. They are convinced of the truth of the gospel, but they trust in their religious works rather than in Jesus alone. They think they are waiting upon God at the doors of his salvation and grace. However, this is not what it mans to truly wait upon God. This is disobedience to God, and to the means of grace he has given. God requires us to be "doers of the word, and not just hearers, and so deceive ourselves" (James 1:22). God calls us to come into his feast (Luke 14:23), and not just stand at the door. If this is all you do, Christ will consider you an eavesdropper, not a true member of his household.

When the Bible speaks of waiting on the Lord, it means that you are believing and hoping in the Lord, and depending on him. "I would have fainted unless I had believed in the goodness of the Lord in the land of the living. Wait on the Lord. Be of good courage, and he will strengthen your heart. Wait, I say, on the Lord" (Psalm 27:13-14). "It is good for a man to hope, and to quietly wait for the salvation of the Lord" (Lamentations 3:26).

What is it that these deluded people are waiting for, before they believe the gospel? Do they need more knowledge of the gospel? The way to get more knowledge is to make use of the knowledge you already have. Believe in Christ for salvation, according to the little knowledge of the gospel you now have. If you do, you will partake of the promise of knowledge that the New Covenant declares: "'They will all know me, from the least to the greatest of them', says the Lord" (Jeremiah 31:34).

Are you waiting for the appointed time of your conversion? If you enter into Christ now by faith, you will find in him waters of life, and the Holy Spirit will heal and give life to your soul. God has already told you in his word that the time for your conversion is **now**: "As the Holy Spirit says, 'Today, if you hear his voice, do not harden your heart'" (Hebrews 3:7-8). You will never know the time God has determined, in his secret council, to give you faith, until you actually believe the gospel.

Are you waiting to feel the love of God in your soul? To obtain it, "believe, that the God of hope may fill you with all joy and peace as you believe" (Romans 15:13). God has already demonstrated his love for your soul by the free promises of life and salvation he has given you in Christ. Trust in the name of the Lord, and rest upon your God. When you walk in darkness and see no light, simply trust in him. If you do not, "you will lie down in sorrow" (Isaiah 1:10-11).

Are you waiting to be a better person, so you will be fully prepared to believe the gospel? If you seek true holiness, you cannot have it before you have faith. True holiness is the fruit of the faith you already have. If you are not seeking true holiness, then I cannot imagine what you are seeking. Perhaps you are waiting to feel a greater sense of God's wrath. Perhaps you would like to have deeper despair. However, I do not recommend it. Greater despair is more likely to give birth to hatred for God. It will not produce holiness. Therefore, put it aside by believing in God's love in Christ. Do not wait for anything else.

To be sure, God often uses thoughts of despair to drive you to Christ. Some people come to hate sin and love Christ when they fall into complete despair over their sins. However, many more people come to Christ without ever falling into this kind of debilitating despair. God gives them knowledge of their sins, and of Christ's salvation, without it. I previously gave you many examples of people who received the gospel with joy right when they first heard it. Do not desire to be filled with despair. Do not think you have to be worse before you get better. You are already bad enough! The best way to spend your time is to get better right now, by believing in Christ!

The fourth main thing I want to say is this: make sure you continue to grow in your most holy faith. Once you have come to saving faith, once you know your name is written in heaven, do not grow careless and lax in your faith. Rather, as long as you live, "continue in your faith, grounded and rooted, not moved away from the hope of the gospel" (Colossians 1:23). Continue to "hold the beginning of your confidence, and your hope, steadfast right until the end" (Hebrews 3:6). "Build yourself up in your most holy faith" (Jude 20), "abounding with thanksgiving" (Colossians 2:7). Even though you have received Christ freely by faith, you are still but an infant in Christ when you first believe (I Corinthians 3:1). Do not think you have already attained the goal, or that you are already mature and complete (Philippians 3:12-13). Strive to be ever more rooted and built up in Christ, until you "come to be a perfect man, to the measure of the stature of the fullness of Christ" (Ephesians 4:13).

If you have really received a new nature through regeneration, you will have an appetite to continue to grow in your faith to maturity – just like a newborn baby craves milk in order to grow (I Peter 2:2). You are not only supposed to receive Christ and your new nature by faith, but you are also supposed to live and walk by that same faith. By faith, you are called to "resist the devil, and to quench all his fiery arrows by it." You are also called to "grow in grace," and to "pursue holiness in the fear of God." For, "you are kept by the mighty power of God through faith unto salvation" (I Peter 1:5). Your Christian warfare is called the "good fight of faith" (I Timothy 6:12).

All aspects of your spiritual life and holiness will either grow or decay in you. It all depends upon whether or not your faith grows or decays in its vigor. When your faith begins to sink under fears and doubts, everything else about you will sink along with it (Matthew 14:29-31). Faith is like the hand of Moses. "As long as it is held up, Israel prevails. When it is let down, the Amalekites prevail" (Exodus 17:11). You must labor and strive to grow in your faith, just as you initially came to faith. Even though you are to give all the glory to God, the author and finisher of your salvation (Hebrews 12:2), you are called to live by faith with all that is in you.

The church will meet great difficulties on her march through the wilderness of this world to heavenly Canaan – just as the Israelites experienced great difficulties in their deliverance from slavery in Egypt. As you move on toward maturity, you will face even greater difficulties than you did when you first became a Christian. God, in his wisdom and mercy, often allows you to face your hardest trials after he has given you the grace to stand in the evil day. The more mature you grow, the more you will face the assaults of your own indwelling sin, and the more you will face the temptations of Satan. Because of this, you must make sure you continue to grow in your faith.

Your faith is imperfect. As long as you live in this world, you will be filled with much unbelief. You will always need to pray, "Lord, I believe. Help my unbelief!" (Mark 9:24). You need to have more faith, so you can receive Christ in a greater way. You will find, as you mature, that your faith is producing good works. When you see them, you will place even more confidence in Christ for his salvation by grace. However, there is a danger you will face as well. You will be tempted to shift from trusting in the merits of Christ to trusting in your own good works – just as the legalists do. This is very subtle, because you will indeed increase in good works as you grow to maturity. As your good works grow, so will the temptation to base your acceptance with God on your good works.

Also, beware of trusting in your faith itself as a work of righteousness, rather than trusting in Christ by faith. If you find that your faith is not producing the fruits of holiness you desire, do not stop believing. Instead, increase your confidence in Christ. The weaker your faith is, the less fruitful your life will be. The more confidence you have in the love of God for you in Christ, the more you will love God and his service. If you fall into some gross sin after you have come to Christ – as David and Peter did – do not throw away your confidence. Do not expect the wrath of God. Do not think you are not allowed to be comforted by Christ's grace for a good long time. If you think this, you will be weaker than ever, and more prone to fall into other sins. Strive to believe even more confidently that you have an advocate with the Father, Jesus Christ the righteous one, and that he is the propitiation for your sins (I John 2:1-2).

Do not let the guilt of any sin stay on your conscience for any length of time. Wash it away quickly in the fountain of Christ's blood. That fountain is always open for you whenever you sin. You need to be humbled for your sins in a gospel-way. This means that you hate your sinfulness, and that you are sorry for it with a godly sorrow, out of love for God. Peter might have been ruined forever after he denied Jesus, just like Judas was, if Peter's faith was not upheld by the prayer of Christ (Luke 21:31-32).

If a cloud comes over your own qualifications, so that you can see no grace in yourself, continue to trust in him who justifies the ungodly. Believe in him who came to seek and to save the lost. If God seems to treat you like an enemy, by bringing you some horrible affliction like he did with Job, do not condemn your faith and its fruit, as if they were not acceptable to God. Rather, say, along with Job, "Though he slay me, I will still trust in him. I will maintain my own ways before him" (Job 13:15). Strive to increase your faith, by trusting in God to build up and increase your faith. Act out your faith frequently. Be confident that "he who began a good work in you will carry it on to completion until the day of Christ Jesus" (Philippians 1:6).

# Chapter 12

### Principle Number 12

**In order to obey the law of God, earnestly live by your most holy faith. Do not walk according to your old nature, and do not put into practice anything that belongs to your old nature. Walk only according to the new nature you received by faith, and live the lifestyle of your new nature. This is the only way to live a holy and righteous life – as much as is possible in this present life.**

Right now I want to tell you how to live by faith so you can keep the law of God. This is the whole purpose of my book, to show you how God has told you to live by faith to live a holy life! In a sense, this chapter gives you the most important principle I have to tell you. Everything I have said up to this point, and everything I will say after this point, must be seen in light of this truth: in order to live a holy life, you must live by faith according to your new nature.

Here is what I have said to you thus far. Your old nature is the nature you received from the first Adam when you were born into the human race. The Bible calls this old nature "the old man." As long as you have only this nature, you are said to be "in the flesh." Your new nature is the nature you receive from the second Adam, Jesus Christ, by being spiritually reborn into union and fellowship with him, by faith. The Bible calls this new nature "the new man." When you receive it, you are said to be "in the Spirit." The lifestyle that belongs to your natural state is what you are able to attain before you are in Christ by faith. The lifestyle of the new state comes from the privileges and qualifications you receive when you come to Christ by faith. Only the new nature Christ gives you can empower you to live a holy life.

You are said to be walking according to either of these states when you are moved and guided by them, or when you act in a way that is agreeable to them. Kings act according to their state when they command with authority. Poor men act according to their state when the act in service and obedience. Children act according to their state when they act thoughtlessly! I am telling you to act according to your state in Christ. Obey God and do the works of the law *by gospel principles and means.* This is the rare and excellent art of godliness, in which every Christian should be a skilled expert. Many people labor for years trying to live a godly life. However, they give it up in shame and confusion because they never understood this holy art. They never tried to attain true godliness in a proper gospel way.

Some worldly arts are called mysteries, but above all, this spiritual art of godliness is "without controversy, a great mystery" (I Timothy 3:16). Why is this the case? Because the means of attaining true godliness are deeply mysterious. You are not a skillful artist until you know them, and can practice them regularly. It is a manner of practice far above the sphere of what you are naturally capable of doing. It would never have entered into the hearts of the wisest people in the world. You can only learn it through the revelation of the Scriptures. And even though the true way of godliness is so plainly revealed in the Scriptures, it remains a dark riddle to those who are not inwardly enlightened and taught by the Holy Spirit.

Many Christians do not fully understand the true way of godliness; it remains obscure to them. They can hardly understand it, and they can certainly not tell other people about the way of life in which they are walking. It is like the disciples who walked with Christ, the only way to the Father, yet they did not perceive that knowledge themselves. "Lord, we do not know where you are going, so how can we know the way?" (John 14:5). The reason why many believers are so weak in Christ, and why they have not advanced in holiness and righteousness, is that they do not self-consciously understand the true way of godliness and sanctification.

I want you to thoroughly understand the mystery of godliness, as much as is possible. I am going to show you what the Bible says about the only way you can actually live a holy life. Then, I am going to give you some very practical principles as to how you can walk in the way of godliness, and move toward maturity in Christ.

The Holy Scriptures clearly tell you to continually grow in holiness. There are many different words and phrases the Holy Spirit uses to teach you this mystery of godliness. Here are some of the ways the Bible tells you to grow in holiness in your heart and life. I will try to group them in some orderly fashion.

First, this way of life is called "living by faith" (Habakkuk 2:4, Galatians 2:20, Hebrews 10:38); "walking by faith" (II Corinthians 5:7); "faith working by love" (Galatians 5:6); "overcoming the world by faith"

(I John 5:4); "quenching all the fiery darts of the wicked one by the shield of faith" (Ephesians 6:16). Some people think "living and walking by faith" means that you merely stir yourself up to live by the principles you believe. The Jews thought they lived by faith because they assented to the doctrine of Moses and the Prophets, and they were moved to have a zeal for God – even though "they sought righteousness not by faith, but as it were by the works of the law" (Romans 9:32). Paul thought he lived by faith while he was a zealous Pharisee. Afterwards, however, he knew that the life of faith consisted in dying to the law and living to God. He knew that not himself but Christ lived in him (Galatians 2:19-20). Just as it is one and the same thing to be justified by faith and to believe in Christ (Romans 5:1), so it is one and the same thing to live, walk, and work by faith. The Bible also speaks of living, walking and working by means of Christ and his saving gifts. You receive these gifts and use them by faith. Faith then guides and moves you to the practice of holiness.

Second, the same lifestyle is commended to you by the terms "walking, rooted, and built up in Christ" (Colossians 2:6-7); "living to God, and not to ourselves but to have Christ living in us" (Galatians 2:19-20); "good conversation in Christ" (I Peter 3:16); "putting on the Lord Jesus Christ, that you may walk honestly as in the day" (Romans 13:13-14); "being strong in the Lord, and in his mighty power" (Ephesians 6:10); "doing all things in the name of Christ" (Colossians 3:17); "walking up and down in the name of the Lord" (Zechariah 10:12); "going in the strength of the Lord; making mention of his righteousness, even of his only" (Psalm 71:16). These phrases occur frequently, and they sufficiently explain one another. They show that you are to practice holiness, not only because of Christ's authority, but also because of the way he strengthens and moves you to holiness. He is the only one who can truly encourage you to live a holy life.

Third, the lifestyle of gospel holiness is also described by the phrases "being strong in the grace that is in Christ Jesus" (II Timothy 2:1); "having our manner of life in the world, not with fleshly wisdom, but by the grace of God" (II Corinthians 1:12); "having or holding fast grace, that we may serve God acceptably, laboring abundantly," in such manner, that the whole work is not performed by us, but "by the grace of God that is with us" (I Corinthians 15:10). By grace you can understand the privileges of your new state given to you in Christ. They should guide and influence you as you seek to live a holy life.

Fourth, the Christian life is also described as "putting off the old man and putting on the new man." You are told to continually do this, even though you have done it to some degree already. You are to avoid your former sinful way of life (Ephesians 4:21-24), because you have put off the old man and have put on the new man (Colossians 3:9-10. I have already showed that this twofold man does not merely consist of sin and holiness. Rather, the old man refers to your natural state, with all of its characteristics, which can only enable you to commit sin. The new man refers to your new state in Christ, which equips you with everything you need to live a holy life.

Fifth, the Bible also speaks of the same thing when it teaches you "not to walk after the flesh, but after the Spirit, that you may be free from the law of sin, and that the righteousness of the law my be fulfilled in you (Romans 8:1-3); and, "by the Spirit to put to death the misdeeds of the body;" and to be "led by the Spirit, because you live by the Spirit, and have crucified the flesh, with its passions and desires" (Galatians 5:24). In these expressions, Paul not only commands you to walk in holiness, he also tells you how you can actually do it. By the flesh, he means your old nature, derived from the first Adam. By the Spirit, he means the Spirit of Christ, the new nature that you have from Christ dwelling in you.

You are said to walk after either of these natures when you make their characteristics the basis of your lifestyle. Paul teaches you to serve in the newness of the Spirit, and not in the oldness of the letter, so that you might bear fruit to God. On the one hand, this means that you are not to live by means of the law. Why? The law is a letter that kills. The flesh is married to it, and the law only stirs up sin within you. On the other hand, you are being taught to live by means of the Spirit, and by the manifold riches he gives you. You receive these spiritual riches when you come into your new state through your mystical marriage to Christ (Romans 7:4-6).

Sixth, Paul also teaches you about this way of living by telling you to look to his own example. The continual work of your life should be to "know Christ, and the power of his resurrection, and the fellowship of his sufferings, being made in conformity to his death – if by some chance you might attain to the resurrection of the dead," and to increase and press forward in this kind of knowledge (Philippians 3:10-14). Certainly he is referring to a deeply experiential and personal knowledge of Christ, and his death and resurrection, which will empower you to die to sin and live to God. Paul tells you to rely upon Christ's death and resurrection to grow in holiness in your heart and life. You must continue in this way of living, until you become mature in Christ.

The second main thing I am going to do is to tell you how to grow in holiness and maturity in Christ. Since you are naturally prone to take the wrong way, you must diligently listen to these instructions that come from the Scriptures. You should also pray that God would give you the Spirit of wisdom and revelation, so you can understand the way of holiness, and walk in it, according to this gracious promise: "The wayfaring men, though fools, shall not err therein" (Isaiah 35:8).

First, remember that even though you have received a new, holy nature through your faith in Christ, your natural state still remains to some degree, with all of its corrupt principles and properties.

As long as you live in the present world, you only know Christ and his perfections by faith. By your own senses and reason, you will see much in yourself that is contrary to Christ, because your faith is so imperfect. True believers will often have to pray to God to "help their unbelief" (Mark 9:24). Therefore, even though you receive a perfect Christ by faith, your degree of enjoying him is imperfect. You should always hope, as long as you are in this world, to enjoy him in a higher degree of perfection than you have already done. You are still only weak in Christ (II Corinthians 13:4). You are just a child in comparison to the perfection you expect in another world (I Corinthians 13:10-11). So, you must grow until you come to be a mature person (Ephesians 4:13). Some are, of course, weaker babes than others; they have received Christ in such a small measure that they may be considered carnal, rather than spiritual (I Corinthians 3:1).

All the blessings and perfections of your new state are seated and treasured up in Christ. They are joined to him inseparably. These are blessings like justification, the gift of the Spirit, your new nature, and the adoption of sons. You can receive them no further than you receive Christ himself by faith – which you can only do in an imperfect way in this life.

The apostle Paul sets himself up as a pattern for all of those who are mature to imitate. And yet he declares that he was not yet made so mature that he no longer needed to "press forward towards the mark for the prize of the high calling of God in Christ Jesus." He labored continuously to "apprehend and win Christ more perfectly, and to be found in him, not having his own righteousness, but that which is from God by faith." He wanted to gain a more personal "knowledge of Christ, and the fellowship of his sufferings, and the power of his resurrection, being made conformable to it" (Philippians 3:8, 10, 14). Believers are justified already, yet they "wait for the hope of righteousness, by faith" – that is, for the full enjoyment of the righteousness of Christ (Galatians 5:5). Believers have received the "first fruits of the Spirit," and they must wait for a more full enjoyment of it. The Spirit testifies now to them that "they are children of God." Yet, they groan within themselves, waiting to enjoy a more full enjoyment of adoption (Romans 8:23).

Your new state is still imperfect in this life. Your natural state, with its characteristics, still remains in you to some degree. It is not yet completely abolished. All believers in this world to some degree partake of both of these two contrary states. Believers have indeed "put off the old man, and put on the new man, where Christ is all and in all" (Colossians 3:10-11). Yet, they are told to put off the old man, and put on the new man, more and more, because the old man still remains in some measure. They are said to be not in the flesh, but in the Spirit, because being in the Spirit is their lasting state. Nonetheless, the flesh is still in them, and they are called to put to death the deeds of the flesh (Romans 8:9,13).

Several things, which are contrary to each other, are frequently attributed to believers regarding these two contrary states. They seem to contradict one another, yet both are true in other respects. Paul can say about himself, "I live, and yet not I" (Galatians 2:20). In the one hand, he did live to God by Christ living in him. Yet, on the other hand, according to his natural state, he did not live to God. Again, he declared that he was fleshly, sold under sin. On the other hand, he did not desire to sin, but hated it. He shows how both of these were true concerning himself in different respects. He says, "In me (that is, in my flesh) lives no good thing;" and, "I delight to do the will of God according to the inward man. With my mind I myself serve the law of God; but, with the flesh, the law of sin" (Romans 7:14-25).

John says, "Whoever says he has no sin deceives himself, and is a liar" (I John 1:8). It is also true, that "whoever is born of God, does not commit sin, for his seed [i.e., Christ, the new nature in him] remains in him. And he cannot sin, because he is born of God" (I John 3:9). It is true that you are weak, and you can do nothing. And yet you are strong, able to do all things (II Corinthians 12:10-11, Philippians 4:13). It is true, that believers are dead because of sin, but alive because of righteousness (Romans 8:10). When they die a natural death, they shall never die (John

11:25-26). They are sons, who have their inheritance by their birthright. Yet, in other respects, they are no different than servants. In one sense they are under the law, and in another sense, they are under grace, and heirs according to the promise, at the same time (Galatians 4:1-2).

Believers are redeemed from the curse of the law, they have the forgiveness of sins, and they have the promise that God will never be wrathful toward them, nor condemn them any more (Galatians 3:13, Ephesians 1:7, Isaiah 54:9). Yet, on the other hand, the curse written in the law is sometimes poured out upon them (Daniel 9:11). They still need to ask God to deliver them from their guilt, and forgive their sins (Psalm 51:14, Matthew 6:12). They may expect God to punish them for all their iniquities (Amos 3:2).

These two seemingly contradictory experiences show that believers partake of two contrary states in this life – the life of the flesh and the life of the Spirit. This is a plain and simple way to reconcile these seeming contradictions. There is no question that the old state remains in believers to some degree, since all evangelical Christians acknowledge that the sinfulness and corruption of our natures – commonly called original sin – remains in believers as long as they live in this world. This does not mean, of course, that this original corruption stays in us as we are in Christ. It stays in us in our old state, derived from the first Adam.

Therefore, the first sin of Adam is imputed, in some respect, even to those who are justified by faith. They remain, in some measure, under the punishment and curse announced in Genesis 2:17: "In the day you eat of the tree, you shall surely die." Because of this, the same original guilt and corruption comes to the children of believing parents, simply because these children are born to sinful parents. Believers still have to live under the curse brought into the world by the first Adam. They still have to face all of the miseries of this life, and death itself, as a result of the punishment for sin that was leveled upon the first Adam.

Now, someone might object and say that this doctrine of the twofold state of believers in this life detracts from the perfection of your justification by Christ. Someone might say that this doctrine diminishes the fullness of grace, the riches of the spiritual blessings given by Christ, and the power of the Holy Spirit. Someone might also say that it also greatly diminishes the comfort of believers in Christ. However, this objection can be answered. Even while believers still have the remnants of the old nature living in them, believers on earth still have all the perfections of spiritual blessings, justification, adoption, the gift of the Spirit, holiness, eternal life, and glory in and with Christ (Ephesians 1:3). In the person of Christ, who is now in heaven, the old man is perfectly crucified. Believers are dead to sin, and to the law and to its curse. They are made alive together with Christ and raised up with him and made to sit in heavenly places in Christ Jesus (Ephesians 2:6). Believers really do receive and enjoy all these perfect spiritual blessings by faith, inasmuch as they receive and enjoy Christ himself who lives in them.

Believers are in a new state, free from the guilt, corruption and punishment of sin. Thus they are free from the wrath of God, and from all miseries, and death itself, while they are in this world. All of the guilt, corruption, and punishments of sin to which they are subject in their natural state, do not harm believers now that they are in their new state; rather, they all work for their good. They are not evils, but they are helpful to them. Why? Because they lead believers toward the destruction of the flesh, and to the perfection of the new man in Christ.

When you receive Christ and all his perfections, you do it imperfectly while you are in this world. Only when you leave this world will your old sinful state, with all of its accompanying evils, be totally abolished. The kingdom of heaven, and the grace of Christ within you, is like yeast in batter. The yeast unites itself to the batter in an instant, but it takes a long time for the whole batch to be leavened (Matthew 13:33). The grace of God is also like the morning light, which gradually expels the darkness, shining more and more unto the perfect day (Proverbs 4:18).

The fact that you remain imperfect in this life does not in any way diminish the merits of Christ's death, or the power of the Spirit. Christ never intended you to enjoy his spiritual blessings unless you are in him, and enjoy him by faith. Christ never intended to make you happy or holy while you are in the flesh. He never intended to reform or repair your old, natural state.

The fact that you remain imperfect in this life also does not diminish the comfort that you have as a believer in Christ. You may be assured that you have the perfection of grace and happiness in Christ, and you can enjoy it in this world as long as you enjoy Christ himself by faith. When you die, you will enjoy God's grace in a perfect way. Then, you will be free from the sinful, miserable state you received from the first Adam.

# Live by Faith to Obey God

This truth is very important if you want to live a holy life by gospel principles -- by the means that belong to your new state, where you have a relationship with Christ by faith. It is true that some Perfectionists will object to this doctrine. They will say, "Which doctrine is most likely to encourage people to live holy lives – ours, which teaches 'that perfect holiness may be attained in this life,' or theirs, which teaches "that it is impossible for you to keep the law perfectly, and purge yourself from all sin, as long as you live in this world, even though you try your hardest'"? They think that in order to encourage people not to sin, they have to teach them that they can become perfect in this life. However, this is not what happens at all. Perfectionist teaching hardens people. They allow themselves to sin, and then they call evil good.

Perfectionist teaching also discourages those who are trying to grow in holiness by walking by faith in Christ. It makes them think they are laboring vain, because they still find themselves to be sinful, and far from perfection -- even though they have done their best to attain perfection. Perfectionist teaching ultimately cannot help anyone live a holy life. You simply have to understand that your old state, with its evil characteristics, will continue to remain in you. You will still have to confess your sins, loathe yourself for them, pray earnestly for the forgiveness of them, sorrow for them with a godly sorrow, accept the punishment of them, give God the glory for his justice, and offer to God "the sacrifice of a broken and contrite spirit, being poor in spirit, working out your salvation with fear and trembling."

Second, give up the idea of purifying the flesh -- your old natural man -- from its sinful lusts and inclinations. Do not think you will be able to attain holiness by your resolutions to do the best you can. Do not trust in Christ to help you keep these resolutions by your own efforts. Rather, resolve to trust in Christ to work in you to will and to do, by his own power, according to his own good pleasure.

Many who are convinced of their own sin and misery commonly try to tame their flesh. They try to subdue and root out its lusts by their own efforts. They try to make their corrupt nature better, and more inclined to holiness, by struggling and wrestling with it. They think that if they can only bring their hearts to resolve to do the best that is in their power, they will be able to conquer their lusts and do the most difficult duties. Many theologians and preachers stir people up to make this resolution to turn from sin to godliness by their own efforts. They do not think this is contrary to the life of faith at all, because they trust in the grace of God in Christ to help them keep their resolutions.

However, here is the problem with this: they are trying to reform their old state, and to be made perfect in the flesh. They are not putting it off and walking according to their new state in Christ. They are trusting in the acts of their own will – their purposes, resolutions, and endeavors – instead of upon Christ. They are trusting in Christ only to help them in this fleshly way. True faith, if they would listen to it, teaches them that they are nothing, and that they are laboring in vain. Trying to purify the flesh is like trying to turn the blackest stain into pure white! They will never be able to purify the flesh from its evil lusts. They will never be able to make the flesh pure and holy. The flesh is desperately wicked, and beyond all cure. The flesh will inevitably lust against the Spirit of God, even in the best saints on the earth (Galatians 5:17). The mind of the flesh is at enmity against the law of God. The flesh is not, and indeed cannot, but subject to the law of God (Romans 8:7).

Those who try to cure the flesh, and make it holy by their own resolutions and endeavors, act totally contrary to the purpose of Christ's death. For, Jesus died, not to make the natural man holy, but to crucify it and put it to death (Romans 6:6). Christ died so that you might live to God, not to yourself. It is not Christ's will for you to live on the basis of the power of your resolutions to do better. Christ wants you to live by Christ living in you, and by his Spirit bringing forth the fruits of righteousness in you (Galatians 2:20, 5:24-25). Therefore, leave the wicked natural man just as you found it. Do not let its wickedness control you. Rather, desire to be delivered from this body of death, and thank God that there is deliverance through Jesus Christ our Lord.

Do not try to put to death your sinful lusts by trying to purge them out of your flesh. Put to death your sinful lusts by putting off the flesh itself by walking in Christ by faith. Walk in the new nature he has given you. Thus "the way of life is above to the wise, that he may depart from hell beneath" (Proverbs 15:24). Do not simply resolve to do the best you can. Resolve to do what Christ and the power of his Spirit will be pleased to work in you. For, "in you (that is, in your flesh) there lives no good thing." You can be sure that God will help you in this kind of resolution to attain holiness, since this is agreeable to the way of living and acting by faith in Christ.

It is very likely that Peter sincerely resolved to die with Christ rather than to deny him. And, it is very likely that he did all that he could by his own power to keep his resolution. However, Christ made him quickly see the weakness and emptiness of such resolutions. You can surely see, by your own experience, what those resolutions made in sickness or in other dangers mostly come to – nothing! It is simply not enough to trust in Christ to help you act and labor. Even the worst of men have this kind of help, for "in him we live and move and have our being" Acts 17:28). It is likely that the Pharisee would trust in God to help him in his duty, since he thanked God after he performed his duty (Luke 18:11). This is all the faith that many use to try to live a holy life. However, this kind of "resolution faith" is not really relying upon God's grace at all. It is relying upon your own strength and willpower.

Trust in Christ to enable you to live far beyond your own natural strength, because you have a new nature from Christ. Christ's Spirit now lives and works in you. Apart from this, your best efforts would be completely sinful. Your efforts will only result in hypocrisy if you are only trusting in God to help you help yourself. You must also beware of making your holiness depend upon any of your resolutions to walk in Christ. You know that the virtue of these resolutions lasts only as long as you continue to walk in Christ, and only as long as Christ lives in you. Keep up your resolutions by the continual presence of Christ in you – just as light is maintained by the continuous presence of the sun. Just as natural light cannot exist without the sun, so you cannot live for God without the presence of Christ in you.

Third, do not try to gain the forgiveness of sins, the favor of God, a new holy nature, spiritual life, or happiness by any works of the moral law. Do not try to gain them through any religious rituals. Instead, work as someone who has already received all these things because of your new state in Christ. Also, work as someone who will only receive them more and more as you live by faith, because they are already treasured up for you in your spiritual head, the Lord Jesus Christ.

If you are still trying to gain these spiritual blessings, that means you presently think you do not have them. You might also think you do not belong to Christ himself, who gives you all these spiritual blessings. If you think that, you will walk according to your old nature, as someone who is still in the flesh. You will think that you have to earn your salvation by your fleshly works and religion, instead of completely resting in Christ by faith.

If you live this way, you are living by a covenant of works. You cannot expect Christ and his Spirit to produce holiness in you this way. Remember who you are! You are dead to the legal covenant, by the body of Christ (Romans 7:4). "If you are led by the Spirit, you are not under law" (Galatians 5:18). When the Galatians were seduced by the false teachers into trying to gain their salvation and life through circumcision and the works of the law, Paul rebuked them for trying to "be made perfect in the flesh." They had begun so well "in the Spirit!" However, they moved to a place where "Christ had no value to them," and where they actually had "fallen from grace" (Galatians 3:3 and 5:4).

When some of the Colossians sought perfection by performing "circumcision, holy food, holy times, and other elementary principles of the world," Paul rebuked them for not "holding fast to the head, Jesus Christ." He rebuked them for living not as people who had died and risen with Christ, but as people who were merely living in the world (Colossians 2:19-20 and 3:1). Paul clearly shows that if you try to gain salvation through these kinds of legal works, you are walking in accordance with your old nature. The true way to live is to live by faith in Christ. You have to walk as someone who already has all fullness in Christ, and who does not have to seek spiritual blessings in any other way.

As a Christian, do not act **for** life but **from** life. Do not try to gain life by your works. Rather, remember that you have already received life from Christ, and live by the power and virtue you have received from him. There are many other religions that will tell you to try to justify, sanctify, and purify yourself by your own works and religious rituals. However, these religions simply promote a fleshly life. These religions can give you no firm, personal relationship with Christ. They will never help their people live in true holiness until they learn a better way of doing religion!

Fourth, do not try to live a holy life by motivating and compelling yourself to do it. Don't "just do it." Instead, continually go to Christ first, by faith. Then, you will receive a gospel motivation to live a holy life. This gospel motivation will strengthen and empower you to live a holy life.

People will offer you many different motives as to why you should live a holy life. People will press you and urge you to live a holy life, for instance, because it is required of you. True enough, but those who tell you this often fail to tell you that you are by nature dead in sin, and under the wrath of God. They tell you what to do, but they forget to tell you that you have no strength or ability to live a holy life!

Here are some other reasons you might be given as to why you should live a holy life:

- ❑ The authority of God as the lawgiver

- ❑ Your absolute dependence upon him as your creator, preserver, and governor, who gives you all of your earthly life, breath, and happiness

- ❑ His all-seeing eye, that searches your heart and knows your thoughts and secret purposes

- ❑ His exact justice, in rendering to everyone according to their works

- ❑ His almighty and eternal power, to reward those who obey him, and to punish forever those who disobey him

- ❑ The unspeakable joy of heaven, and the awful damnation of hell

These motivations are all true to a certain degree. They will compel you to live a holy life if you really believe them and meditate on them. They are so powerful, in fact, that some people think they are all you need if you want to live a holy life and become a virtuous person. However, these alone are not enough. Paul spoke of something deeper when he talked about living a holy life. He said, "I live, yet not I, but Christ lives in me. And the life I live in the body, I live by faith in the Son of God, who loved me and gave himself for me" (Galatians 2:20).

A non-Christian might use the motivations I have listed above to try to live a holy life. A non-Christian has enough knowledge of the Bible that they might try to obey God out of fear. However, they have no personal relationship with Christ. They live as if Christ never came into the world. God does not want you to live in this way. The motivations and principles I have listed above should stir you up to go to Christ for the strength to live a holy life. If they do not do that, your life will be no different than a non-Christian who tries to live the same lifestyle.

# The Gospel Mystery of Sanctification

Non-Christians may make some progress in becoming virtuous people. They may try very hard to live holy lives. However, because they do not know Christ, they are left to their own natural strength – or, I should say, they are left to their own natural weakness! They have absolutely no assurance that God will give them strength to live holy lives (and of course, they have no right to have this assurance, because they do not know Jesus!). They will not be able to do anything right, until they come to a precious saving faith. When they do, they will receive life and strength from Christ to live a holy life.

You would not need the gospel of Christ if the motivations listed above were enough to enable you to live a holy life. You would not need to receive new life and strength from Christ if you were able to live a holy life by your own power and ability. If you live according to these motivations only, you are simply walking according to the flesh, according to your old corrupt nature. You are trying to be made perfect in the flesh.

Paul was very diligent in trying to become a better person while he was a Pharisee. Many pagan philosophers in our own day will attain some level of goodness by the light of common reason and virtue. The devils themselves understand morality – although of course morality does them no good! The world has a kind of natural wisdom, but it is a wisdom in which the world does not know God. The world does not understand the wisdom of God, revealed in the gospel. This wisdom is the only wisdom that can save you and sanctify you.

What will you be able to produce in your life if you try to live a godly life by your own strength and wisdom? Nothing but corruption. However, once you come to understand your own sinfulness and the deadness of your old nature, you will realize that you will never be able to bring yourself to holiness by worldly wisdom or moral principles. You will come to understand that moral principles place obligations upon you, but they give you no power, life, or strength to keep them. And, what are mere obligations to someone who is dead in sin? If you do not have any spiritual life in your soul, moral obligations and laws will only stir up your sin all the more! "Our sinful passions are aroused by the law." "Sin, taking occasion by the commandment, produces in us all kinds of covetousness" (Romans 7:5, 8).

However, all of these principles I have been talking about can be good for you if you use them in the right way. They will help you if you use them in a gospel way. It is just as Paul said about the law: it is good, if you use it lawfully (I Timothy 1:8). What he means, of course, is that the law is good if you use it in light of the gospel. A sinner who has become humbled understands his obligations before God very well. But, what he really wants is life and strength to do them. He knows he can never keep these obligations until he receives his life and strength from Christ. These principles and motivations move him to go first to Christ. Then, when he is strengthened and made alive by God's grace in Christ, he will be able to live a holy life.

Fifth, stir yourself up to live a holy life because you are completely assured that you have a personal relationship with Jesus Christ. Live for God because you have already received every spiritual and eternal blessing through him.

Do not try to keep the law as if you were a person who has no solid personal relationship with Jesus Christ. You will be continually tempted to fall into unbelief. You will think that God does not love you. You will think that you are still under the curse of the law, and the power of sin and Satan. You will think you are no better off than a non-Christian. You will think you have no more strength than what you are able to muster up by the resolutions of your own will. If you give in to this kind of unbelief, you are in fact acting according to your old natural state. You will be moved to yield yourself to the dominion of sin and Satan. You will also withdraw yourself from God and godliness – just as Adam tried to hide himself from God (Genesis 3:10).

If you truly want to live a holy life, you must first conquer and expel this kind of haunting unbelief. Trust confidently in Christ, and assure yourself that Christ's righteousness, Spirit, glory, and spiritual blessings are all yours. Remember that he lives in you, and you in him. In this confidence, you will go out and keep the law of God. You will be strong against sin and Satan. You will be able to do all things through Christ who strengthens you. You absolutely must have this confident assurance in your heart if you are going to walk in your new state in Christ. Faith is the hand that not only receives Christ, but which works by Christ. Your faith can only work powerfully in your sanctification if you know you have a personal relationship with Christ.

Act as a person who is in union and fellowship with Christ. Paul maintained in his heart the absolute assurance that Christ had loved him and had given himself for him. By this assurance he was able to live to God in holiness, through Christ living in him by faith. You also must have this assurance if you are going to live in holiness in Christ. You must understand that your old man is crucified with him. You must consider yourself "dead to sin and alive to God, through Jesus Christ your Lord" (Romans 6:6, 11). This is the way that you become "filled with the Spirit, strong in the Lord, and in his mighty power" (Ephesians 6:20). Remember, God would not require this of you without also giving you the means to do it! Jesus himself walked in the constant assurance of his excellent state. He "set the Lord always before him." He was assured that because "God was at his right hand he would not be shaken" (Psalm 16:8).

How can you expect to act in accord with your new state in Christ if you are not sure you are actually in this new state? It is a common principle that in your earthly profession, you have to know what your state is. Then, you have according to it – neither above it in pride, nor below it in false humility. It is very hard to bring some people to a right understanding of their earthly condition! The same is true in spiritual matters: you have to know your state in Christ if you are going to walk in it! If Christians could just understand the glory and wonder of their new state in Christ, their hearts would be lifted above the sordid slavery to their own lusts. They would be encouraged and motivated to "run cheerfully in the way of God's commands." If Christians knew the strength that they have in Christ, they would attempt greater things for the glory of God!

However, I recognize that it is very hard to attain this knowledge of what you have in Christ. It can only come by faith and spiritual illumination. Even the best only understand it in a very small way. That is the reason why the lifestyles of Christians usually fall so far below their holy and heavenly calling.

Sixth, consider the privileges of your new state in Christ that will most enable your heart to love God, to renounce sin, and to obey God's commandments with all your heart. Then, continue to assure yourself of these truths. Then, you will be able to live a holy life before God.

I am joining all these aspects of obedience together, because the first and greatest commandment is that you "love the Lord your God with all your heart, soul, mind and strength." This is the command that influences you towards all other true obedience. If you love God, you will obey him. If you love God, you will hate and detest sin, and you will run away from everything that is contrary and hateful to God.

# Live by Faith to Obey God

How do you actually do this? The blessings of your holy nature will empower you to love and obey God. You can only live out of your new nature when you live by faith. Particularly, you must believe that all your sins are blotted out, that you are reconciled to God, that you have access into his favor by the blood of Christ, that God is your Father, that he loves you, and that you have all you need for your eternal happiness in Christ.

If you meditate on these wonderful truths of the gospel, God will be very lovely to your heart. These precious truths will sweetly draw you and win you over. You will not be forced to "love God" by commands or threats. You will love God because these precious realities of the gospel will draw you to love God. If you truly want to love God, you cannot harbor the secret suspicion that he is really your everlasting enemy. "There is no fear in love, but perfect love casts out fear. Fear has to do with punishment. He who fears is not made perfect in love. We love him because he first loved us" (I John 4:18-19).

David loved the Lord, because he was assured that God was his "strength, rock fortress, his God, and the horn of his salvation" (Psalm 18:1-2). Love that produces obedience to the law must proceed from a good conscience, which has been cleansed from sin. This good conscience can only come from an unhypocritical faith, through which you apprehend the merits of the blood of Christ (I Timothy 1:5, Hebrews 9:14).

If you want your heart to be prepared to live a holy life, the Bible tells you to walk in the assurance of what you have received in your new state in Christ. The Bible gives you many assurances, such as:

- ❑ You have fellowship with the Father, and with his Son Jesus Christ (I John 1:3)

- ❑ You are the temple of the living God (II Corinthians 6:16)

- ❑ You live by the Spirit (Galatians 5:25)

- ❑ You are called to holiness, and created in Christ Jesus to do good works (Ephesians 2:10)

- ❑ God will sanctify you through and through, and make you perfect in holiness at the very end (I Thessalonians 5:23)

❑ Your old man is crucified with Christ, and through him you are dead to sin, and alive to God. And, being made free from sin, you have become servants of righteousness, and have fruit unto holiness, the end of which is everlasting life (Romans 6:6,22).

❑ You are dead, and your life is hidden with Christ in God. When Christ, who is your life, shall appear, then you shall also appear with him in glory (Colossians 3:3-4).

Such assurances as these, when they are deeply rooted and established in your heart, will empower and encourage you to obey God. They will encourage you to repent of every sinful lust. You will consider it not only your duty, but also your great privilege to do all things through Christ who strengthens you. God will work in you both to will and to do according to these principles, because they belong to the gospel. The gospel is the "ministry of the Spirit," and "the power of God for salvation" (II Corinthians 3:6-8, Romans 1:16).

Seventh, in order to keep the law of God, continually meditate upon the privileges of your new position in Christ. In addition, give special attention to the blessings that are specifically designed to motivate and empower you to keep the law of God. Continually assure yourself of them by faith, so you will be empowered to obey the law of God.

Let me give you some examples of what I mean, and then you will be able to guide yourself in all the rest. Consider the first table of the law, the first five of the Ten Commandments. If you want to draw near to God in worship with a pure heart, you must do it in full assurance of faith in Christ and his salvation.

Do you want to trust in the Lord with all your heart, and cast your cares upon him? Do you want to give all your concerns over to him? If you do, you have to be assured that in Christ, God has promised that he "will never fail you or forsake you," that he will take fatherly care of you, that he will "withhold no good thing from you," and that he will make "all things work together for your good." If you believe these things, you will be able to trust in the Lord and give all of your worries over to him. However, if you live in uncertainty about whether or not God cares for you, you will be enslaved to fleshly fears and cares in your heart. You will trust in the arm of flesh, even though your conscience tells you that when you do this you are guilty of idolatry.

Live by Faith to Obey God

Do you want to be strengthened to submit to the hand of God, with a joyful patience, even when you face trouble or death itself? The way to strengthen yourself is to believe with complete assurance that your "afflictions, which are but for a time, are working for you a far more exceeding and eternal weight of glory;" that Christ is your gain in death and life; that his "grace is sufficient for you, that his "strength is made perfect in your weakness;" that he will not "allow you to be tempted beyond what you are able;" and that he will "at the end make you more than a conqueror" over all evil. Until you are completely assured of these truths of the gospel, you will worry and grumble under the burden of your troubles. You will use other means to try to deliver yourself from them, even though you know you should not try to do this!

Do you want to faithfully worship God in the way that he has commanded you to? You must believe that you are complete in Christ, and that you have all the spiritual blessings in him that you need. You must trust that God will build you up through the elements of worship that he has given you. If you believe this, you will understand that God's elements of worship are sufficient for you. The ordinances and traditions of men are absolutely unnecessary for the worship of God. If you do not understand your fullness in Christ, you will be like the legalistic churches that multiply superstitions and rituals endlessly. Why? Because they think they need these man-made rituals to supply their spiritual needs.

Do you want to confess your sins to God, pray to him, and praise him from your heart for all his goodness to you? Do you want to praise God for suffering as well as for prosperity? Then believe with assurance that "God is faithful and just to forgive your sin" through Christ. Believe that you have become "a holy priesthood" able "to offer spiritual sacrifices" of prayer and praise. Believe that you are "acceptable to God through Christ." Believe that God hears your prayers and will answer them so far as they are good for you. Believe that all "God's ways are mercy and truth to you," whether he chooses to prosper you or make you suffer in this life. If you are in doubt about any of these gospel blessings, all your confessions, prayers, and praises will simply be heartless lip-labors, just slavish and pharisaical works.

Do you want to hear and receive the Bible as the Word of God? Do you want to meditate on it with delight? Do you want to understand the strictness and the spirituality of the commands of God? Do you want to test and examine your life impartially by the word of God? Then believe with assurance that the word of God is "the power of God for salvation." Believe that Christ is your Great Physician, willing and able to heal you, no matter how bad your case is. Believe that where your sin abounds, his grace towards you abounds all the more. If you do not believe these gospel truths, all of your effort in hearing, meditating, and self-examination will just be heartless works. You will do them carelessly and half-heartedly, or hypocritically, or out of slavish fear. You will do them reluctantly, without any good will or readiness of mind.

Do you want to receive the sacraments properly? Then be strengthened by believing that you can have communion with God in Christ through them. Believe that you have a Great High Priest who bears your sins, and who has made you forever acceptable to the Lord.

The same principle is true if you want love your neighbor, the matter about which the second tablet of the Ten Commandments speaks. In order to do these things, you have to be assured of the privileges and blessings you have through your new state in Christ. Only this will encourage and empower you to love your neighbor as yourself. Consider the responsibilities you have towards your neighbor:

- ❑ Love your neighbor as yourself

- ❑ Do to others as you would have them do to you, without any partiality or self-seeking

- ❑ Give him his due honor, and do not injure his life, his marriage, his worldly goods, or his good name

- ❑ Do not covet anything that is his

How can you possibly do these things? You certainly have to understand that you are required to treat others in this way. It is certainly true that these things are just and equitable towards your neighbor. However, if you really want to love your neighbor, you have to live by the gospel. Believe that these commands are the will of your heavenly Father, who has recreated you in his own image, in righteousness and true holiness. Believe that they are the mind of Christ, who lives in you, and in whom you live. Believe that God and Christ are kind, tenderhearted, longsuffering, and full of goodness to men – whether they are good or bad, friends or enemies. Believe that Christ came into the world, not to destroy but to save. Believe that the injuries done to you by others cannot harm you. Believe that you do not need to seek any good for yourself by injuring others, because all your happiness and satisfaction come from Christ. Believe that all things, even if your enemies intend them to hurt you, work for your good through Christ. If you believe these things by faith, you will be empowered and equipped to love and do good to your neighbor.

Do you want to have a pure love towards your brothers in Christ? Do you want to live with them in all humility, meekness, patience, forgiveness and love? Then believe that you are inseparably joined with them through Christ. Believe that there is "one body and one spirit, one hope of your calling, one Lord, one faith, one baptism, one God and Father of all, who is over all through all and in all" (Ephesians 4:4-6).

Do you want to be free from fleshly and worldly lusts that war against your soul and hinder you from godliness? If you do, do not just believe that gluttony, drunkenness, and immorality are filthy abominations (although they certainly are!). Do not just believe that the pleasures, profits, and honors of this world are vain and empty things (although, again, they certainly are!). Go beyond this. Believe that you are "crucified to the flesh and to the world." Believe that "you have been made alive, raised, and seated in heavenly places together with Christ." Believe that you have pleasures, profits, and honors in Christ, to which the best things in the world are not worthy to be compared. Believe that you are a "member of Christ, the temple of his Spirit, a citizen of heaven, a child of the day, not of the night, nor of darkness." Believe that it is simply below your royal estate and dignity in Christ to practice the deeds of darkness. You do not need to give your attention to fleshly and worldly things. You have much better riches in Christ.

I have given you several examples to show you how you have to live by faith in the gospel if you want to obey the law of God. You have to understand the privileges and blessings of your new position in Christ that you received through the gospel of grace. It is the gospel that empowers your new nature to live a holy life. You have to be stirred up by faith in the gospel to carry out the duties of holiness – both to God and to other people. When you walk in this way, your heart will be comforted and established in every good word and work. You will grow in holiness, until you attain maturity in Jesus Christ.

Eighth, if you desire to grow in grace and in holiness, trust with assurance that God will enable you to do everything that is necessary for his glory and for your eternal salvation. He will be very gracious to you.

He will accept your obedience through Christ, according to the measure of faith that you have. He will also pardon your failings – because you will indeed offend him in many ways. You will fall short of holiness all the time.

If you want to live a holy life, it is very important for you to understand how to deal with your failures to obey God – which will indeed be many! When you fail, you will be tempted to handle your failures in the wrong way. On the one hand, you will be tempted to fall into despair: "I cannot believe I committed that sin again!" On the other hand, you will be tempted to return to using fleshly self-reliance to fight against your ever-recurring sins. You will fall into the same old trap of thinking that living and acting by faith are insufficient for your salvation and sanctification. I can guarantee you that you will continually look for something other than Jesus and the gospel to fight against your indwelling sin and corruption.

Again, go back to the truth of the gospel in your battle against your indwelling sin! Paul told the Galatians to "walk in the Spirit, even though the flesh lusts against the Spirit, preventing them from doing the things that they want to" (Galatians 5:16-17). Understand that even though the law of God requires perfection, the gospel makes an allowance for your weakness. Christ is so meek and lowly in heart that he accepts what your weak faith is able to attain by his grace. He does not require of you any more for his glory or your salvation until you grow stronger in grace.

God was very patient with his people in the Old Testament. Moses the lawgiver allowed them, "because of the hardness of their hearts, to put away their wives, even though from the beginning it was not so" (Matthew 19:8). God also tolerated the customary practice of polygamy. To be sure, God will not tolerate such practices in his church – especially since his Spirit is so much more plentifully poured out upon us now that the Gospel has come. Do not think Christ tolerates sin and wickedness! However, what I am saying is that God is as patient as ever. He will bear with the failings of his weak saints who desire to obey him sincerely.

There is another Old Testament example of God's patience. He commanded that the fearful and the faint-hearted should not be forced to go to war against their enemies. He allowed them to return home to their houses. To be sure, God commanded his people to fight against their enemies without fear and faint-heartedness. Nonetheless, because of his great patience and kindness, he allowed the fearful and faint-hearted to go home (Deuteronomy 20:3, 8).

So it is now under the gospel. It is an eminent part of the service of Christ to fight against afflictions, and to endure death courageously for the name of Christ. However, if anyone is so weak in faith that they do not have sufficient courage to enter into battle, no doubt Christ allows them an honest way to escape from their persecutors without denying their faith. Jesus accepts them in this weaker kind of service. He would much rather them do this, than take the risk of denying his name by putting themselves through the trial of potential martyrdom. This is what happened to Peter. He fell into sin and shame because he ventured beyond the measure of his faith. He walked right into the hands of his persecutors when he followed Christ into the High Priest's hall. He should have just done what Jesus very patiently allowed him and the other disciples to do: "Let these ones go their way" (John 18:8).

Christ deals with his people as a good and careful shepherd. He does not drive his sheep too hard. "He shall gather the lambs, with his arm, and carry them in his bosom, and he shall gently lead those that are with young" (Isaiah 40:11). Jesus does not want his disciples urged to rigorously fast, when their spirits were unfit for it. He knew that imposing duties beyond their strength would be like "putting a piece of new cloth on an old garment, and new wine into old wineskins" (Matthew 9:14-17).

The command of Solomon, "do not be overly righteous" (Ecclesiastes 78:16) is very useful and necessary, if you understand it correctly. You are to beware of being too rigorous in exacting righteousness from yourself and others beyond your, and their, measure of faith and grace. In other words, do not expect others to do what God has not yet equipped them to do! **Overdoing** usually ends up in **undoing**! Children who try to walk on their feet beyond their strength will have many falls. So it will be with infants in Christ. When they unnecessarily try to do things that are beyond the strength of their faith, they will have many falls.

Be content at the present time to do the best you can according to the measure of faith and grace God has given you – even though you know that others are enabled by God to do much more. "Do not despise the day of small things," but praise God that he enables you to do anything that is pleasing in his sight. You can have the sure hope that he will sanctify you through and through, and at the end he will bring you to perfection in holiness through Jesus Christ our Lord. Carefully observe, in all things, this good lesson of the apostle Paul: "Do not think of yourself more highly than you ought to think. Rather, think soberly, according to the measure of faith God has given you" (Romans 12:3).

# Chapter 13

## Principle Number 13

**Now that the Holy Spirit has renewed you, God calls you to live a holy life. To live this obedient life, you must continue to believe in Christ and walk in him by faith. To live this life of faith, God calls you to diligently use all of the means of grace he has given you in his Word.**

The only way to grow in holiness is by living a life of faith in Christ. However, this does not mean you should not use the means given to you in the word of God for attaining and growing in holiness. Living by faith **establishes** your need of using these means given to you in the word of God.[1] Some of these means of growing in your faith are: reading and meditating upon the word of God; examining yourself and repenting of your sins; partaking of the sacraments of baptism and the Lord's Supper; praying, fasting, and worshiping God; and being involved in a local church. When you live by grace through faith, you know you must give yourself to these things more than ever!

You must clearly understand this because of the pride and misunderstanding of some people who supposedly live out the gospel. They actually only practice cheap grace, because they do not think they need to pursue holy living now that they have been forgiven of their sins. However, their faith is phony, and they are puffed up with conceit. They think they are already so perfect that they are above all commands and disciplines except singing praise songs!

You also have to watch out for what the Legalists do. They run to the other extreme – they heap together a multitude of rules for holiness that God never commanded you to do. They viciously criticize the doctrine of faith and free grace. They say that grace destroys peoples'

---

[1] By the term "means," Marshall is referring to the "means of grace" that God has given in his word for believers to use to grow in their faith in Christ. The modern term for these means is "the spiritual disciplines," but Walter Marshall uses a more biblical term, "the means of grace." These "means of grace" are not what you do to attain holiness; they are what bring you into a deeper fellowship with Christ who makes you more holy.

motivation to pursue holiness through the commands and means of grace God has given in his Word. They say that free grace will only produce a bunch of lazy, "faith-only" Christians![2]

Do not believe either of these two extremes — the extremes of sanctification by doing nothing at all or sanctification by your own efforts. I have been saying to you that a true and living faith in Christ alone is sufficient, through the grace of God, to receive Christ and all his fullness. This faith is necessary in this life for your justification, sanctification, and eternal salvation. However, God has given several means for creating, maintaining, and increasing your faith. Use these means to exercise your faith, to attain holiness of life.

True Christians find, by experience, that their faith needs such help. They do not see themselves above any need for help in their faith. Anyone who thinks he does not need these helps for his faith rejects the counsel of God against himself – like the proud Pharisees and Lawyers, who thought it beneath them and refused to be baptized by John (Luke 7:30).

The only means you are to use to attain holiness are those specifically given by God in his word. You do not need to invent any human traditions to live a holy life. God has given you everything you need in his word. However, you must guard your heart, even when you use the God-given means of grace. If you are not careful, you will make them an end in themselves. You will forget about the Christ who gave them to you. It will be easy for you to fall into the legalism the Pharisees fell into. Remember what Jesus said about them — they "draw near to God with their mouths, and honor him with their lips, yet their hearts are far from him. In vain do they worship him, teaching the doctrines and commandments of men" (Matthew 15:7-9).

---

[2] Here, the word I have rendered "faith only" is literally "Solifidians." "Solifidian" is a word that literally means "faith alone." In Marshall's day, it was a word coined by legalists and other enemies of the gospel as a term of insult – much like in our own day how legalists speak of true Christians as "born-agains" or "cheap-gracers." This term of insult and contempt again reflects the idea on the part of legalists that the gospel of grace cannot produce true godliness, but can only result in licentious living. Marshall, of course, dispels this false notion, as he explains the true way of the gospel, as opposed to either legalism or lawlessness.

# Live by the Means of Grace

To avoid this empty spirituality, make sure you use the means of grace in the right way. The only way to grow in holiness is by believing in Christ, and walking in him by faith, as a renewed person. Use these means of grace to help you live this life of faith. These means help your faith to begin, to continue, and to grow. They are subservient to faith; faith alone is the principal way your soul receives Christ. Be very careful that you do not use these means in opposition to, rather than in submission to, the way of salvation and sanctification by free grace through faith in Christ. If you abuse these means of grace, they will become hindrances rather than helps to your faith. Do not idolize any of these means, and put them in the place of Christ, as some do, by trusting in them. Some people fall into the error of thinking that these means automatically impart grace to their souls when they merely practice them!

Also, do not use these means of grace as works of righteousness you must perform to attain the favor of God and the salvation of Christ. You cannot consider them so absolutely necessary for salvation that someone who is not able to practice some of them is not a Christian. The Holy Scriptures, which contain all of the means of grace, are able to make you wise for salvation in no other way other than by faith in Jesus Christ (II Timothy 3:16). Therefore, you must be wise in how you use the means of grace. Do not use them in opposition to the grace of God in Christ.

The means of grace are like the cherubim of glory, who were made with their faces looking toward the mercy seat. The means of grace are given to guide you to Christ for salvation by faith alone. If you turn them from this and use them in any other way, it is a great violation of what God has given you. That would be just like some sacrilegious person turning the faces of the cherubim away from the mercy seat in another direction!

Many people are simply unwise about how to use the means of grace. Many use them with great zeal and diligence, but they lose their benefit because they pervert them to their own destruction. The Jews, under the Law of Moses, had many more means of grace from God regarding worship than you do under the gospel. But what happened? These means became a trap and a snare to them. They fell miserably from God and Christ, because the veil of ignorance was on their hearts. They simply could not see the real purpose of the means of grace God had given. They were supposed to see that all of these commands and rituals were meant to point them to the Lord Jesus Christ. However, they did not seek salvation by faith. They sought salvation through their own works of righteousness, by trying to keep the law.  They stumbled terribly at this stumbling stone of their own righteousness (Romans 10:4-5).

I do not want you to fall into this same, terrible mistake. Therefore, I am going to show you how to properly use the means of grace God has given you in his Word.

## 1.    Read, study and know the Word of God (II Timothy 3:15)

There are other means of grace that are just as necessary to the health of your faith and your new state in Christ, but the word of God is absolutely necessary to the very existence of your faith!  Why?  Because faith comes by hearing the word of God, and faith receives Christ who is revealed in the Word.

Think about Rahab the Canaanite.  She was justified by faith, even though she did not have any membership in the Old Testament Church, and she had no contact with any of God's commands or means of grace. Yet, she was not without the Word of God.  True, she did not have the Bible.  She had never even heard any preaching by a minister!  However, she did hear the report about God by the pagans (Joshua 2:9-11).  That was enough to kindle real faith in her heart.

Gain such knowledge of the Word of God that it will guide you to receive Christ and to walk in him by faith.  Do not think that simply knowing the Ten Commandments is sufficient to save you.  Also, do not be like those who only listen to preachers who tell them what they want to hear.  Do not just listen to people with whom you agree.

Strive to know the mystery of the Father and the Son, as it is revealed in the Gospel — in which is hidden all the treasures of wisdom and knowledge (Colossians 2:2-3).  If you know the gospel you know eternal life; if you do not know the gospel, you know eternal death (John 17:3, II Corinthians 4:3).  You must know that Christ is the end of the law (Romans 10:4).  Therefore, diligently strive to know the commands of the law.  However, do not do this to gain your salvation by your own good works as you try to keep these commands.  Rather, know God's commands so you will become aware of your inability to keep them.

When you read the word of God, you will also become aware that in your heart you really hate the commands of God.  You will see that you are under God's wrath for breaking his commands, and that it is impossible for you to be saved by your own works. Once you realize all these things, you will run to Christ for safety, and trust only in the free grace of God for your justification. Once you are a Christian, you will continue to run to Christ for the strength to keep the law in your daily Christian life.

Learn how high the standards of God's law really are. Realize the exact perfection and the spiritual purity they require. The more you know this, the more you will be convinced of your sin. The more you know your sin, the more you will seek Christ for the forgiveness of your sin. You will also seek a more pure heart and a more deeply spiritual obedience. As you come to see that your heart is more sinful than you ever imagined — and that the blood of Christ covers all of your sin — you will enjoy Jesus more than ever! Remember the Scribe who understood the greatness of the command to "love the Lord with all your heart and soul." Jesus said he was not far from the kingdom of God (Matthew 12:34).

In order to be saved by God, you must understand these two points. First, you must understand the desperate sinfulness and misery of your own natural condition. Second, you must understand how the grace of God in Christ is alone sufficient for your salvation. When you understand this you will put no confidence in your own efforts. You will exalt Christ alone.

There are certain basic things you must learn if you are going to come to this deeper understanding of both your own sinfulness and of the free grace of Christ. First, learn how the first Adam was a pattern of the second Adam, Jesus Christ (Romans 5:14). When Adam disobeyed God by eating the forbidden fruit, sin and death came upon the entire human race (Romans 5:14). When Jesus obeyed his Father even to death on the cross, righteousness and everlasting life came to all of those who truly believe in him.

Next, learn the true difference between the Old Covenant and the New Covenant, or the law and the gospel. The Old Covenant imprisons you under the guilt and power of sin, and under God's wrath and curse, by its rigorous requirements. It says, "Do all the commandments, and live; but, if you do not do them all, if you fail at the smallest point, you are cursed." The New Covenant opens the gates of righteousness and life to all believers by its gracious requirements: "Believe in the Lord Jesus

Christ, and live." If you believe, all your sins will be forgiven. His Holy Spirit will give holiness and glory to you freely by Christ's work.

Furthermore, learn the principles of the gospel by which you must live, so you truly live in holiness in Christ. If you really want to understand this, study Romans chapters 6, 7, and 8. In those chapters, Paul tells you about the really powerful principles of sanctification -- not those weak and ineffective principles by which you naturally tend to live.

At this time, I do not need to tell you about any other matters of our faith. If you come to understand these main points, and if you use them to live and walk by faith, your renewed mind will learn all the other things you need to know about life and godliness as you study the rest of the Bible. However, let me warn you about something. Do not put your knowledge in the place of Christ. If you do, you will lose Christ, because you will be trusting in your knowledge for your salvation. Make sure that as you gain knowledge of the Bible, you are constantly gaining knowledge of Christ!

Remember why many of the Jews perished. They rested on their knowledge of the truth of the law (Romans 2:20), without ever having saving faith. Many Christians will, by all of their knowledge, only earn a more strict judgment by God. Why? Because they make their religion and their salvation a matter of only knowing the Lord's will and being able to argue about it. They do not prepare themselves to do God's will (Luke 12:47). They never allow the Word of God to bring them to true conviction and real repentance.

Do not place your hope of salvation in your daily Bible reading, or in how many sermons you hear. There are many people who are very disciplined about hearing and reading the word of God, but who do not know the saving truth of the gospel. Just as Isaiah said, "in hearing, they shall hear, and not understand" (Mathew 13:14-15). Do not let this happen to you. As you read the word of God, pray that God will bring you to repentance and to the obedience that comes from faith.

## 2.  Examine your ways and your life by the Word of God

This is important whether you are presently a non-Christian or a Christian. If you are a non-Christian, in a state of sin and wrath, you need to come to know your sickness. Come to the great Physician while you still have a chance, while it is still called today! If you are a Christian, in a state of grace, you need to know that you are of the truth. You need to assure your heart before God, with greater confidence, by the testimony of a clear conscience (I John 3: 19, 21). You need to have your heart more strongly comforted by faith, and established in every good work. If your ways are evil, you must turn from them to the Lord God through Christ, apart from whom no one comes to the Father (John 14:6).

Above all, there is one thing to be very careful of when you examine yourself. Do it in such a way that it strengthens your life of faith. Do not let it hinder and destroy your life of faith. Make sure that you do not trust in your self-examination rather than in Christ. Some people think they have made their peace with God merely because they have examined themselves on their sick bed, or before they receive the Lord's Supper. They find themselves lacking before God, but they do not depend on Christ to make them better. Instead, they depend upon their own deceitful purposes and resolutions.

Do not think that when you examine yourself, you have to doubt whether or not God will be merciful to you and save you. This is a very common error, and it is really the great sin of unbelief. When you give in to this kind of unbelief, it destroys all of your peace, hope, joy, and love to God and his people. Why? Because you spend all your time wondering whether or not you really are a Christian, instead of thinking about God and others. This will also make you think your own qualifications for salvation are really better than they are. After all, no one wants to completely despair of having salvation. Everyone needs something to trust in! These errors completely ruin the good work of self-examination, and they actually make it harmful to your soul.

When you examine yourself, do it with great assurance of faith. Even though you presently find your heart more wicked and deceitful than you ever imagined (as **all** of God's greatest servants have **always** found), the door of mercy is open for you. God will certainly save you forever if you put your trust in his grace through Christ. This confident assurance is what true saving faith is all about. You can have true confidence of God's favor because of the free promises of the gospel – even when you walk in darkness, and you can see no shining light in your own qualifications.

If you will examine yourself with this kind of confidence, it will make you impartial — you will not be afraid to find out the worst about yourself. You will be willing to admit that your own heart is more deceitful than anything else, and desperately wicked, beyond what you can even imagine (Jeremiah 17:9). You will also be able to see that any holiness you do have is because you are presently in a state of God's grace.

Understand the difference between these two questions: "Even though I am a vile sinner, will God save me through Christ?" and "Have I already come into a state of salvation?" The former question you must answer "Yes," with confident faith in Christ. The latter question you must answer by examining yourself.

Do not waste your time, as many do, looking into your heart, trying to find out whether you are good enough to trust in Christ for your salvation. Also, do not try to find out whether you have any faith, before you dare to be so bold as to believe in Christ! Even though you cannot find any faith or holiness in yourself, if you now believe on him who justifies the wicked, it will be credited to you for righteousness (Romans 4:5). If you love Christ, and your own soul, do not waste your time examining whether or not you have committed the unforgivable sin – unless it is to reassure yourself that you are not guilty of it! Thinking about this will only harden you in your unbelief.

Remember, you should only try to answer one question: *Am I presently in a state of grace?* In order to answer this, be willing to recognize what is best about yourself, as well as what is worst about yourself. True humility does not mean that you have to overlook what is good in you, and notice only what is bad! Your great challenge is to find if there is some drop of saving grace in the ocean of your wickedness. True humility means that you will notice any spark of true holiness that is in you. However, when you see it, you will admit that all the praise and glory for it belongs to God alone and not to you at all.

Being in a state of grace does not mean you have to deny there are fleshly, sinful desires within you. You know how the flesh lusts against the desires of the Holy Spirit, and how the Holy Spirit fights against the flesh within you. Do not think you are a mere infant in Christ because you find yourself to actually be more fleshly and sinful than you ever thought, and that sometimes you see the old man to be bigger than the new man (Galatians 5:17).

Examine yourself and test whether or not you are in the faith. If you make sure of this, you will make sure of all the things that are

198

important for life and godliness. However, if you doubt this, you will think everything else about you is counterfeit as well. It is true that to the unbelieving there is nothing pure. Everyone who has not truly received Christ by faith is at present in an unregenerate state, no matter how pure and godly they might appear (II Corinthians 13:5, Titus 1:15).

Do not let the result of this examination depend at all upon whether or not you know the exact time, or know the exact sermon you heard, when you were first converted to Christ. If you do know it, that is fine. However, do not let your assurance of faith rest on it. Some people lived terrible lives before they became Christians. They lived in terrible ignorance of the gospel, and they may even have opposed the true faith! Such people usually know the circumstances of their conversion to Christ. Take the Apostle Paul, who was suddenly turned from his persecuting rage to become a disciple and an apostle of Christ.

Yet there are other sincere believers who have no idea of the time of their conversion – such as John the Baptist, who was filled with the Holy Spirit right from his mother's womb (Luke 1:15). Others have been raised very religiously, and they know the Holy Scriptures from their childhood, as Timothy did (II Timothy 3:15). Still others at first turn from living terrible lives to some kind of external change in their lives. Over a period of time, they come nearer to the kingdom of heaven by smaller degrees. Then, at some point, they are born again and have true faith. However, they never know the exact time of their conversion.

Some people actually deceive themselves in this matter. They know the exact time, and by what text of Scripture, they were converted. They can talk a long time about the working of God in their hearts. However, they become unreasonable, because they glorify their own experiences. The time inevitably comes when their experiences are not sufficient evidence for them. They never get the least bit of assurance that they really have true saving faith!

The best thing to do is to always keep before you the absolutely necessary elements of true saving faith. Focus on these major elements by asking yourself the following questions:

❑ Am I fully convinced of my sinfulness, and of the deadness and misery of my nature and state apart from Christ?

❑ Have I given up all hope of ever attaining any righteousness, holiness, or true happiness, while I continue in the state of my sinfulness?

❑ Have the eyes of my understanding been enlightened, so that I now see how wonderful Christ is?

❑ Do I see Christ and his grace as the only thing I really need for my salvation?

❑ Do I enjoy Christ above everything else?

❑ Do I desire Christ with my whole heart as my only happiness – no matter what I might suffer for his sake?

❑ Do I desire with my whole heart to be delivered from the power and practice of sin, as well as from the wrath of God and the pains of hell?

❑ Does my heart come to Christ and lay hold of him for salvation, by trusting him only?

❑ Do I strive to trust him confidently, even though I have fears and doubts that constantly assault me?

You may find you only have a grain of faith as small as a mustard seed. You may also find you still have much unbelief and sin in your soul. However, if you find that your faith has these qualities in it that I have listed above, you may rightly conclude that you are presently saved. Your challenge now is to continue to grow in your faith, and walk worthy of it.

In addition to examining whether or not you are in the faith to begin with, you should also examine the fruits of your faith. Test and see whether or not you can show your faith by your works, as you are taught to do (James 2:18). Make sure that you are not deceived in your opinion about your faith. Make sure your faith is real. Ask whether or not your inclinations, purposes, affections, and actions are good. However, ask something else: "What principle is giving birth to and influencing the basic direction of my life? Am I being driven by the slavish fears of hell? Do I hope that, like a paid worker, I will get to heaven by my own good works?"

If in fact you are driven by these influences, they are legalistic and fleshly principles. They will never bring about true holiness. True holiness only comes from gospel principles. Do you have them? Ask yourself: "Am I driven by love for God, because God has loved me first? Am I driven by love for Christ, because he has died for me? Am I motivated by the hope of eternal life, as the free gift of God through Christ? Am I depending upon God to sanctify me by his Spirit, according to his promises?" You may know that you have passed from death to life, if you love your brothers and sisters (I John 3:14). The grace of faith can truly be seen by the love it produces in you towards all true believers.

Let me conclude this point. You are very blessed if you can find even a moderate amount of fruits from your faith. It is a great blessing to be able to say, "Pray for us; for we trust we have a good conscience, in all things willing to live honestly" (Hebrews 13:8).

## 3. Meditate upon the Word of God

Meditation upon the Word of God is very important for living a holy life through faith in Christ. When you meditate, your soul feeds, chews, and digests the word of God as your spiritual food. The word becomes your nourishment, by which you are strengthened for every good work. Your new nature is rightly called the mind (Romans 7:25), because it lives and acts by thinking about and meditating on spiritual things. Therefore, meditate on God's Word, not only at certain limited times, but all the day (Psalm 119:97), even day and night (Psalm 1:2). Do this in your activities both at home and abroad. Knowledge of the Word of God will not profit you, unless you frequently listen to it and meditate upon it.

Some people think preaching is not necessary for people who already know what they need to know to be saved. However, those who are born again by the word find by experience that their spiritual life is maintained and strengthened by meditating on the very same word. Therefore, like newborn babies, they desire the sincere milk of the word, that by it they may grow up (I Peter 2:21). If you want to live this way, you will want to be reminded by your preacher of the things you already know! You will want to remember them, and feed on them by meditation, even though you do know them already and are established in them (II Peter 1:12).

# The Gospel Mystery of Sanctification

Here is the greatest skill to develop when you meditate upon the Word of God.  Make sure it is an integral part of your life of faith, and not opposed to your life of faith.  Do not rely upon your daily meditation as a work of righteousness that will gain you the favor of God.  Rely on Christ alone.  You will always tend to trust in something other than the free grace of God in Christ for your salvation.  Do not meditate to merely speculate, or to just gain more knowledge of the truth.  Meditate upon God's Word so he will convict your conscience, and stir your heart up to practice the truth.

Be very careful that you do not fall into the trap that some people fall into.  Do not think that you will love God or live a holy life merely by reading about God in his Word.  You can read the word of God and learn much about God, such as:  God's eternal power and nature; his sovereign authority, omniscience, perfect holiness, and exact justice; the equity of the law and your need to obey it; and, about heaven and hell.  However, just learning about these things will not automatically mean you live a godly life.  There is a deeper dynamic you must understand.

When you meditate upon all of God's truth, and upon his character, your conscience will understand how high God's standards of holiness really are.  As you see this, you will go in faith to Christ for life and strength to live in holiness.  However, in order to receive this life and strength that enables you to obey God's commands, you must mediate believing on Christ's salvation as it is revealed in the gospel.  The gospel is the only doctrine that is the power of God for your salvation.  Through the gospel, the enlivening Spirit comes to you.  He alone is the one who is able to build you up, and give you an inheritance among all of those who are sanctified (Romans 1:16, II Corinthians 3:6, Acts 20:32).

Be very careful that you act in faith in your meditation.  Mix the word of God's grace with it, or else it will not profit you (Hebrews 4:2).  If you set the loving kindness of God frequently before you, and meditate upon it, you will be strengthened to walk in the truth (Psalm 36:3).  By beholding as in a mirror the glory of the Lord, you will be changed into the same image, from glory to glory, by the Spirit of the Lord (II Corinthians 3:18).  This kind of meditation is sweet, and very delightful to those who are guided to it by the spirit of faith.  You do not need any artificial, hard-to-learn methods to guide your meditation.  In your meditation, you can simply let your thoughts run at liberty.  You will find that your soul will be made alive by it, and you will be enriched with the grace of God.  No other kind of meditation will be so valuable to you as this kind of meditation on the word of God and the grace of God.

## 4.  The Sacrament of Baptism

The sacrament of baptism is very important for the growth of your faith — as long as you use baptism in the way God intended you to use it. Baptism is a seal of the righteousness you have by faith, just as circumcision was formerly a seal of this same thing (Romans 4:11). Be very careful not to make baptism a seal of a righteousness that comes by your own works. This is what the non-believing Jews did, when they tried to be justified by the Law of Moses. This is exactly what many Christians do -- they transform the new covenant into a covenant of works, by requiring sincere obedience to all the laws of Christ as the condition of their justification. They think they enter into this newly devised works covenant by their baptism.

I will say the same thing about this kind of abuse of baptism that the Apostle Paul said about the abuse of circumcision: Baptism indeed profits you if you keep the law. However, if you are a lawbreaker, your baptism is made to be no baptism at all (Romans 2:25). If you are baptized, if you continue in the abuse of that holy sacrament, Christ will profit you nothing. Christ has become of no value to you; you have fallen from grace (Galatians 5:2, 4).

Beware of making baptism an idol by putting it in the place of Christ, as some churches do. Some people think baptism automatically imparts grace to a person when they are baptized. Many people trust in their baptism for their salvation, rather than in Christ. This is just like the Pharisees, who placed their confidence in their circumcision, and their other external privileges (Philippians 3:4-5). The time will come when God will punish the baptized with the unbaptized, as well as the circumcised with the uncircumcised (Jeremiah 9:25).

Be careful also not to make your baptism an equal partner with faith in your salvation. Some people make baptism too important. One of the ways they do this is by putting too much emphasis on the time you are baptized. They say baptism is only valid if you are an adult, and if you know what you are doing when you are baptized. They also say that if you were baptized when you were a baby, but have not been re-baptized as an adult, your baptism does not count. Even if you have faith in Christ, they say, you have no right to call yourself a Christian. They also say that you have no right to consider yourself a member of the true church of Christ if you were not baptized as an adult. This is a tragic misunderstanding and abuse of baptism. These people say that if you have only been baptized when you were a baby, you have missed salvation and church membership – all because you were not baptized at the right time of life!

Let us just suppose, for the sake of the argument, that infant baptism is not a valid baptism before God. Suppose that only an adult baptism is a valid baptism. (The Bible does not teach this, but let me be hypothetical for a moment.) Even if this were true, if you were baptized as a baby but were never baptized as an adult, this would not mean that you are not a true Christian! Remember, in the Old Testament, circumcision was as necessary as baptism. Yet, the Israelites failed to practice circumcision for forty years in the desert. They were not afraid that they would fall short of salvation because they lacked circumcision (Joshua 5:6-7). Many precious Christians, in former times of persecution, have gone to heaven through a baptism of suffering for the name of Christ. They never had any opportunity to be baptized with water! In ancient times, church leaders delayed baptism for new Christians for too long a period of time. However, we cannot think such people were not Christians because their baptism was delayed or neglected!

My point is, do not get hung up on the time of baptism! If you were baptized as an infant, and you now believe in Christ, your baptism is a valid baptism! You do not need to be re-baptized. Those who think you need to be re-baptized are, in effect, turning baptism into another work of righteousness you must do to be truly acceptable to God.

Not only must you avoid these errors in the way you think about baptism, you must also use your baptism to accomplish the purpose for which God gave it to you. Let me ask you this: What good use do you make of your baptism? How often do you think about it? Or, do you rarely think about it at all? Many Christians think so little about their baptism, and make so little use of their baptism, it is as if they had never been baptized at all.

Even though you were baptized only once, reflect upon your baptism frequently. Frequently ask yourself this question: Unto what was I baptized? (Acts 19:3). What does baptism seal? What did my baptism obligate me to? Stir yourself up and strengthen yourself by your baptism. Lay hold of the grace that it seals to you, and fulfill what it calls you to be and do before God – to live as one who has died and risen with Christ.

You have been made Christ's disciple by baptism, and you have been obligated to listen to him, rather than Moses, and to believe on him for your salvation. John baptized with the baptism of repentance, telling people to believe in him who was coming after him, Christ. Your baptism sealed your putting on Christ, your being a child of God by faith in Christ, and your being no longer under the former schoolmaster, the law (Galatians 3:25-27). Your baptism sealed to you the putting off of the body of sin, your burial and resurrection with Christ by faith, the forgiving of your trespasses (Colossians 2:12-13), and your being made members of one body and being given of one Spirit to drink (I Corinthians 12:12-13).

Baptism points you to the central truths of the gospel. Baptism guides you to faith in Christ alone for the forgiveness of sins, for holiness, and for all salvation, through union and fellowship with him. When you make good use of the sacrament of baptism, it will be a great help to your life of faith.

## 5.  The Sacrament of the Lord's Supper

The sacrament of the Lord's Supper is a spiritual feast to nourish your faith. It strengthens you to walk in holiness as Christ lives and works in you. This will happen as long as you use the Lord's Supper according to the pattern Christ gave you when he first instituted it, which the gospel writers record (Matthew 26:26-28, Mark 14:22-24, Luke 22:19-20). Christ also revealed instructions about the Lord's Supper from heaven in an extraordinary way to the Apostle Paul (I Corinthians 11:23-25). God gave these instructions to encourage you to keep this feast properly!

The purpose of the Lord's Supper is not only to help you remember Christ's death in the history of it, but in the mystery of it. His body was broken for you, and his blood was shed for you as the blood of the New Covenant for the forgiveness of sins. God wants you to receive and enjoy all the promises of the new covenant that are recorded (Hebrews 8:10-12). The purpose of the Lord's Supper is to remind you that Christ's body and blood are bread and drink, a totally sufficient food to nourish your soul to everlasting life. Take, eat, and drink of him by faith. This will assure you that when you truly believe in him, he is as closely united to you by his Spirit as the food you eat and drink is united to your body. In John 6, Christ himself more fully explains this mystery.

This sacrament not only reminds you of the spiritual blessings you have by faith in Christ, the Lord's Supper is one of the ways God holds forth Christ and his salvation to true believers. God's purpose is to stir you up and strengthen you to receive and feed upon Christ through active faith, while you partake of the outward elements of bread and wine. When Christ said, "Eat, drink, this is my body, this is my blood," Christ meant that he truly gives his body and blood to you in the Lord's Supper, as he gives the bread and the cup. You receive Christ's body and blood by faith, just as truly as you receive the bread and the cup.

Let me illustrate. It is just like a prince who gives one of his subjects a very honorable position. To do this, he gives to this subject his staff, his sword, or his signet ring. Then, he says to him, "Take this staff, sword, or signet ring; this is the position I am giving you." Or, suppose a father gives a deed to transfer ownership of a piece of land to his son. He gives his son the deed and says to him "Take it as your own; this is now your land." What do these expressions mean? They mean that the office and the land are actually being given through the means of these outward signs. In other words, when the king gives his signet ring, and the father gives the deed, he is giving away an actual royal position and an actual piece of land!

Even so, the Apostle Paul says the bread in the Lord's Supper is the communion of the body of Christ, and the cup is the communion of his blood (I Corinthians 10:16). Christ's body and blood are really communicated to you, and you really partake of them, just as you partake of the bread and the cup. This sacrament is indeed a wonderful, symbolic picture of the fact that you must constantly live upon a crucified Savior. However, the Lord's Supper is much more than this. The Lord's Supper is also a precious means by which Christ, the bread and drink of life, is really given to you. When you come to the Lord's Table, you receive Jesus spiritually.

In other words, Christ is spiritually present in the Lord's Supper. You receive him, through faith, when you partake of it! The Lord's Supper is a love-gift from God. Christ's heart was filled with love for you when he first instituted the Lord's Supper. Christ first gave the Lord's Supper when he was right at the point of finishing his greatest work of love, by laying down his life for you (I Corinthians 11:23). Use this sacrament properly, and receive its spiritual benefits.

Some people disregard the Lord's Supper. They rarely ever partake of it, and they never seem to get anything out of it when they do! Why? They think that in the Lord's Supper, God is only holding out bare signs and symbols of Christ and his salvation. They do not think they have any need of help from signs and symbols! If they only understood that in the Lord's Supper God really gives Christ himself to their faith by and with those signs and symbols, they would look at it much differently. They would cherish the Lord's Supper as a most delicious feast. They would want to partake of it every opportunity they could (Acts 2:42, 20:7).

There is another reason why many rarely ever partake of the Lord's Supper, and why they do not receive much benefit from it: they are afraid to partake! They think that if they partake of it, they will be brought into a greater danger of eating and drinking their own damnation. They know those terrifying words of the Apostle Paul, "For whoever eats and drinks unworthily, eats and drinks damnation to himself, because he does not discern the Lord's body" (I Corinthians 11:29). They think that coming to the Lord's Table is like walking through a mine field. God is ready to destroy them if they make one false move when they come. Therefore, they only come to the table once a year. However, they think it is safest just to wholly abstain from this dangerous sacrament. They do not want to be judged and destroyed by God!

When they do come to the Lord's Supper, their slavish fears take away all the benefit they might receive in it. Instead of joyfully receiving Christ and his salvation in the Lord's Supper, they consider they have succeeded if they partake of the Lord's Supper without receiving the sentence of damnation! They literally think they are "risking their life" when they come to the Lord's Table. This is just like the Old Testament High Priest, who only risked his life by entering once per year into the Holy of Holies. When he came out alive, the people held a feast of thanksgiving because he was delivered from the judgment of death!

There is no reason you should be terrified by these words of the Apostle Paul. Paul aimed these words at the Corinthian Church because they were terribly abusing the Lord's Supper. You can easily avoid this same error if you simply listen to what Paul told them to do. He told them they were not discerning the Lord's body when they ate the Lord's Supper. They had turned the Lord's Supper into a regular meal, where they came together to eat and drink. When they did this, some went hungry, and others got drunk. They had forgotten about Christ when they ate together! So, Paul told them to discern the Lord's body when they came together to eat the Lord's Supper.

Consider this also: the word "damnation," or judgment, does not refer to eternal condemnation in this context. It means a temporal judgment upon the people.  In I Corinthians 11:31, Paul himself interprets what he means when he says, "we are chastened by the Lord, so that we should not be condemned with the world."  You are indeed prone to sin, and you will very often receive this sacrament in an unworthy manner.  However, this is no different than anything else.  You pollute every other holy thing with which you come into contact!

Remember, you have a great High Priest who has born all of your sins, including how you treat holy things!  This means you do not have to participate in any of the means of grace -- the Lord's Supper included – with this kind of slavish fear.  Under the covering of Christ's righteousness you can draw near to God, without slavish fear, in the full assurance of faith, when you partake of the Lord's Supper, and when you participate in any other holy activity.  You are to rejoice in the Lord in this spiritual feast, as the Jews were bound to do in their solemn feasts (Deuteronomy 16:14-15).

There are other abuses of the Lord's Supper, just as there are with baptism.  Some people set the Lord's Supper in opposition to the life of faith, rather than making it an integral part of the life of faith.  Some people put the Lord's Supper in the place of Christ.  How?  They trust in it as a work of righteousness to gain God's favor, or they see it as a ceremony that will automatically impart grace to their soul by merely partaking of it.  Other people think that the Lord's Supper is so necessary, you really cannot have true faith with it.   Still other people think that somehow the bread and the wine actually become the physical body and blood of the Lord.  Always remember that the true body and blood of Christ are given to you, with the bread and wine, in a spiritual and mysterious manner, by the unsearchable work of the Holy Spirit.  He unites Christ and you together by faith, without any kind of physical change in the outward elements.  Christ is spiritually present, and you commune with him by faith.

## 6.  Prayer

Prayer is an important way of living by faith in Christ, as a new person in Christ.  When you pray, you make your requests known to God with supplication and thanksgiving.  It is obviously important because God requires it (I Thessalonians 5:17, Romans 12:12).  Prayer is your priestly work (I Peter 22:5).  Prayer is the basic privilege of every believer (I Corinthians 1:2).  God is a God of hearing prayer (Psalm 65:2).  God wants his people to pray to him, because of the blessings he wants to pour out upon them once he has enabled them to pray.  At first, God is found by those who do not seek him (Ezekiel 36:37, Philippians 1:19-20).  But then, he prepares them for thanksgiving, and gives them double the blessings.

It is not that God's sovereign will is ever changed when people pray.  However, ordinarily, God's purpose is to accomplish his will through prayer.  Faith should not lead you to neglect prayer, but to pray all the more (II Samuel 7:27).

It is the gospel that makes prayer possible.  Christ, the Mediator of the new covenant, by whom justification and sanctification are promised, is also the Mediator who makes your prayers accepted by the Father (Hebrews 4:15-16).  The Holy Spirit, who gives you the new birth, who unites you to Christ, who sanctifies you, and who shows you the things of Christ, is a Spirit of prayer (Zechariah 12:10, Galatians 4:6).  He is like a fire inflaming your soul, and he makes you mount upward in prayer to God.  Prayerless people are dead to God.

Prayer is such an important responsibility that if it is done, everything else will be done well.  In fact, nothing else can be done without prayer!  All other aspects of worship are a help to prayer (Isaiah 66:7).  When you pray, you come to God in faith and pour out all of your holy desires and affections (Psalm 62:8).  Prayer is your continual incense and sacrifice, whereby you offer yourself, your heart, your affections, and your life to God (Psalm 141:2).  You put grace into practice through prayer.  Indeed, you must act in this way, or else you are not likely to put grace into practice in any other way.  As you put grace into practice, you obtain more grace, and all holiness (Luke 11:13, Hebrews 4:16, Psalm 81:10).

Your riches come by prayer.  Israel prevails while Moses holds up his hands (Exodus 17:11).  Prayer strengthened Hannah against her sorrows (I Samuel 1:15-18).  By prayer peace continues (Philippians 4:6-7).  By prayer the distressed soul is comforted, as it was with Hannah (I Samuel 1:18, Psalm 32:1-5).  Incense (symbolizing prayer) was always burned, and the lamps were always trimmed (Exodus 30:7-8).

Prayer is added to your spiritual armor — not as a particular piece of the armor, but as a means of putting it all on and making right use of it all, so you might stand in the evil day (Ephesians 6:18).  Prayer is a means of transfiguring you into the likeness of Christ in holiness, and making your spiritual face to shine – just as Christ was transfigured in the body while he prayed (Luke 9:29). Moses' face shined while he talked with God (Exodus 34:29). Hence you are called to pray frequently (Ephesians 6:18).

Pray always, in all seasons and opportunities, both in private and in public with the congregation, as the early Christians did (Acts 2:42, 10:30-31). Set apart times for prayer daily (Matthew 6:11), even several times in a day, as a morning and evening sacrifice (Daniel 6:10). Pray also on special occasions (James 5:13-15). Pray briefly, throughout the day, when it does not hinder your other appointed business (Psalm 129:8, II Samuel 15:31, Nehemiah 2:4). Pray in your solitary rooms (Matthew 6:6), and in your families (Acts 10:30-31). There were many sacrifices on the Sabbath day, on the day of Atonement, and at other appointed times of worship (Numbers 28). In the same way, you should pray at specially appointed times of worship.

In a word, give yourself enthusiastically to prayer, without any limits (Psalm 109:4, Psalm 119:164). But, again, the real challenge is to pray in the right way, to bring about holiness by faith in Christ. Here you must say, "Lord, teach us to pray" (Luke 11:1). You need to be taught, not only with regard to the matter of prayer, but also with regard to the manner of prayer. Christ teaches both. He gave you a brief pattern of prayer, which he taught to his disciples. However, in order to really understand prayer, you must consult the whole word of God. You also need the Spirit of Christ to guide you in your prayer life. Therefore, you need to be taught to pray by the Holy Spirit (Jude 20, Ephesians 2:18). It is only the Spirit of God who can guide and enable your soul to pray correctly.

When you pray, remember the following guidelines:

First, pray with your heart and spirit (Isaiah 26:9, John 4:24) – where the Spirit of Christ, and of prayer, principally reside (Galatians 4:6, Ephesians 1:17). Pray with your understanding (I Corinthians 14:15-16). Praying without understanding will do you no good, since you are being renewed in knowledge (Colossians 3:20). Pray with a sincere and hearty desire for the good things you ask for in prayer, for God sees your heart (Isaiah 62:8).

Prayer is chiefly a heart-work. God hears the heart without the mouth, but he never hears acceptable prayer from the mouth without the heart (I Samuel 1:13). Your prayer is a terrible hypocrisy, and a mocking of God. You are taking his name in vain when you say "your kingdom come, your will be done," and you hate godliness in your heart. This is lying to God. You are flattering him with your lips, but you are not truly praying. God will not receive it as true prayer (Psalm 78:36).

You must also have a sense of your wants and needs, and that only God can supply them for you (II Chronicles 20:12). Be fervent in those desires (James 5:16). Pray with attention, being very mindful of what you pray for, or else you cannot expect God to be mindful of it (Daniel 9:3). Watch your prayer (I Peter 4:7). Set yourself to prayer intently. God sees where your heart wanders, when you pray without attention (Ezekiel 33:31).

When you pray many prayers without any understanding, attention, or feeling, you are sinning by being a hypocrite. Some people say their form of prayers in church, mouthing words that they cannot understand – just like a parrot would do! Then, they think they have done their duty of prayer well – even though their heart did not pray at all, and they were thinking about other things. This is mere lip-labor. This is just plain deceit (Malachi 1:13-14), a form of godliness that denies its power (II Timothy 3:5). Some people think that God hears and approves their prayers, even though they do not understand what they are saying. The reality is, God judges them to be hypocrites, and profane persons, because they do know what they are saying.

Second, pray in the name of Christ. The Holy Spirit glorifies Christ (John 16:14). He leads you to God through Christ (Ephesians 2:18). Walking in the spirit, and walking in Christ, is the same thing. So is praying in the Spirit, and praying by and through Christ. Just as you are to walk in the name of the Lord, and to do all things in his name, so you must pray in his name, as he commanded (John 14:13-14). It is not enough to simply conclude your prayers by saying "In Jesus name, Amen." Come for your blessings in the garments of your elder brother. Come in his worthiness and in his strength for everything.

Praise God for all things in his name, as things received for his sake, and by him (Ephesians 5:20). Lay hold of his strength only. Do not place you confidence in anything other than Christ for your acceptance. Do not arrogantly plead your own works, like the proud Pharisee (Luke 18:11-12). See them as fruits of grace, and rewards of grace.

Praying in the spirit means that you pray based upon the gospel, not upon legalistic principles (Romans 7:6, II Corinthians 3:3). Praying in the spirit means that you pray with great humiliation, and a sense of unworthiness (Psalm 51). It means that you pray with a broken spirit. It means that you pray with no hope of acceptance except through Christ (Daniel 9:18). You can struggle in prayer all you want, but without these things your prayers are not true prayers to the Father. Without the gospel, prayer is just an abomination before God.

Third, do not think that you will be accepted because your prayers are so good! Do not trust in your prayers as works of righteousness. This turns prayer into an idol, and puts it in the very place of Christ himself. Some people hope to be saved by how many prayers they offer. Even some true Christians trust their prayers as works of righteousness.

Some people also think one prayer is more acceptable than another because of the holiness of the form of the prayer. They especially view the Lord's Prayer in this way. They use it like a good luck charm when they are in danger, and they make an idol of it. Other people use the Lord's Prayer as a spell or a charm to drive away the devil. Still other people think their prayers are more acceptable because they are offered in one place rather than in another, because of the holiness of the place (John 4:21-24, I Timothy 2:8). Still others trust in speaking many words (Matthew 6:7). They think that if they pray to God, they will appease him so they can live any way they please.

Fourth, pray to God as your Father, through Christ your Savior. Come to prayer in faith that your sins really are forgiven, that you are accepted by God, and that you have obtained all other things you need for your salvation (James 1:5-7, James 5:15, I John 5:14, Mark 11:24, Hebrews 10:14, Psalm 62:8, 86:7, 65:16, 67:1, and 17:6). This is what it means to pray in Christ (Ephesians 3:12), and by the Holy Spirit, the Spirit of adoption (Romans 8:15, Galatians 4:6). Without him, your prayer is lifeless and heartless, and just a dead carcass (Romans 10:14, Psalm 78:1-2). Remember, your prayer is not effective because of how emotional or how expressive you are. You cannot be sure you will receive everything you ask for, but you can be sure you will receive everything you ask for that is good.

If there are any sins on your conscience, first ask for forgiveness of them (Psalm 32, 51). Ask for the purification of them by faith, so you can lift up holy hands without anger or disputing (I Timothy 2:8). This sin of anger is especially mentioned here, because anger is contrary to loving and forgiving others. Here is where the strength, life, and power of prayer lie: Set your faith to work, and you will receive power, and prevail.

Fifth, ask God to enable you to live by faith, so that his grace will sanctify you. Seek the Spirit himself, in the first place (Luke 11:13), and all spiritual things (Matthew 6:33). Praying only for worldly things reveals that your heart is very worldly, and this kind of prayer leaves your heart worldly. Pray for faith (Mark 9:24), and pray for those things that will glorify God the most (I Chronicles 1:11-12). When you pray for all other outward things, act in faith in submission to his will. This prayer sets you in a holy mindset (Matthew 26:42, Luke 22:42-43). Make it your chief aim to hallow God's name (Matthew 6:9), and not indulge your own fleshly lusts (James 4:3).

Sixth, bring your soul into order by prayer, no matter how distressed you are by guilt, anguish, inordinate cares, or fears (Philippians 4:6-7). A watch must be wound up very often. Even so, you will often have to wrestle in prayer against your unbelief, doubts, fears, cares, and weaknesses of the flesh, and pray for what is good. You will wrestle against evil lusts and desires, the coldness of you heart, impatience, and trouble in your spirit. You will wrestle against everything that is contrary to a holy life. You will often have to ask God to produce holy desires in you and in others (Colossians 4:12, Romans 15:30).

Stir yourself up to prayer (Colossians 2:1, Isaiah 64:7). Your flesh will be unwilling and very reluctant, but do not yield to it. Resist it by the Holy Spirit (Matthew 26:41). In this way you will find the Spirit helping you in your weakness (Romans 8:26-27). Even though God seems to make you wait a long time, do not give up or be discouraged (Luke 18:1-7). The greater your agony, the more earnestly you should pray (Psalm 22:1-2, Luke 22:42). Continue in constant prayer (Romans 12:12, Ephesians 6:18). You will thus find that prayer is a great heart-work. Prayer is not something you can do while you think about other things. Prayer requires all the strength of faith and emotional energy you can possibly stir up. This is how you get a holy frame of mind.

Seventh, use the whole matter and manner of prayer to bring your heart and soul into a holy frame of mind. Wrestle in prayer to bring this holy frame of mind about. When you confess your sins, condemn yourself as you are in your flesh, but not as you are in Christ. Do not deny that you have grace, as if you were a non-Christian, or as if you were just now beginning your Christian life. This way of thinking hinders praise for the grace you have already received now that you are a Christian. Have in your heart a godly sorrow, a holy sense of your own sin and misery (Psalm 38:18, 51:3,12). Sorrow is one of the great parts of prayer.

You must also plead with God. Pleadings are based upon God's attributes (Numbers 14:17-18), God's promises (II Samuel 7:26, 28), and the justness of your cause (Psalm 17:2-3). They are also based upon your understanding that what you are asking for will promote the glory of God (Psalm 115:1-2). Christ's long prayer in John 17 is made up of much pleading, and very few petitions.

Pray in praise and thanksgiving, to stir up peace, joy, love etc. (Genesis 32:10, Psalm 18:1-3, 33:1, 74:14, and 104:34). Spend much time praising God for the mercies of your new state in Christ (Ephesians 1:3). Then, you will be more able to give thanks for all the other benefits God has given you (Ephesians 5:20, I Thessalonians 5:18). You will also plead for those benefits, in order to stir up your faith and duty. It is very good to pray that very brief prayer, "God, have mercy on me." However, it is not the only thing you should pray. Some lazy people think this, and they harden themselves in their neglect of praying.

Eighth, do not confine and limit your prayers to prescribed forms of prayers. There is no way you can come up with a set form of prayer to fit all of the conditions and needs of your soul at all times and occasions. I am not necessarily condemning all forms of prayer. Christ gave us a form of prayer, the Lord's Prayer. However, Christ never intended to bind you to the precise form of words. The Holy Spirit himself expressed it in different words in Mathew 6 and Luke 11. However, it is better to pray by that form, or other forms, than to not pray at all. It would be very unloving to take away the crutches or wooden legs from lame people!

It is absolutely wrong to bind yourself to a form of prayer, because no form will fit every particular occasion when you need to pray (Ephesians 6:18, Philippians 4:6, John 15:7, I Thessalonians 5:18, Ephesians 5:20). Make the whole Bible your common prayer book, as the early church did. The Bible is the language of the Holy Spirit; it applies to all occasions and situations, and it gives you language to help you properly speak to God. If you use a prescribed form of prayer, follow it by the Holy Spirit farther than the form goes, just as he will guide you by the Word. If you do not, you will quench the Spirit (I Thessalonians 5:19).

If you know the principles of prayer, and if have a real sense of your great need and a heartfelt desire for God's grace and mercy, you will be able to pray without any prescribed prayer forms. Your own emotions will bring forth words out of the fullness of your need. You do not need to be overly scrupulous about what words you use. There is no doubt that the Holy Spirit, who is there to help you when you speak to men, will also much more help you speak to God, if you desire it (I Corinthians 1:5, Mark 13:11, Luke 12:11-12). God has no regard for eloquent words or artificial composure. You do not need to have any regard for them either when you pray in private (Isaiah 38:14). If you limit yourself to prescribed prayer forms, you will simply grow formal, and you will limit the Spirit.

## 7. Singing

Another means of grace is that of singing of psalms, hymns, songs of praise, and spiritual songs of any spiritual matter — in short, songs of any sacred subject composed to a tune. God has commanded this in the New Testament (Colossians 3:16, Ephesians 5:19). The Old Testament people were commanded to sing a great deal (Psalm 144:1-3, 96:1 etc.). Moses and the children of Israel sang before David's time (Exodus 15). David composed psalms by the Spirit, to be sung publicly (II Samuel 23:1-2), and in private (Psalm 40:3, II Chronicles 29:30, Psalm 105:2).

Other songs also were composed on several different occasions, and used whether they were part of the Scripture or not. Solomon composed one thousand and five (I Kings 4:32). They composed songs on many occasions, and this shows that it is lawful for us to do so – as long as these songs are according to Scripture (Isaiah 38:9,14). The subjects of Scripture should be sung (Psalm 64:54). Christ and his disciples sung a hymn (Matthew 27:30) – probably one of David's psalms. Psalms were written for our instruction, as well as other parts of Scripture (Romans 15:4), which now can be used for singing. The psalms speak about matters contained in the New Testament, either figuratively or quite clearly. We can understand what they mean now, better than the Old Testament believers could, under the Old Covenant (II Corinthians 3:16, Galatians 2:17).

The early Christians also practiced this form of worship through song (Acts 16:25). Even Pliny, a pagan philosopher, noticed the hymns they sang before daylight. These songs or hymns may be used at all times, but especially for rejoicing (James 5:13). However, this text does not apply exclusively to singing, any more than it applies exclusively to prayer (Psalm 38:18, II Chronicles 35:25).

Make sure you sing in the right way. First, do not trust in the melody of your voice, as if that pleased God, who only delights in the melody of the heart (Colossians 3:16). Also, singing is not simply a matter of music, which can simply remain fleshly. "Not a musical string, but the heart; nor crying, but loving sounds in the ear of the Lord." This spiritual music was symbolized in the Old Testament by the musical instruments that were used.

Second, use singing for the same purpose as meditation and prayer, according to the nature of what is sung – to kindle your faith (II Chronicles 20:21-22, Acts 16:25-26), to take joy and delight in the Lord, and to glory in God (Psalm 104:33-34, 105:3, 144:1-2, and 33:1-3). The purpose of singing is to help you be heartily joyful in the Lord, and to act with a holy joy (James 5:13, Ephesians 5:19). Through song, you receive knowledge and instruction in heavenly mysteries, and you learn more about your duty through teaching and admonishing (Colossians 3:16). Many psalms are psalms of instruction.

Third, particularly use the psalms for singing. You can easily sing the psalms that speak in the first person. Even though you cannot claim that you originally composed them about yourself, you are not lying when you sing them. David speaks of Christ as if it were of himself, as a pattern of suffering and virtue, in order to instruct others. You can sing such psalms in the same way— not as your own words, but as words to instruct you. When you do this, you are not lying, any more than the Levites, the sons of Korah, or Jeduthan, or other musicians who were called to sing them (Psalms 5, 35, and 42). You have a certain liberty when you use the psalms. Even though you cannot apply all of them to yourself – i.e., you cannot think and speak exactly what they say – you should sing them for your instruction, as in Psalms 6, 26, 46, 101, and 130.

The psalms are particularly useful. They are filled with God's wisdom for teaching and instructing. They also have a very pleasant meter, which helps you to remember them whether you say them or sing them (Deuteronomy 31:19,21). For instance, there are some alphabetical psalms, such as Psalms 25, 34, 37, 111, 112, 119, and 145.

When you put these words to a good melody, you can more easily receive instruction in God's word with great delight – just like when you eat food with sugar on it! Your sorrow is naturally dispelled, and you become spiritually joyful when you sing the word of God to a pleasing melody (II Kings 3:15, I Samuel 16:14-15). Even non-Christians understand that music brings improvement and culture to other people.

## 8. Fasting

Fasting is a practice given by God to be used for the same purpose as in the New Testament (Matthew 9:15, 27:21, I Corinthians 7:5). There are many examples of it in the New Testament (Acts 13:2-3, 14:23, I Corinthians 7:5). In the Old Testament, there were many fasts that were commanded by God. Usually, fasts took place in times of great affliction (I Samuel 7:6, Nehemiah 9:1, Daniel 9:3, 10:2-3, II Samuel 12:16, Psalm 35:13, Joel 2:13). The great fast day was the Day of Atonement (Leviticus 16:29-31), when everyone was commanded to fast. There is also the prophecy of fasting for the times of the New Testament (Zechariah 12:12). Fasting was used mostly on extraordinary occasions. It is a great help to holiness by faith. When you fast, you set aside special time for fervent prayer, humility, and repentance (Joel 1:14, 2:12).

When you fast, make sure that you follow these guidelines:

First, do not trust in fasting as meriting the grace or favor of God. This is exactly what the legalists and the Pharisees did (Luke 18:11). They put fasting in the place of Christ. Other people use fasting as a direct means to attain grace, or as a way to kill off their lusts. These people will kill their bodies before they kill off their lusts! Also, do not use fasting as a purifying ritual. Do not think that fasting in and of itself is acceptable to God (I Timothy 4:8, Hebrews 12:9, Colossians 2:16-23).

Do not think your prayers are acceptable only if you have fasted; this is against faith in Christ. Fasts, as well as feasts, are not substantial parts of worship, because they are not spiritual; they are simply matters of the body. In the Old Testament, they were instituted as ceremonies that were meant to teach you. However, they are no longer used for that purpose. On the Day of Atonement, there were many figurative rites given in addition to fasting, such as sackcloth, ashes, rending garments, pouring out water, and lying upon the earth. The kingdom of God does not consist in these things (Romans 14:17). Your soul will become hardened if you trust in them (Isaiah 58:3, Zechariah 7:5-10).

Second, use fasting to help you in special, extraordinary times of prayer and repentance. Fasting is valuable only to help your soul. It removes impediments, the earthly things that normally consume your time and energy, such as eating, drinking or bodily pleasures (Joel 2:13, Isaiah 22:12-13, Zechariah 12:10-14). The best fasting takes place when your mind is taken off these delights, as it was in John the Baptist's case (Matthew 3:4), and when heaven and godly sorrow take over your soul (Zechariah 12:10-14).

Third, only use fasting to accomplish its right purpose. If fasting becomes an end in itself, it becomes worth nothing at all. If you abstain from food, and then you get a gnawing appetite, you should eat sparingly, as Daniel did in his great fast (Daniel 10:2-3). Some people are not spiritually minded enough to give themselves to fasting without being distracted by it. Such people are better off eating, than going beyond their own strength in trying to do something that is not absolutely necessary. This only results in a slavish performance, as in the case of those who thought they had to abstain from marriage (I Corinthians 7:8-9, 34-36). Christ does not want his weak disciples feeling obligated to fast (Matthew 9:14-15). If you find yourself having difficulty fasting, become aware of the weakness and fleshliness behind this problem. Then, you will be able to take full advantage of this excellent help to your faith.

## 9. Vows

You may expect me to say something about vows. However, I will only say this about them. Do not think you will bring yourself to be a better person, or to good works, by vows and promises – as if the strength of your **own** law could do it when the strength of God's law cannot do it. We tell children to make promises to change their ways, but we know how well they keep their promises! The devil will urge you to make a vow, and then break it, so he may frustrate you and torment your conscience all the more.

## 10. Fellowship and relationships with other Christians in the Church of Christ

Another means of building your faith is fellowship and communion with other Christians (Acts 2:42). Whoever is saved should join some visible church, and come into fellowship with other Christians.

If for some reason they have no opportunity for this, their heart should desire it. Sometimes the church is in the wilderness and hindered from visible communion and sacraments. However, those who believe in Christ always want to join themselves to the church of Christ. They continued steadfastly in fellowship (Acts 2:42-47).

God bids his people to leave the fellowship and society of the wicked as much as they can (II Corinthians 6:17). When we do spend time in their company, they must be charitable to their spiritual and physical needs (I Corinthians 5:9). This communion with other Christians is to be carried out in private relationships (Psalm 101:4-7), and in public assemblies (Hebrews 10:25, Zechariah 14:6-7). It will help you attain holiness in many ways.

God ordinarily saves people through or in a church. When God brings people to faith in Christ, he usually does it in one of two ways: he either brings people into the fellowship of a church, or else he holds forth the light of truth by his churches to the world. A church is the temple of God, where God lives (I Timothy 3:15). He has placed his name and his salvation there, as in Jerusalem of old (Joel 2:32). He has given to his churches those officers and sacraments that he uses to convert others (I Corinthians 12:28).

He uses all of the members of a church to convey his grace and fullness to others, as the members of a natural body convey to each other the fullness of the head (Ephesians 4:16). All the newborn in the faith are brought forth and nourished by the church (Isaiah 64:8-11, 44:20, 60:4). Therefore, everyone who wants to be saved should join a church. Those who love the church, who unite as members, brothers, and companions, will prosper. God pronounces his wrath against those who are not members of the church. No one can have God for his Father if he does not have the church for his mother. The gospel makes those who desire fellowship with God take hold of the garments of his people (Zechariah 8:23).

Fellowship with other Christians promotes holiness in many ways. In the church, you have the word and the sacraments (Acts 2:42, Isaiah 2:3, Matthew 28:19-20). You also have pastors who watch over your soul (Hebrews 13:17, I Thessalonians 5:12-13). None of these helps will have any value if you do not have fellowship with other Christians. If you live as a solitary Christian, and do not pursue fellowship with other Christians, you cannot have any of these things – the word, the sacraments, and care by church officers.

You have mutual prayer. Prayer is far more powerful when everyone prays together (Matthew 18:19-20, II Corinthians 1:10, James 5:16, Romans 15:30).

You have mutual admonition, instruction, and consolation, to help others when they are ready to fall, and to promote the good work in each other (I Thessalonians 5:14). "He who walks with the wise shall be wise" (Proverbs 13:20). Woe to him who is alone when he falls (Ecclesiastes 4:9-12). In a church fellowship, there are many helpers, many to watch over each other. Soldiers have their security in a company; so it is with the church. For making hearts alive, iron sharpens iron (Proverbs 27:17). Likewise the counsel of a friend, like ointment and perfume, rejoices the heart (Proverbs 27:9). The wounds and reproofs of the righteous are like a precious ointment (Psalm 141:5).

You have external supports, which are meant to reduce suffering. These things are to be a mutual ministry (Ephesians 4:28, I Peter 4:9-10). The affliction is greatly increased when no one cares for your soul (Psalm 142:4).

You have church discipline, or the ministry of restoration. This is used only when sins are exceedingly bad, or when people are obstinate in their sin. This procedure is appointed for the destruction of the flesh, that the spirit may be saved (I Corinthians 5:5). It is better and more hopeful to be cast out by the church, so you might repent, than to be completely without the church at all times. It is better to be a lost sheep, than a goat or a pig! Excommunication cuts off an unrepentant sinner's actual fellowship only, until he or she repents.

Excommunication does not completely abolish the title and relation of a brother and church member — though it judges the disciplined person to be an unnatural brother, and a member who is not fit for acts of communion. A person in this situation still needs to be admonished (II Thessalonians 3:15). We are to use any means we can to cure and restore him to repentance. The church reaches forth a hand to help such a person, even though it does not join hands in fellowship with him. However, if he does not have enough grace to repent, it would be better if he had never known the way of righteousness (II Peter 2:21).

Live by the Means of Grace

You have the living examples of other Christians before your eyes in a church fellowship, to teach and encourage you (Philippians 3:17, 4:9, II Timothy 3:10, II Corinthians 9:2).

You have godly discourse – the teaching, admonishing, and comforting of others in Christ. You can only teach and encourage those with whom you have close fellowship in Christ. Some people, like pigs, trample these jewels under their feet. Christians, therefore, are supposed to refrain from godly discourse in their company (Amos 5:10-13, 6:10). However, Christians gladly receive fellowship, and you should have fellowship with them (Malachi 3:16). This will greatly help you in your growth in holiness (Proverbs 11:25).

You have mutual ministry to other members of the body of Christ. You do good to Christ in his members in a church fellowship. Just as you yourself are a member of Christ, so also you must do good to others who are his members as well. It is just as if you were doing it to him. You have the great privilege of being able to serve all the other members of the body of Christ (Matthew 25:35-49, Psalm 16:2-3). However, you cannot serve them if you are separate from them, just as a member of a physical body cannot perform its function to the other members of the body if it is separate from them.

It is also important that you correctly use church fellowship to attain holiness in Christ. There are many principles to keep in mind for your life in the church of Christ:

Do not trust in church membership in and of itself, or in any kind of a relationship with any church, to commend you to God. A church is simply a way to have fellowship with Christ, and for walking in what that fellowship requires. The Israelites stumbled over Christ, because they trusted in their external privileges rather than in Christ alone. They trusted in their membership in the community of God's people. They set the church in opposition to Christ. They should have made this privilege of church membership subservient to Christ! They should have abandoned their confidence in this privilege just as Paul teaches (Philippians 3:3-7).

You must not glory in Paul, Apollos, or Cephas, but only in Christ. If you do not glory in Christ alone, you glory in the flesh and in men (Corinthians 1:12-13, 3:21). Trusting in church privileges is an inroad to both religious formalism and licentiousness (Jeremiah 7: 4-10). This mistake will eventually lead to the corruption of churches (Isaiah 1:10, II

Timothy 2:20).

Do not follow any church further than you may follow in the way of Christ. Stay in fellowship with a church only because of Christ — because it follows Christ, and has fellowship with Christ (I John 1:3, Zechariah 8:23). If a church rebels against Christ, do not follow it, however old and established the church might be. The Israelite church persecuted Christ and his apostles, and as such no one should have followed it. Many people who stayed with that church fell from Christ (Philippians 3:6, Acts 6:13-14, 21:28). You are indeed to listen to the church, but not to every church that **calls** itself a church. Do not listen to any church any further than it speaks as a true church. It must speak following the voice of the true shepherd (John 10:27).

Subject yourself to ministers of Christ, who are stewards of his mysteries (I Corinthians 4:1). However, you must give yourself first to Christ absolutely, and then to the church according to the will of Christ (II Corinthians 8:5). Your faith must not rest upon the precepts of men (Matthew 15). You must test the doctrines of men by scripture, whatever authority they pretend to have (Acts 17:11). Whenever people completely and mindlessly follow church guides, they inevitably sink the church into all kinds of spiritual adultery and abominations. You are not baptized into the name of the church, but into the name of Christ (I Corinthians 1:13).

Do not think you must attain a certain level of grace before you join yourself in full communion with a church of Christ. When you have given yourself to Christ, and have learned the responsibility of communion, you can give yourself to a church of Christ. You can join it even though you find much weakness and incompetence in that church. Church membership, and all that goes with it, are meant to strengthen you! How can you get warm when you are all alone? Whenever any disciple was first converted to Christ, the first thing he did was to join a church fellowship (Acts 2:42). Churches must be willing to receive Christ's weak ones, in order to bring about holiness in themselves and in others. They must feed his lambs as well as his more full-grown sheep. How else will Christ's weak ones grow strong, except by being nourished by the other members? Christians should never think that they can "grow out of" church fellowship, by "moving on" to a higher degree of grace and to greener pastures!

Do not be unwilling to receive people into your fellowship just because you know they will be irritating to you! Yes, you will have to bear with them; but remember, patience and longsuffering are essential parts of church fellowship (Ephesians 4:2-3, Romans 14:1). The weakest members have the greatest need to be strengthened by church fellowship. You are obligated to receive them, just as Christ has received you (Romans 15:7). You should not reject or be separate from the weaker parts of the body (I Corinthians 12:23-24). You should place more honor and attractiveness on them.

In the New Testament church, people were admitted to the church by making a credible profession of faith. It is true, some weeds got in with the wheat. Within the church, many scandals did arise and reproached the ways of Christ. However, being stricter about who can join the church will not keep all hypocrites out of the church. Be very careful that you do not hinder any who have the least truth of grace from joining the church.

Keep fellowship and communion with a church for the sake of fellowship and communion with Christ (I John 1:3, Zechariah 8:23). You must keep communion in Christ's pure ways only. Seek Christ by faith in these pure ways. When you enjoy the great blessings Christ gives you, you will receive him more fully, and you will begin to act in a holy and godly way. You will also flourish spiritually and grow in grace. Choose fellowship with the most spiritual churches. Judge other churches and people according to the rule of the new creation (II Corinthians 5:16-17). Test them (Revelation 2:2, 3:9), so they do not corrupt you!

Make sure your fellowship with a church builds you up in your faith, and does not tear you down. You should have fellowship not only in the church where you are a member, but also with other churches into which God will occasionally send you. Why? Because your fellowship with a particular church obliges you to have fellowship with all true churches of Christ. It is wrong to say, "I am a member of a church in the city; therefore I will not have any fellowship with a church in the country." If you belong to Christ, you belong to other Christians. This includes both individual Christians and other churches.

Make sure you join in fellowship with the godly in the place where you live, so you will have more frequent and constant fellowship with them. Onesimus, though converted at Rome, was a member of the church of the Colossians, because he lived there (Colossians 4:9 and Philemon 10). The union of Christians together where they lived was the practice of the apostles of Christ. You cannot violate it without sinning. People who live near each other can best watch over, admonish, comfort, and build up one another. This is the benefit of fellowship. These who join a church where they will not have this benefit of mutual ministry destroy true fellowship. They will only harm themselves spiritually.

Any church fellowship that does not practice the ways of Christ is simply a conspiracy to take his name in vain. It is a counterfeit church fellowship, and an assembly of hypocrites. It is pure arrogance for people like this to invite others to join their church. It is tyranny for hypocrites to compel others to come to their church. Every Christian is required to try to make their church better by reforming it, according to the power of the gospel and the Word of God. Those who do this are the best sons of Christ's church. They are always asking in their church, "Is this the way to enjoy Christ?" They understand that God has established the church for Christians to enjoy Christ!

Finally, do not leave your church during a time of persecution. During a time of persecution, you need your church's help the most. When you are most severely tested, you will cling to it most dearly. Leaving the church during persecution is a sign of apostasy – of falling away from the faith (Hebrews 10:25-26, Matthew 24:9-14). You must cling to other Christians in your church as one flesh, even to prisons and death. If you do not do this, you deny Christ in his members (Matthew 25:43).

These are the means of grace that God commends to you in his word. In themselves they do not make you holy; they draw you into deeper fellowship with Christ, the True Vine, who makes you holy as you abide in him. What good reason to diligently make use of these means of grace to the glory of God!

# Chapter Fourteen

### Principle Number Fourteen

**I have been telling you up to this point that you must seek to live a holy life by believing in Christ, and by walking in him by faith. If you are going to do this, you must understand why living by faith in Christ is so important and beneficial to your soul.**

It is time to conclude our discussion about sanctification by grace through faith. I know you may find it hard to believe that living by grace will really empower you to live a holy life. Very few people will tell you that the Christian life is a life of joy. However, this is what God plainly tells you in his word. I want you to be excited about living, each day, by grace through faith in Christ! All around you, people are giving up the quest for godly living, because they do not know how to do it. They grow weary in their fight against sin, and they just give up. Why is this? Most people think godliness is an unpleasant, joyless, and discouraging way to live. They think that living a holy life is like the wearisome journey through the desert the Israelites had to take on their way to Canaan, where they constantly grumbled (Numbers 21:4).

This is not the case as all! Living by grace through faith is a wonderful way to live. Once you understand it, if you really want to live a godly life, you will never give it up! I want to show you how important living by grace really is. However, let me first remind you of what I have been saying to you. I have been talking about the gospel – how through faith in Christ you come into union and fellowship with Christ. You cannot possibly be in union with Christ as you are in your natural state, trapped in the guilt and corruption of sin. You cannot come into fellowship with Christ through the law, or by your own good works.

However, this is the good news: you do not have to swim upstream by trying to be a good person before you are allowed to come to Christ in faith. All you have to do is believe in Christ, and receive the free gift of his salvation. Then, you are called to continue to live and walk by faith in Christ, as a renewed person, and as a new creation. As you live in Christ, you are to use all of the means of grace God has given you to live by faith, which I have told you about in the previous chapter.

# The Gospel Mystery of Sanctification

Now, why is it that living by grace through faith in Christ is so crucial to the health of your spiritual life? There are many reasons for this.

Sanctification by grace through faith humbles you and exalts God alone because of his grace and power given to you in Jesus Christ. Sanctification by grace through faith is in accord with the great purpose of all that God does. God's glory is the purpose of all creation (Romans 11:6, Isaiah 2:17, Ezekiel 36:21-23, 31-32). You are called to hallow and glorify God's name in all things, which indeed is the first petition of our Lord's Prayer (Matthew 6:9). You are also called to make the glory of God the prime purpose of everything you do (I Corinthians 10:31). The glory of God is the reason why he gave his law (Romans 3:19-20). God made all things for Christ, and gave him the pre-eminence in everything (Colossians 1:17-18).

Salvation by grace through faith alone is the only way of salvation that gives God alone **all** the glory. When Paul talks about justification by grace through faith in Christ, he makes the point that it excludes all boasting and pride on your part (Romans 3:27-28, Ephesians 2:8-9). This is also true in your Christian life. The glory of God shines forth ever more brightly because your sanctification comes also by faith in Jesus Christ. Why is this so?

Sanctification by grace through faith shows that you can do nothing by your natural ability, or by any power of your flesh. God simply will not enable you to do anything good by your own abilities – no matter how hard you try in the flesh to keep his law (Romans 7:18). This truth will really humble you! Your own nature is desperately wicked, beyond all cure, and totally unable to be reformed or repaired. The only way it can be put off is by putting on Christ! Your flesh remains wicked and powerless even after you have put on Christ. You simply cannot look to anything in yourself to make you holy.

Sanctification by grace through faith shows you that all of your good works, and living for God, are not by your own power or strength at all. They only come by the power of Christ living in you, as you live by faith. Whenever you do anything good, it is not because of your own natural power. It is because God is enabling you to act above and beyond your natural power. Why? Because Christ is united to you, and he lives in you, through the Holy Spirit.

226

# The Benefits of Living by Faith

All men live, move, and have their being in God. It is because of his universal support that they act (Hebrews 1:3). Even for non-Christians the glory of their actions belongs to God. God acts even more immediately and intimately with his own people, who are one flesh and one Spirit with Christ.

If you are in Christ, you do not act by your own power, but by the power of the Spirit of Christ in you. You are in union with him, and you are a living temple for his Spirit. Christ is the one who empowers you for all your good works. We might even say that these works you do are Christ's works, because he is the one working in you and through you. Yet at the same time, they are your works, because you are in fellowship with Christ, in whom you live (Galatians 2:20, Ephesians 3:16-17, Colossians 1:1).

The result of Christ living in you is that you are to give all the glory for your good works to God, and thank him for them as if they were free gifts (I Corinthians 15:10, Philippians 1:11). God enables you to act, not by yourself, but by himself. Non-Christians act only according to their own nature, and therefore they always act wickedly. However, God enables you to conquer sin, not by yourself, but by himself. All the glory belongs to him. Remember how the proud Pharisee could not give any glory to God for his "good" life. He kept it all for himself (Luke 18:11). If you do not understand that your good works all come from Christ himself, you will inevitably keep all the glory for yourself. You will not give all the glory to God the Father through Christ.

The glory truly is his for anything good that you do! You work as one with Christ, even as he works as one with the Father, by the Father working in him. You live as a branch by the juice of the vine, you act as a member by the power of the head, you bring forth good fruit by marriage to Christ as your husband, and you work in the strength of him as the living bread that you feed upon. Christ is all in the new creation (Colossians 3:11), and all the promises are fulfilled in Him (II Corinthians 1:20).

Sanctification by grace through faith is consistent with all of the other main teachings of the gospel. No other scheme of holy living is truly consistent with the entire gospel. Sanctification by grace through faith in Christ is truly in harmony with the truths of the gospel, and it is in the same golden chain with them in the mystery of godliness. When men misunderstand this true way of sanctification, they twist the rest of the

227

The Gospel Mystery of Sanctification

Scriptures in other points of faith. They soon decline from the truth into legalism and man-centered doctrines. Men will always deny teachings of Scripture if they do not think these teachings are in accord with godliness.

When you understand sanctification by grace, you will see that many other teachings of Scripture match up with the teaching about true godliness and holiness. You will also understand that many of the teachings that men embrace in their blind zeal for holiness are actually in opposition to true holiness. Remember, Satan always appears as an angel of light. False teachings always look good! In this case, men have set up many legalistic schemes to attain true holiness. However, I want you to see that whatever men say, it is the legalists who are in fact the Antinomians, the *lawlDss <sup>c</sup>nDs*.

Note the following truths of the gospel that the doctrine of sanctification by grace through faith affirms:

First, sanctification by grace through faith is the only way of holiness that truly affirms the doctrine of **original sin.** By original sin, I mean not only the guilt of Adam's sin, but also the total corruption of human nature. This corruption leaves all men absolutely powerless to do anything that is spiritually good, and it leads them in a direction that is always prone to sin, which always leads to death (Psalm 51: 5, Romans 5:12). Men are totally and completely unable to truly keep the law in any point.

Many people deny the doctrine of original sin. They think that if people believe in original sin, they will use the doctrine to excuse their sins. "I cannot help it. My original sin made me do it." They say that the doctrine of original sin will destroy people's motivation to do good works. They say that the only way to motivate people to godly living is by denying the truth of original sin! They think that if you tell people that they are not totally sinful, but that there is some good in them, they will try to be godly in their lives. The message is, "You are really not so bad, there is some good in you, so get out there and be good. You can do it!"

People will always find ways to get rid of the doctrine of original sin. In some churches, this denial of original sin is actually part of the church's official teaching. The churches may simply deny original sin flat-out. They may say that baptism takes away original sin. Or, they may tell people that they have a free will to do good. There are many ways that people deny original sin. Make sure you understand why people deny original sin. They are trying to compel people to godly living by telling them they have the inherent power in themselves to be good and to do good.

I understand the reasoning behind this denial of original sin, but it can only end in disaster. Denying original sin will never produce true holiness in anyone. I have labored to tell you that in your natural state, you cannot do anything good, because your natural state, your flesh, is totally corrupted by sin. Indeed, we all might fall into despair if it were totally up to us to produce good lives out of a corrupt nature.

However, you need not despair! Even though you were ruined by the fall, God has given you a new way to attain holiness. Through the gospel, you can receive a new birth and a new heart. You become a new creation. That is why I have been telling you to seek holiness by the Spirit of Christ. If you want to desire what is good, and do what is good, you have to come into a relationship with Jesus Christ. He will give you a new spiritual power. He will make you a new creation, and a partaker of the divine nature. He will give you joy in obeying God.

You must know the first Adam in order to know the second Adam, Christ (Romans 5:12). You must truly believe in the fall, and in original sin. If you do, you will be stirred up to run to Christ by faith for holiness by free gift, knowing that you cannot attain it by your own power and free-will (II Corinthians 1:9, Mathew 9:12-13, Romans 7:24-25, II Corinthians 3:5, Ephesians 5:14). There would be no need of a new man, or a new creation, if the old man still had strength and life (John 3:5-6, Ephesians 2:18).

Do not be afraid of the doctrine of original sin! It magnifies God's grace all the more! This original sin and deadness cannot stop God's work in the lives of his people. God will work faith in those whom he has chosen to walk before him in holiness and blamelessness. He will give them a hunger and thirst for Christ, by the Spirit, through the gospel. Even though all his people were once totally dead in sin and corruption, they have been made alive through connection to a new head, they have become branches of another vine. Therefore, they live to God by the Spirit, not by the power of their own natures.

Second, sanctification by grace through faith also confirms the doctrine of **predestination**. Many people deny predestination, because they say that it discourages men from any effort. They think people who believe in predestination will say, "My effort is fruitless, because all events are predetermined anyway." This argument would indeed have some force if in fact we had the power to live good lives by the power of our free wills. However, this argument has no force at all when you consider that holiness comes only by the working of God. God is the one who gives you faith and holiness by his own Spirit working in you through Christ. You are to trust in Christ for the grace of the elect, and God's good will towards men (Matthew 3:17, Luke 2:14). To be sure, the doctrine of election destroys seeking holiness by works, but not by grace (Romans 11:5-6).

God is telling you to seek salvation only in the way of the elect. True holiness can come only by God's will, and not by your own. If you believe this truth, it will move you to seek holiness by the will of God (Romans 9:16). Sanctification through faith in Christ tells you that you are God's workmanship, because it is only God who brings about anything good in you (Philippians 2:12, Ephesians 2:10). When you see this, you can easily admit that God has done according to his good pleasure and will from all eternity. He has not in the least bit infringed upon the natural liberty of your corrupt will! If you do not have a relationship with Christ, you can and will do all the evil you want! However, when you are chosen by God in Christ to become a new creation, he moves you by his Spirit to will and to do what is good.

Third, sanctification by faith in Christ confirms the true doctrine of **justification and reconciliation with God by faith**. When you are truly saved, you rely totally on the merits of Christ's blood, and not upon any works of your own. Faith is not a work that procures the favor of God because it is an act that is so righteous in and of itself. Faith is simply a hand that receives a gift, it is the eating and drinking of Christ himself. Faith is not a condition that entitles you to have Christ as your spiritual food! Faith receives Christ as your spiritual food.

Many people hate this great doctrine of the gospel, because they say that it will remove all the boundaries of holiness and open up the way for all kinds of licentious and godless living. They say that if you make works a condition to earn the favor of God, people will be compelled to live good lives; they will work hard, so they can avoid the wrath of God and earn eternal salvation! They believe and teach that free grace in Christ, totally apart from works, will open up the flood gates to all kinds of unrighteous living. They think it will remove all compelling motivation for people to live good lives.

# The Benefits of Living by Faith

Again, this point of view would make sense if people truly could become good through legalistic motivation. It would make sense to use the law to get people working for God if they were indeed just paid workers working their way to heaven. It would make sense to motivate people to godliness through slavish fear if they indeed had to get into heaven by paying off a hard master! However, the true doctrine of justification by grace through faith totally abolishes all of these motives and reasons for trying to live a godly life!

I have previously showed you that people who are guilty and dead before God cannot serve God out of love if they are forced to do so. You simply cannot compel people to love God out of the motivations of slavish fear and works righteousness. You cannot be sanctified by any of your own endeavors. You cannot produce holiness in yourself. You can only attain holiness by faith in Christ's death and resurrection -- the very same faith that justifies you. The law only stirs up sin in you. You must be freed from the law if you are going to attain any holiness at all, as the Apostle Paul teaches (Romans 6:11-14, 7:1-6).

This way of sanctification by faith confirms the doctrine of justification by faith, as Paul says (Romans 8:1). How do we know this? If you are being sanctified and restored to the image of God by the Spirit, one thing is obvious: God has already taken you into his favor, and pardoned your sins, by the same faith, apart from the law. If you were not already forgiven, you would not have any fruit of God's favor for your eternal salvation (Romans 8:2). In other words, holy living proves that you have already been saved. Only those who have been forgiven and justified by faith are filled with the Spirit of Christ. They are the only ones who can produce any fruits of holiness at all!

You will not receive any holiness from Christ unless you have already trusted in Christ for the forgiveness of your sins. Guilty, cursed people cannot do any good because of the deadness the curse of sin has brought about in their lives. They cannot love God unless they apprehend that he has first loved them first, totally apart from their works (I John 4:19).

Why do so many people object to this doctrine of free grace? They think if salvation is by grace, then it does not matter how they live. However, this is a false objection to free grace. Sanctification is an effect, a result, of justification. Sanctification flows from the same grace as justification. You must trust for both justification and sanctification by the same faith. You must trust in Christ by faith for justification in order to have any sanctification at all. Justification must precede sanctification.

Be absolutely sure and confident of this: this kind of faith in Christ does not motivate believers to licentiousness and ungodliness, but to holiness! I grant you this: justification by faith will destroy your attempts to attain true holiness by your own slavish, legalistic endeavors. It will keep you from trying to do anything apart from Christ. However, this is exactly what you want to have happen in your life! There is no need to live as a legalist, and die as a lawless, ungodly Antinomian.

Fourth, the doctrine of sanctification by faith in Christ confirms the doctrine of **real union with Christ**, which Scripture speaks about so much. Many people consider this doctrine of union with Christ to be an empty notion. They cannot endure it at all, because they do not think it promotes and produces true holiness. They think it only promotes presumption. I have already shown you how important this real union with Christ is. You can only enjoy spiritual life and holiness through faith union with Christ. True holiness is so inseparably treasured up in Christ, you cannot possibly have it apart from a real union with him (II Corinthians 13:5, I John 5:12, John 6:53, John 15:5, I Corinthians 1:30, Colossians 3:11). The members cannot live without union with the head. The branches cannot live without union with the vine. The stones cannot be part of the living temple unless they are really joined to the cornerstone.

Fifth, the doctrine of sanctification by faith confirms the doctrine of **the certain, final perseverance of the saints** (John 3:36, 4:14, 5:24, 6:37, 10:23; I John 3:9, I Thessalonians 5:24, Philippians 1:6). Many people think that this doctrine of eternal security will make people careless about doing good works. My answer is this: the doctrine of eternal security will make people careless about trying to do good works by their own natural strength, with a motive of slavish fear! The doctrine of eternal security will make people careful and courageous about doing good works by trusting in the grace of God!

God's people, because they have been born anew and given new hearts by the power of the Holy Spirit, want to do good works (Romans 6:14, Numbers 13:30). By the power of grace, they labor to do them (I Thessalonians 5:8-11). I have already shown you that the fear of hell and damnation will never bring anyone to good works from a heart of love. Only a comfortable, comforting doctrine will motivate people to obey God out of love. The doctrine of the eternal security and perseverance of the saints is the most comforting doctrine that I know!

Sanctification by grace through faith is the never-failing, powerfully effective, totally sufficient, and sure way to attain true holiness. Those who find the truth find it. Those who are truly humble find it. People labor in vain when they seek holiness in any other way. All other ways to attain holiness either stir up more sin, or increase your despair. If you seek holiness by the law alone, you are working under a curse. This attempt at holiness brings about, at best, slavish and hypocritical obedience. It restrains sin to a certain extent, but it does not put sin to death (Galatians 4:25). The Jews sought to attain holiness in another way, apart from Christ, and they could not find it (Romans 9). All who seek holiness apart from Christ shall lie down in sorrow (Isaiah 1:11). Why is this the case?

In your natural state, under the law, you are dead, and a child of wrath (Ephesians 2:1-3). The law curses you, it does not help you (Galatians 3:10). Its commands can give you no life. You cannot produce holiness in yourself (Romans 5:6). A person who is truly humble does not seek holiness through the law, or through his own strength. Why? The law is weak because of the flesh. If you seek a pure life without having a pure nature, you are building without a foundation. The law cannot give you a new nature. It tells you to make bricks without straw. The law says to the cripple, "Walk!" but it gives him no strength.

Sanctification by grace through faith is the only way that God is reconciled to you in Christ (II Corinthians 5:19, Ephesians 1:7). God loves you, and you should love him (I John 4:19). This is the only way you can have a new and divine nature by the Spirit of Christ in you. He carries you on to holiness of life (Romans 8:5, Galatians 5:17, II Peter 1:3-4). You have a new heart that is designed to keep God's law. You will be able to serve God from your heart out of your new nature. You cannot help but serve him (I John 3:9).

The gospel gives you a sure foundation for godliness. You now have the power to love God with all your heart, might, and soul. Through the gospel, sin is not only restrained, but put to death. Not only is the outside made clean, but also the inside. The image of God is renewed in you. Because of what God has done in you, holy living surely follows. You are not perfect, because of the remnants of the old nature within you; however, you are no longer a total slave to sin like you once were.

# The Gospel Mystery of Sanctification

Sanctification by grace through faith in Christ is very pleasant to those who are seeking holiness in this way. There are several reasons for this:

Sanctification by faith in Christ is a very plain way to go. In other words, anyone who knows he is dead and powerless under the law will easily find it. Those who see this about themselves are renewed in the spirit of their minds, and they accept the truth of the gospel. Such people will indeed be troubled and pestered with many legalistic thoughts and actions from time to time. However, when they seriously think about it, they know that holiness through faith in Christ is so plain to them, it is madness to go in any other direction! A soul that is truly enlightened cannot think of any other way of holiness, once it is truly humbled.

When you are in Christ, you have his Spirit to be your guide in this way of holiness (I John 2:27, John 16:13). You do not need to be filled with distracting thoughts, like legalists are. They have thousands of rules for thousands of situations. They have so many rules, so many doubts, and so many intricacies in their system of religion, they despair of ever finding the true way of religion. You can be sure that God will teach you your duty, so you will not be led into error to your own destruction.

What an awful thing it is for a traveler to be filled with doubt about his way. What an awful thing for him to have no guide, when he is on a journey of great importance! How much more so when his journey is a matter of life and death! It is absolutely heart breaking! However, this is not the case with you. Those who are seeking holiness through faith in Christ may be sure that even though they sometimes err, they shall never fall so as to be destroyed. They will always find their way again (Galatians 4:7,10).

Sanctification through faith in Christ is easy for those who walk in it by the Spirit – even though it is difficult to get into it in the first place. The flesh and the devil will both try to scare you and seduce you away from it. Here, holiness is a free gift which you receive by faith. Whosoever will may come, take it, and drink freely, and nothing is required but a willing mind (John 7:38, Isaiah 55:1, Revelation 22:17).

The law, on the other hand, is an intolerable burden (Matthew 23:5, Acts 15:10), if you allow it to place its duty upon you by its own terms. Fortunately, you are not left to conquer your lusts by your own endeavors. You cannot possibly succeed if you try to do this. In Christ,

234

# The Benefits of Living by Faith

God gives you the power to do your duty, and the law is turned into promises (Hebrews 8:6-13, Ezekiel 36:25-26, Jeremiah 31:33, 32:40). You now have everything in Christ (Colossians 3:11 and 2:9, 10, 15, 17). The gospel of Christ is one universal medicine. You do not need a thousand different medicines.

If you only really understood your own desperate need, inability, and sinfulness, the free gift of holiness through faith in Christ would be so pleasant to you! Some people actually punish their body in a depressing, legalistic way, trying to attain holiness so that they might not perish forever! How much more ready you should be, when God has said to you, "Take and have. Believe, and be sanctified and saved" (II Kings 5:13). Christ's burden is light by his Spirit's bearing it (Matthew 11:30). There is no weariness here, but only renewing of strength (Isaiah 40:31).

The way of holiness through faith in Christ is a way of peace (Proverbs 3:17). It is free from the fears and terrors of conscience that those who seek salvation by their own works inevitably experience, because the law produces wrath (Romans 4:15). Holiness through faith in Christ is not the way of Mount Sinai, but the way of Jerusalem (Hebrews 12:18, 22).

Whenever people place works as a condition between Christ and themselves, doubts about the certainty of their salvation inevitable arise. However, you walk by faith, which rejects such fears and doubts (John 14:1, Mark 5:36, Hebrews 10:19, 22). This way is free from the fear of Satan, or any other evil (Romans 8:31-32). It is free from the slavish fear that you will perish because of your sins (I John 2:1-2, Philippians 4:6-7). When your faith lays hold of God's infinite grace, mercy, and power to secure you, God's free and powerful grace answers all objections. The Lord is your keeper and the shade on your right hand (Psalm 121:5).

The way of sanctification through faith in Christ is paved with love, like Solomon's chariot (Song of Solomon 3:10). You are to set God's loving kindness, and all the gifts of his love, always before your eyes (Psalm 26:2). Set Christ's death, resurrection, and intercession always before your eyes, for they bring about peace, joy, hope and love (Romans 15:13). You must believe the gospel in order to receive justification, adoption, the gift of the Spirit, your future inheritance, and your death and resurrection with Christ. When you believe the gospel for these things, your whole path is adorned with flowers. It has these fruits growing on either side of your way. It is through the Garden of Eden, rather than through the wilderness of Sinai (Acts 9:31).

It is the work of the Holy Spirit to be your guide and your comforter. He is not a spirit of bondage, but he is the Spirit of Adoption (Romans 8:15). Peace and joy are plentiful on this path of holiness (Philippians 4:4-6). God does not drive you along with whips and terrors, or by the rod of the schoolmaster, the law. Rather, he leads you and draws you to walk in his ways by pleasant attractions (Hosea 11:3-4). The love of Christ, of course, is the greatest and most pleasant attraction to encourage you to godly living (II Corinthians 5:15, Romans 12:1).

When you walk in holiness through faith in Christ, your very moving, acting, and walking is a pleasure and a delight. You do all of your good works with pleasure. The labor along this path is pleasant! Worldly men wish they had no duties, because they are so burdensome to them. However, duties are pleasant for you, because you do not have to try to attain holiness through your own fleshly wrestling with your lusts. You do not have to use fleshly fear, regret, and grief to try to hinder your sinful propensities. You do not have to use the law to try to stop sinning.

Through the gospel, you act naturally, according to your new nature. You live out of your new spiritual desires by walking in the ways of God through Christ. Your lusts, and the pleasures of sin, are not only restrained, they are taken away in Christ. The pleasures of holiness are freely given to you, and implanted in you (Romans 8:5, Galatians 5:17, 24, John 4:34, Psalm 8:5, 40:8). In Christ, you have a new taste, and a new love, that comes from the Spirit of Christ. You can look upon the law, not as a burden, but as your privilege in Christ.

The way of sanctification by faith in Christ is a high and exalted way, above all other ways. The prophet Habakkuk rejoiced in this way of life. He saw that all visible helps and supports would fail, and so he resolved to rejoice in the Lord, in the God of his salvation. He made God his strength by faith. When he did, his feet became like the deer's feet, and he walked in high places (Habakkuk 34:18-19). God has also set you in a high place. He has set you in the heavenly places Jesus Christ. God has made you alive, and has raised you up together with him (Ephesians 2:5-6).

You live very high with sanctification by faith, for you live not according to the flesh, but according to the Spirit. Christ is in you, with all his fullness (Romans 8:1-2, Galatians 2:20, 5:25). You walk in fellowship with God. God lives in you and walks in you (II Corinthians 6:16, 18). Your works are of higher price and excellence than the works of others, because they are produced by God (John 3:21). They are the fruit of God's Spirit (Galatians 5:23, Philippians 1:11). You may be sure that they are accepted by God and are considered good, because you live by gospel principles. Non-Christian people simply cannot live this way (Romans 7:6).

When you live by sanctification by faith, you are enabled to do the most difficult duties (Philippians 4:1-3). Nothing is too hard for you. See the great works done by faith in Scripture (Hebrews 11, Mark 9:23). When you live by faith, you can work and suffer for Christ with all joy.

In sanctification by faith, you walk in an honorable state with God, and on honorable terms. You are not a guilty person, you do not have to attain your pardon by works, you are not a paid servant, and you do not have to earn your food and drink. Rather, you are a son and an heir, and you are walking towards the full possession of the happiness to which you are entitled by Christ. Therefore, you can have great boldness in God's presence (Galatians 4:6-7). You can approach nearer to God than others, and you can walk before him confidently, without any slavish fear whatsoever – not as a stranger, but as a member of God's own family (Ephesians 2:19-20). This prompts you to do greater things than others, because you walk as a free person (Romans 6:17-18, John 8:35-36). This way of life is a royal way. For you, the law of God is a royal law, a law of liberty. It is your privilege to keep the law. The law of God is not a chain of slavery or yoke of compulsion.

The way of sanctification by faith is only for those who are honorable and precious in the eyes of the Lord – his elect and redeemed ones, whose special privilege it is to walk in this way of holiness. No non-Christian, fleshly person can walk in this way, but only those who are taught by God (John 6:44-46). This way of holiness can only come into your heart by divine revelation.

The way of sanctification by faith is a very costly way (Hebrews 10:19-20, I Peter 3:18). It cost Christ very dearly to prepare this way of holiness for you.

This way of sanctification by faith is a good, old way. When you walk in it, you are following the footsteps of all of the true flock of God.

# The Gospel Mystery of Sanctification

This way of sanctification by faith in Christ is the way to perfection. It leads to such holiness that will, in a little while, be absolutely perfect. This holiness differs only in degree from the holiness of heaven. In heaven the saints live by the same Spirit as we do on the earth. The same God is all in all (I Corinthians 15: 15:28, John 4:14). They have the image of the same spiritual man (I Corinthians 15:49). Here, on this earth, you have only the first fruits of the Spirit (Romans 8:23). You live by faith, and not by sight (II Corinthians 5:7). You are not yet full-grown in Christ (Ephesians 4:13). Sanctification in Christ is the beginning of your glorification. When you are glorified in heaven, your sanctification will be completely perfected. All glory to God for his indescribable gift!

# Appendix

## The Doctrine of Justification Explained and Applied
## A Sermon by Walter Marshall

*[23]for all have sinned and fall short of the glory of God, [24]being justified freely by His grace through the redemption that is in Christ Jesus, [25]whom God set forth as a propitiation by His blood, through faith, to demonstrate His righteousness, because in His forbearance God had passed over the sins that were previously committed, [26]to demonstrate at the present time His righteousness, that He might be just and the justifier of the one who has faith in Jesus.*

In the verses prior to Romans 3:23-26, the Apostle Paul has overthrown every attempt by anyone, Jew and Gentile alike, to be justified by their works. Now, Paul more directly proves this point. He shows from these verses that there is no difference between Jews and Gentiles. When God justifies either one of them, he reveals his righteousness totally apart from the law. He proves this by showing what the gospel teaches about how people are justified before God. Only the gospel reveals the righteousness of God. "I am not ashamed of the gospel of Christ. For in the Gospel, the righteousness of God is revealed from faith to faith" (Romans 1:16-17).

These words declare how the gospel justifies people by the righteousness of God. Justification is a grand and glorious benefit! It is, in fact, the first benefit you receive through your union with Christ. Justification is the foundation of every other spiritual benefit you have. This text from Romans 3 is considered the "gospel of gospels." It is one of the most important expressions of the gospel in the Bible. It explains the gospel as briefly, yet as fully, as any other passage in the Bible.

Note the subject of the text: the justification of people, or how they are justified. What this means is quite clear in the text. Justification means to "make just," just as sanctification means "to make holy," and glorification means "to make glorious." However, Paul is not talking about God making people holy and just by infusing grace and holiness into them. This view confuses justification and sanctification. No, he is talking about being just in a legal sense, being just in the judgment. He is talking about a judicial sentence, where God discharges your guilt, frees you from blame, and clears you from every accusation. When God justifies you, God approves, judges, owns, and pronounces you to be righteous.

The word "justify" is used in different ways in the Bible. It is a judicial term, a term from the law courts. It often refers to trial and judgment. Consider I Corinthians 4:3-4: "It is a very small thing to me if I am judged by you or by anyone else. I do not even judge myself. For I know nothing by myself, but that does not justify me. The Lord is the one who judges me." "Justification" is the opposite of being condemned in the judgment. See Deuteronomy 25:2: "If there is a disagreement between men, and they come to the judgment so that the judges may judge them, the judges shall justify the righteous and condemn the wicked." See also Matthew 22:37: "By your words you will be justified, and by your words you will be condemned."

Justification is also the opposite of both accusation and condemnation. "Who shall lay any charge against God's elect? Who is the one who condemns?" (Romans 8:33-34). "If I justify myself, my own mouth shall condemn me" (Job 9:20). "I will maintain my own ways before him" (Job 13:15). "I have ordered my cause. I know that I will be justified" (Job 13:19). In these cases, justification is the opposite of being accused, or at fault.

Justification is also the opposite of being condemned. "Go and judge your servants. Condemn the wicked, and bring his way upon his head. Justify the righteous, and give them according to their righteousness" (I Kings 8:32). It is a sin to justify the wicked (Isaiah 5:23, Proverbs 17:15, Job 27:5). Certain actions are brought to trial, and they are justified (Job 33:32, Isaiah 43:9, 26).

Justice or righteousness means at least two things. First, the basic nature of an action can be righteous: "He did a righteous deed." Second, an action can be righteous before the law, and thus before a judging body. In this second case, righteous actions are considered righteous because God the judge deems them to be righteous. In other words, an external standard of law judges the action. Someone does something, and the law either approves of it or disapproves of it. The law either justifies the action, or condemns it. The law considers the action sinful, or not sinful. The action either breaks the law, or it does not break the law.

Apply this principle to people. People are either righteous or unrighteous before the judgment tribunal of God. When people appear before God, he judges them. If they are considered righteous, we consider them to be **justified** before God. It is just as if they were righteous. They are declared to be righteous because they **are** righteous before God. It is just like the situation with Jesus. He was, and is, in fact the eternal Son of God. However, when he rose from the dead, he was declared to be the eternal Son of God (Acts 13:33, Romans 1:4). God declared to the world what was already true of him. In justification, God declares Christians to be righteous because he considers them righteous.

This explains what certain verses mean that say that God is justified (Job 32:2, Psalm 51:4, Luke 7:29). You cannot add anything to the infinite righteousness of God. He is as righteous as he can possibly be! However, when you "justify" him, you declare that you consider his actions to be righteous. You are declaring what is already in fact true about him. Jesus said "wisdom is justified by her children" (Matthew 11:19). What did he mean? He meant that the followers of true wisdom continually declare that wisdom is supreme.

Now, apply this to Christians who are justified. When you are justified by faith in Christ, there is no real change that takes place within you as a sinner. You are still sinful. The change that takes places involves the way God judges you. (To be sure, once you are justified, your life will begin to change. However, this is the process of sanctification, not justification.) This is the way Paul is using the term "justified" in Romans 3. It is a legal term. It means that you are no longer condemned by the law of God and the justice of God. Your status before the law of God is now one of righteousness, as if you had kept the law perfectly. The text means that you are considered and accounted just, or righteous, in the sight of God.

Many people fall into confusion about what justification really means. Many people think that when they are justified, they actually become righteous in their character. This, of course, is impossible. You are still sinful! The change involves your legal standing before God the lawgiver and judge. In Christ, your status is one of perfect righteousness.

I would like to bring out eight principles about justification by faith from this text.

- ❏ Who is justified? Those who are justified are sinners, who have all fallen short of the glory of God.

- ❏ Who is the justifier? God himself.

- ❏ Why does God justify anyone? He does it freely by his grace.

❑ What makes justification possible? The Redemption of Jesus Christ.

❑ What is the result of justification? The complete forgiveness of sins.

❑ How do you receive justification? By faith alone.

❑ When does God declare that you are righteous? Right now, in the present time.

❑ What is the purpose of God justifying sinners? His purpose is to declare that he is just in forgiving sins, and that he is the justifier of all of those who believe in Jesus Christ.

These principles will lead into several practical applications of the doctrine of justification by faith.


**Principle Number One: Who is justified? Those who are justified are sinners, who have all fallen short of the glory of God.**

The people who are justified by God are all sinners. They have fallen short of his glory. They are under God's condemnation (John 5:44). They do not have God's image of holiness (II Corinthians 3:18, Ephesians 4:24). They have no right to expect eternal happiness (I Thessalonians 2:12, Romans 5:2, II Corinthians 4:17).

The law of God condemns all sinners. It strikes them dead like a thunderbolt (Romans 3:20). When the law of God judges them, their state is one of shame, confusion, and misery. Their state is not one of glory and happiness by the strict terms of the law (Romans 2:6-12). No one can possibly fulfill the law (Romans 8:7), whether they are Jew or Gentile. They have absolutely no hope, apart from the free grace of God.

Christ came for sinners. He died for this purpose. "While we were still powerless, at the right time, Christ died for the ungodly" (Romans 5:6). "This is a faithful saying, worthy of full acceptance: Christ Jesus came into the world to save sinners, of whom I am the worst" (I Timothy 1:15). "I have not come to call the righteous, but sinners to repentance" (Matthew 9:13). "The Son of man came to save what was lost" (Matthew 18:11). To be saved, you must believe in a God who "justifies the ungodly." You must believe in him who "justifies the wicked" (Romans 4:5). You must not try to earn your justification by your works.

Note also that God justifies sinners of all kinds. God's salvation comes to Jews and Gentiles alike. Everyone who believes will be justified before God. Just as Jews and Gentiles are universally condemned by the law of nature and the written law of God, so "the righteousness of God is upon all of those who believe" (Romans 3:21-22). There is no difference regarding nationality.

Paul needed to make this point very clear in his own day. Many of the Jews thought that only Jews could be justified. They set up a system of works, and anyone who wanted to be saved had to enter their system. Anyone who wanted to join with them to be justified had to be circumcised and keep the Law of Moses. God then revealed to the Apostles that the Gentiles could be accepted by God without becoming Jews. This was a very glorious revelation to them! (Acts 10:28,45, Ephesians 3:4-8, Colossians 1:25-27).

How does the Bible teach this?

❑ Even though the Jews had great privileges, they needed to be justified by grace as much as the Gentiles did.

God gave the law to the Jews, but the Jews continually broke his law. The Jews were no more acceptable to God than the Gentiles were. In fact, in one sense, they were greater sinners, because they had the revealed law of God (Romans 2:23-24). When both Jews and Gentiles are equally needy, God can righteously justify them both (Romans 3:9).

❑ God is the God of the Gentiles as well as the God of the Jews (Romans 3:29). This is exactly what God had promised all along (Romans 4:9-12, Galatians 3:8, Isaiah 19:25, Zechariah 14:9).

❑ Abraham was justified before he was circumcised, so that he might become the Father of all those who believe. Even if they are uncircumcised, they can inherit the same blessing as he did (Romans 4:10-12).

- Justification is by faith, and not by the works of the law. Justification depends upon the righteousness of another, not upon your own righteousness. Therefore, both Jews and Gentiles are able to receive it. The Jews have no inherent qualifications to be justified.

**Principle Number 2: Who is the Justifier?  God himself.**

Justification is an act of God. "God is the one who justifies" (Romans 8:33). He is the only one who can justify in a way that is authoritative and irreversible.   Why is this so?

- God is the lawgiver. Therefore, God has the power to both save and destroy (James 4:12).

  Justification involves God's law, and thus you can be tried only at the judgment seat of God. God is the judge of the world (Genesis 18:25). It is a very small and worthless thing to only be judged by yourself, or by other people (I Corinthians 4:3-4).

- Sinners owe God the lawgiver a debt. They are required to act righteously, but since they have not done it, they deserve to suffer for their sins. Only God can discharge their payment. Only God can release them from their debt of sin (Psalm 51:4, Mark 2:7).

**Principle Number 3: Why does God justify anyone?  He does it freely by his grace.**

Paul emphasizes the reason why God justifies anyone. He explains why God freely justifies people. God simply gives his free, undeserved favor upon sinners. This is totally opposite of earning salvation by your own works of righteousness. You can never say that God owes you salvation, because you did not work for it. "To the one who works, his wages are credited not as a gift, but as an obligation" (Romans 4:4). "If it is by grace, then it is no longer by works. Otherwise, grace would no longer be grace. But if it is by works, then it is no longer by grace. Otherwise, work is no longer work" (Romans 9:6). "It is by grace you have been saved, through faith – and this not of yourselves, it is the gift of God, not by works, so that no one can boast" (Ephesians 2:8-9). "He has saved us and called us to a holy life, not by our works, but by his own purpose and grace, which was given in Christ Jesus, but is now made know by the appearing of our Savior Jesus Christ…" (II Timothy 2:9-10).

What is grace? Grace is when God freely shows mercy and love. He shows mercy to you because he shows mercy to you. He loves you because he loves you (Romans 9:15). Consider the implications of grace:

❑ There is nothing in you that makes you worthy of grace. The only things you can bring to God are worthy of his condemnation, for "we have all sinned" (Ephesians 2:3, Ezekiel 16:6).

❑ God wants to remove any reason for boasting on your part.

God wants you to glorify and exalt his grace alone for your salvation. God desires to have all the praise and glory, even though you receive the blessedness of the gospel, "…that in the ages to come, he might show the exceeding riches of his grace, and his kindness to us, through Christ Jesus" (Ephesians 2:7-9, Romans 3:27).

**Principle Number 4: What makes justification possible? The Redemption of Jesus Christ.**

God justifies sinners because of the redemption that is in Jesus Christ, whom God made to be a propitiation through faith in his blood. This is the way that God can justly justify sinners: the redemption that Jesus accomplished by shedding his blood. Redemption is found in and because of Christ.

What do we mean by redemption? By redemption, we mean a deliverance that is made by paying a price. The words redeem and redemption are frequently used in this way in the Bible (Exodus 13:13, Number 3:48-51, Leviticus 25:24,51, Jeremiah 32:7-8, Nehemiah 5:8). It sometimes came to mean deliverance without a price (Luke 21:28, Ephesians 1:14, 4:30). Sometimes the state of glory is called redemption, because the state of glory is the crowning result of Christ's redemption.

Paul also uses the term propitiation. Propitiation is something that appeases and satisfies the wrath of God for sin, and wins his favor. In the Old Testament, the propitiation of Christ was symbolized in two ways. First, it was symbolized by the propitiatory sacrifices, where blood was shed. Second, it was symbolized by the mercy seat. The mercy seat was actually called the **propitiation**, because it covered the ark of God which contained the law of God. The blood of the sacrifices for atonement was sprinkled upon the mercy seat by the High Priest on the Day of Atonement. This mercy seat was a sign of God's favor to a sinful people. It resided among them, and thus it was called the propitiation, or the mercy seat (Hebrews 9:5).

Here is what the Bible teaches about this principle:

❏ Christ gave himself, by the will of God, to be a ransom for you, to redeem you from sin and punishment, and from the wrath and curse of God.

"He gave himself for us, to redeem us from all wickedness" (Titus 2:14). He gave himself over to death for you. He was delivered for your offenses. His death was the price of your redemption, so that you might be justified in his sight. God have him up to death, and did not spare him, so that he might be made righteousness (I Corinthians 1:30). "He gave his own life as a ransom for many" (Matthew 20:28). "He bought us with a price" (I Corinthians 6:20). "He redeemed us not with silver and gold, but with his precious blood, a lamb without blemish or defect," "He suffered the penalty due to us for sin" (I Peter 1:18-19, II Peter 2:1, Revelation 5:9). "He bore our sins in his won body on the tree" (I Peter 2:24). "He was made a curse for us" (Galatians 3:12), and as a result he redeemed us from the curse of the law. So that he might be made a curse, he was made "sin for us" (II Corinthians 5:21, Isaiah 53:6).

Jesus also subjected himself to the law in active obedience, as well as passive obedience (Galatians 4:4). His passive obedience refers to his suffering the curse of the law. His active obedience refers to the fact that he completely kept the law in his own life. He obeyed his Father even to death, doing what he commanded (John 14:31, Hebrews 10:7). His obedience was for our justification (Romans 5:19, Philippians 3:8-9).

Christ did two things: he satisfied our debt of righteousness, and he satisfied our debt of punishment. He made satisfaction for our lack of righteousness, and he made satisfaction for our guilt and liability to punishment. He did this so that we might be freed from

God's wrath, and credited as righteous in God's sight. Christ's suffering was the final act of redemption, and so all of our blessings are attributed to it (Hebrews 2:9-10). We are righteous through Christ just as we are guilty through Adam (Romans 5:12).

❑ God accepted this price to satisfy his justice.

God raised Jesus from the dead. By this, he showed that he accepted the sacrifice of Christ for all of our sins. "He was justified by the Spirit." It was "for us" (I Timothy 3:16). He was "raised for our justification" (Romans 4:25). "God is the one who justifies. Who is he who condemns? Christ, who died, rather, who was raised to life" (Romans 8:33-34). "By one sacrifice he has perfected forever those who are sanctified" (Hebrews 10:14). Christ's "sacrifice was a sweet-smelling savor to God" (Ephesians 5:2).

If Christ had sunk under weight of our sins, and had not been raised from the dead, he would not have accomplished the full payment. The debt would not have been discharged. However, he did not sink under the weight of our sins. "I have come to convict the world in regard to righteousness, because I am going to my Father" (John 16:10).

❑ This redemption is in Christ. You cannot have it unless you are in Christ, and unless you have Christ.

Christ is the propitiation, and since he is, he is "our righteousness" (I Corinthians 1:30). We have redemption and righteousness in him (Ephesians 1:7, II Corinthians 5:21), and thus we have our freedom from condemnation (Romans 8:1). Christ died so that his "descendants might be justified" (Isaiah 53:10-11). This only includes those who are in him because of a spiritual rebirth (I Corinthians 4:15).

**Principle Number 5: What is the result of Justification?  The complete forgiveness of sins.**

When God justifies you, he not only removes your guilt and your punishment, he also removes your fault. He clears your fault, because it is a pardon grounded upon justice. "By him we are justified from all the things with which the law charges us" Acts 13:39).

Justification involves two aspects: your sins are completely forgiven, and you are reckoned as righteous in God's sight. Sometimes justification and the forgiveness of sins are used interchangeably, as it is in Acts 13:38-39: "Through this man the forgiveness of sins is preached, and by him all who believe are justified." Forgiveness and justification are also used interchangeably in Romans 4:6-8, II Corinthians 5:19-21, and Romans 5:17.

Why is this the case? For human beings who are subject to a law, there is no middle ground. You are either guilty before the law, or you are not guilty before the law. If you are guilty, it is because you have broken the law. If you are not guilty, it means you have not broken the law. When you stand before God, it is the same thing. If you are in Christ, God cannot forgive your sins without accrediting you as righteous in his sight. If you are forgiven, it is because he considers you righteous before the law. Forgiveness by its very nature implies that the penalty of the law has been satisfied, and that your status is now as if you had kept the law perfectly. That is why forgiveness and justification are sometimes used interchangeably. You cannot have one without the other.

**Principle Number 6: How do you receive justification? By faith alone.**

God justifies sinners through faith in Christ's blood. The only way you can receive the blessing of justification is to receive it by faith in the blood of Christ. What can we say about faith?

❑ Faith is described as believing in Christ, so that you may be justified by him.

"We know that a man is not justified by the works of the law, but by faith in Jesus Christ. We have believed in Jesus Christ, that we might be justified by the faith in Christ, and not by the works of the law" (Galatians 2:16). You must believe in Christ for your justification, because you know you are absolutely unable to gain your justification by your works.

❑ Faith in itself is not an act of righteousness that earns your justification.

Faith is not a work that gains your salvation. If faith were a work, then salvation by faith would in reality be salvation by works of the law. It would be diametrically opposed to grace, and the free gift of salvation. Salvation by grace means that you do not look to any of your works to be your righteousness. Salvation by grace excludes a penny's worth of work on your part (Romans 11:6). In salvation, faith is considered to be a matter of **not working** (Romans 4:5). Your faith does not give you the righteousness required by the law. The righteousness of Christ gives you the righteousness that is required by the law of God.

❑ When we say that God justifies by faith, we are saying that faith is the means by which you receive Christ and his righteousness. Faith is the instrument by which you are justified.

The only reason we speak of "justification by faith" is because you receive justification through faith. It is one and the same thing to say that you are justified "by faith" and "by Christ" (Galatians 3:8, Romans 5:19). By faith you receive the forgiveness of sins (Acts 26:18, 10:43). Faith means that you **receive** justification; you do not work for it. It is just like when we say that a man is maintained by his hands, or nourished by his mouth. We know that his hands and his mouth do not maintain and nourish him! We are saying that his hands and his mouth receive the things that nourish him – namely, his food and drink. His hands hold the food he eats, and his mouth receives drink from the cup which he holds. Christ lives in you by faith (Ephesians 3:17). By faith, you receive him, you eat of him, and you drink of him (John 1:12, 6:51-54).

❑ Justification excludes all your works. Against all legalistic teaching, we maintain that justification is by faith alone. The Scriptures are quite clear about this (Romans 3:28, Galatians 2:16, Philippians 3:8-9).

❑ Being justified by faith means that your sins are forgiven, and that you are no longer liable for the punishment that you deserve.

God no longer holds you responsible for the smallest sin. Every single sin is forgiven. When faith is said to be credited for righteousness, it is because of what your faith receives (Romans 4:4-8, II Corinthians 5:19-21): when you believe, Christ's righteousness is credited to your account, and your sins are credited to his account. If both of these things do not happen, you cannot consider yourself forgiven. Sin would be charged to your account. In the gospel, two things happen. First, God removes the charge of sin against your account. Second, God gives you the gift of righteousness from Christ (Romans 5:17). You receive this double-gift when you receive Christ's redemption through the shedding of his blood (Ephesians 1:7, Matthew 26:28).

**Principle Number 7: When does God declare that you are righteous? Right now, in the present time.**

When God set forth Christ to be a propitiation through faith in his blood, his goal was to declare his righteousness **now** through the gospel. His purpose was to forgive sins that are **past** as well as sins that are **present**.

God aimed to forgive all of the sins that were committed in the past, during the Old Testament. This was the time of God's forbearance. He forgave sins long before his justice was actually satisfied by Christ's atonement (Hebrews 13:8, Revelation 13:8, Matthew 28:26). How could God forgive those sins? Upon what basis? The basis for the forgiveness of those sins was revealed when Christ came (Isaiah 51:5-6, 55:1, Daniel 9:24, II Timothy 1:9-10). Now that the justice of God has been satisfied through Christ, those pardons cannot be considered a blemish upon the justice of God. Here are some important considerations:

❑ By righteousness, Paul means the righteousness of God (Romans 3:21-22).

Paul does not mean God's righteous character in this instance. Rather, he means the righteousness of God that comes upon "everyone who believes." He is referring to Christ's righteousness, which is "the end of the law" (Romans 10:3-4). It is called "God's righteousness" because Christ obtained it for you. He gives it to you when you receive it by faith. In other words, Christ satisfied the law for you.

The reason this righteousness is called God's righteousness is because God produced it. He accepts it and approves of it because it comes from him to begin with. Christ is called the Lamb of God, because God provided him and accepts him as a sin offering (John 1:29). Christ's kingdom is called the kingdom of God because God himself establishes it, maintains it, and rules it (Ephesians 5:5). Christ became obedient to death to provide this righteousness for us. Since Christ is the God-Man, we can accurately say that his righteousness is **from God**. Paul sets this righteousness from God through Christ in opposition to his own righteousness, that which he could achieve by trying to keep the law. Paul calls it "the righteousness from God, which comes by faith," (Philippians 3:9).

❑ God's purpose was to declare, in the present time, that he justly and righteously forgave the sins that were committed during the time of the Old Testament.

Romans 3:25 calls the time period of the Old Testament the "time of God's forbearance." Someone might accuse God of being unjust in forgiving sins committed during the Old Testament time period, because Christ had not yet come. However, God is not unjust. God could justly forgive those who committed sins during the Old Testament just as he can forgive those who believe in Christ during the present time. How? Because he forgave sins based upon the righteousness of Christ – the same Christ upon whom he bases the forgiveness of sins at the present time!

Christ was the "lamb slain from the foundation of the world" (Revelation 13:8). During the Old Testament time, Christ's righteousness was not yet actually fully fulfilled and revealed. God spoke of it through shadows and symbols, through the Old Testament sacrifices, ransoms, redemptions, ceremonies, etc. This was therefore the time of God's forbearance. In a sense, he forgave sins without having the present payment and satisfaction. He had patience – he did not demand the debt until Christ came and paid the debt (Matthew 18:26). However, during this whole time, God promised that he would reveal his righteousness in due time (Isaiah 56:1, 51:5-6, Psalm 98:2, Daniel 9:24). God has fully accomplished his promise, now that Christ has come (II Timothy 1:10).

**Principle Number 8: What is the purpose of God justifying sinners? His purpose is to declare that he is just in forgiving sins, and that he is the justifier of all of those who believe in Jesus Christ.**

This principle gets to the heart of the issue: justification by faith is consistent with the character of God. God's justice is revealed when he justifies sinners through Christ. In addition, God's glory is revealed when he graciously justifies sinners by his own mercy.

❑ God justifies people freely by his grace.

Salvation is by grace, but God cannot rightly justify you without a payment for the debt of your sin. God would be unjust if he ignored the debt of your sin. God must maintain the justice of his character when he justifies sinners. He is able to do this by accepting the sacrifice of Christ on your behalf. Even though God is gracious and merciful, he cannot and will not by any means "clear the guilty" (Exodus 34:7, Genesis 18:25, Exodus 23:7). In the Old Testament, believers declared that God forgave sin and redeemed sinners in righteousness – even though God had not yet fully revealed his plan of redemption in Christ (Psalm 51:14, 130:7-8, 143:1-2). God must combine both justice and mercy in our salvation (Psalm 85:10).

❑ God wants to make known to everyone that only he is just. Therefore, he saves you, not by your own righteousness, but by his righteousness. God would not be unrighteous if he gave people the condemnation they deserve (Romans 3:4-5, Daniel 9:7). However, when he saves them, his righteousness is exalted even more by their unrighteousness.

❑ God wants you to know that he is the only one who can provide and establish your righteousness. He justifies you by a righteousness of **his** own, not by a righteousness of **your** own (Isaiah 54:17, 45:222-25). Why does he do this? So that you will "glory in the Lord only" (I Corinthians 1:30-31).

Having looked at the biblical teaching on justification by faith, let us consider some of the practical applications of the doctrine of justification by faith.

## Application Number 1: Justification by faith gives you great encouragement and comfort.

If you are a Christian, the greatest joy you have is that your sins are forgiven! Nothing should make you happier than this truth: you are considered righteous before the judge of the whole world! You have been redeemed by the blood of Christ. Every other blessing that you have flows from this truth.

The "one to whom God credits righteousness apart from works" is greatly blessed. You share in the blessings of Abraham. "Those who are of faith are blessed, along with Abraham, the man of faith" (Galatians 3:9). The righteousness which God has revealed by faith is the most fundamental blessing you can have. If you have been justified by faith, you are called to live by faith. You must continue to believe the gospel, and be strengthened and comforted by the gospel of grace (Romans 1:17).

Why are you so blessed? Consider these things:

❑ You are delivered from the charge of sin and blame before God (Romans 8:33-34).

"Who shall bring any charges against God's elect? It is God who justifies. Who is he that condemns?" God has justified you. Christ has died and rose again for you. You are redeemed from among all people. You are one of the first fruits of God and of the Lamb. In your mouth there is no guile. You are without fault before the throne of God (Revelation 14:4-5, Colossians 1:22).

❑ You have been delivered from all condemnation before God.

You are no longer under the curse and wrath of God. You are no longer under the sentence of condemnation, and you will therefore not face the punishment of condemnation. "Christ has redeemed us from the curse of the law, having been made a curse for us" (Galatians 3:13). "Jesus, who delivers us from the wrath to come" (I Thessalonians 1:10). "You have turned away all you wrath. You have turned away the fierceness of your anger" (Psalm 135:3).

The wrath of God is a burden you cannot bear. It is the foundation of all misery in life. If you are in Christ, this miserable foundation is knocked down, and God lays a foundation of blessedness. You now have peace with God, because you are fully reconciled to God through Christ (Romans 5:1-2). "At one time you were alienated from God, and enemies in your minds because of your wicked deeds. But now, God has reconciled you, through the body of Christ, and through his death, to present you holy, without blame, and without fault in his sight" (Colossians 1:21-22). Since God does not blame you any more, you can no longer be under his wrath.

❑ You no longer need to seek your salvation through the works of the law.

You are delivered from a yoke that you could never bear anyway. You are delivered from the endless religious ceremonies that Pharisees and Legalists continually want to heap upon you. You are free from continual fright, doubt, fear, and terror from the law of God (Acts 15:10, Romans 8:15). You are free from the wrath that the law pronounces upon unforgiven sinners (Romans 4:15). You are free from the law that stirs up sin within you (Romans 6:5). You are free from the law that puts you to death, the law as a "ministry of death and condemnation" (II Corinthians 3:6-9). You are free from the law of "Mount Sinai, which gives birth to children in slavery" (Galatians 4:24).

❑ You are delivered from a conscience that condemns you.

Your conscience no longer gnaws away at you like a worm. "The blood of goats and bulls and the ashes of a heifer sprinkled on those who are ceremonially unclean sanctify them so that they are outwardly clean. How much more, then, will the blood of Christ, who through the eternal Spirit offered himself unblemished to God, cleanse our consciences from acts that lead to death, so that we may serve the living God! (Hebrews 9:13-14).

A guilty conscience is a polluted conscience. A guilty conscience makes all of your service and obedience dead works. They will be unfit for the service of the living God. The blood of Christ, which you receive by faith, takes away the pollution of guilt from your conscience. The blood of Christ is the only thing that can clear your conscience of its sin and guilt (Hebrews 10:1-4). If you are in Christ, you have a "good conscience" (I Peter 3:21). Your conscience is "void of offence toward God" (Acts 24:16).

☐ You have received an everlasting righteousness through Christ.

Christ has secured you forever! (Daniel 9:24). Christ has obtained for you an "eternal redemption" (Hebrews 9:12). If you live under the law, you are justified today and condemned tomorrow. Every day the Old Testament people had to offer yet another sacrifice for their sins. They had no real way of cleansing their consciences. The sacrifices could not clear their consciences of guilt in any lasting way. In Christ, it is much different. Christ's redemption is total, complete, and perpetual. Christ cleanses all of yours sins, **past**, **present**, and **future** (I John 1:7).

☐ Your righteousness in Christ is of infinite value.

Why is this so? Because it is the righteousness of God himself. His name is "The Lord our righteousness" (Jeremiah 23:6, Hebrews 9:14). God's righteousness is more powerful to save you than Adam's sin was to destroy and condemn you (Romans 5:12-21). Christ is the "power of God" (I Corinthians 1:24). Therefore, you are powerful, and you conquer by faith. You have received an infinite amount of mercy and grace from "the Lord our righteousness." You have received a "plenteous redemption" (Psalm 130:7). Your redemption is so plentiful because it is infinite! No human being could pay the penalty for your sin, but the Lord himself could do it abundantly. In Christ, God's mercy prevails far above your sins (Psalm 103 11-12).

☐ Both God's grace and God's justice come into play in the righteousness you have by faith.

The justice of God seems terrible. It seems to be against mercy. It is a dreadful thing for non-Christians to think about God's justice. However, you as a believer do not need to fear the justice of God. God's justice has been satisfied and pacified through the righteousness of Christ. Christ has satisfied the justice of God by dying for your sins. Justice has become your friend, and joins together with grace. Instead of accusing you, God's justice is altogether for you. It says something totally different to you than it says to non-Christians (Joshua 24:19-20). You may also plead

justice for forgiveness, through God's mercy to you in Christ
(Romans 3:26).

❑ Because you have been justified, you will also receive holiness
and glory.

Not only are you delivered from the penalty and guilt of your sin,
you are delivered from the power of sin as well. Not only is your
conscience now free from guilt, you are also now free from the
dominion of sin in your life. This is why Christ died, to deliver
you from evil (Titus 2:14, Romans 6:6,14, 8:3-4). "Those whom
God has justified, he has also glorified" (Romans 8:30). The law
is what gave sin its power. Because of the curse of the fall, sin
had the right to rule over you in your life. Satan also ruled over
you. However, through Christ, you have been delivered from sin,
from Satan, and from death (Hebrews 2:14-15, Hosea 13:14). In
the same way, through the righteousness of Christ, you have been
raised up into a better state than you first had in Adam. Christ
died so that you might receive "the adoption of sons," and the
Spirit. Christ died so that you might be brought into a new
covenant. Christ died to enable you to live a holy life, serving out
of love (Galatians 3:14, I John 4:19, Galatians 4:5, Hebrews 9:15,
Romans 5:11, Luke 1:74, Colossians 2:13).

❑ Because you have been justified, you can be sure that all things
work together for your good.

All things will work together for your good, because by his grace
God is bringing you to glory. God, the creator and ruler over all
things, is for you (Romans 8:28-33). God will never be angry with
you, nor rebuke you in anger any more" (Isaiah 54:9, Romans 5:2,
5).

❑ Because you have been justified, you can come before God
without any fear.

You can come with boldness before the throne of grace in the
name of Jesus. When you come, you can expect everything good
from him (John 14:13-14)."In him we have boldness and access
with confidence through faith in him" (Ephesians 3:12). "Let us
draw near with full assurance of faith" (Hebrews 10:22-23).

Christ's blood pleads for you in heaven (Hebrews 12:24). You can boldly come before him at any time.

❑ You now live in the time when God's righteousness has been fully revealed.

Sin has been atoned for through Christ (Romans 3:21-22). You have a greater blessing than those who lived before the first coming of Christ. They lived under the types and shadows of this righteousness by faith. You have the reality, now that Christ has come. You are no longer under the law, as they were, as under a schoolmaster. You are not a servant, but a son, called to freedom (Galatians 3:23, 26, 4:7, 5:13). You are not to look to the law for your justification (Romans 10:5-8, II Corinthians 3:6-7, Galatians 3:13, 24).

**Application Number 2: Examine yourself, to make sure you are in Christ. Make sure you have received this gift of justification by faith with all your heart.**

❑ Ask yourself: have you really come to understand the depths of your sin? Do you understand that the law of God condemns you?

If you understand these things, you will run to Christ. This is why God gave you his law – to lead you to Christ (Galatians 3:22, Matthew 9:13, Acts 2:37). If you do not understand your sin, you will neither value Christ nor desire holiness. You will, rather, abuse grace by giving yourself a false security, and by living any way you please. In the Old Testament, those who were bitten by the poisonous snakes looked up to the bronze snake that Moses put upon a pole.

❑ Are you trusting only in God's free mercy for your justification in his sight? Have you given up the idea that your works can give you any standing before God whatsoever? Have you said, along with the tax collector of the New Testament, "God, have mercy on me, a sinner?"

Perfectionists and self-righteous people do not do this (Luke 18:13-14). They see no need of God's mercy. Paul was a man whom the world considered righteous. However, he considered all of his works and accomplishments but "rubbish, that he might gain Christ, and be found in him, not having his own righteousness which comes from the law, but the righteousness that comes from faith in Christ, the righteousness which comes from God and is by faith" (Philippians 3:6-9). He was talking about the redeeming and propitiating righteousness of Christ. In order to be justified, he only wanted Christ's righteousness. He put his trust in Christ's righteousness. He did not put his trust in anything inherent in his own life. He gave up any hope in his own righteousness.

❑ Are you trusting in Christ with confidence? Or are you unsure, still in suspense about whether or not Christ can save you?

If you continuously doubt, you will receive no good thing from God (James 1:6-7). If you remain in doubt, your conscience will not be freed from the guilt of your sin (Hebrews 10:22). Doubt will leave your soul in fear. Abraham's confidence gives you an example of what justifying faith can do in your life. You should seek to have this same confidence, believing with full assurance, in "hope against all hope" (Romans 4:20-24). To be sure, if you are a believer, you will be assaulted with many doubts. Yet, you will fight against those doubts. You will not give in to those doubts (Psalm 42:11, Mark 9:24). True faith always opposes doubt, and strives against doubt.

❑ Have you come to Christ to be forgiven of your sins for the right reason? Have you come to Christ so that you may be freed from the slavery to sin before the living God? (Hebrews 9:14, Titus 2:14, I Peter 2:24).

If you do not desire to be delivered from the dominion of sin as well as the penalty of sin, you have come to Christ for the wrong reason. You really do not desire the favor of God, or the friendship of God. You cannot receive the forgiveness of sin without also receiving freedom from the slavery to sin!

❑ Are you walking in holiness? Are you seeking to demonstrate your free justification by bearing fruit in your life? Are you living out your faith by a life of good works?

If you are not, your faith is a dead faith. True faith purifies your heart (Acts 15:9). If Christ is yours, he will be your sanctification as well as your righteousness (I Corinthians 1:30, Romans 8:1-9, John 13:8). If you God has taken you into his favor, he will also cleanse your life. To be sure, you are justified through faith alone. Your works play no part in your justification before God. However, justifying faith is never alone. It will always be accompanied by good works. It is like this: your eye is the only part of your body that can see. Yet, your eye is never alone. It is always connected to the other parts of your body. In the same way, you are saved by faith alone, but your faith is never alone. It is always connected to good works which flow from it.

The apostle James declares that if your faith is alone, it is dead. He tells you to demonstrate your faith by your works. In other words, your works are not the **condition** of your justification. Your works are the **evidence** of your justification that you received by **faith**. Good works are a very necessary result of true faith (James 2:14-15). Now remember, the gospel is not a covenant of works. The gospel does not require you to attain righteousness by what you do in order to live. However, your good works demonstrate to others that you have a true and living faith.

Just as good fruit on a tree tells you that the tree is good (Matthew 12:33-37), so your good works tell the world that you have true faith. They will be strong evidence against those who accuse you, and say you are not justified by faith. However, always remember, your good works are not your righteousness! Your good works do not earn you the right to have the righteousness of Christ. Your good works do not qualify you to receive free grace from God. Your good works are simply the evidence that you already have Christ's righteousness and Christ's Spirit in your life.

**Application Number 3: Justification by faith will encourage you to carry out your responsibility, no matter who you are**

❏ **If you are presently a non-Christian:**

If you are not yet a Christian, it is very important for you to understand justification by faith. Do not continue in your sin. Do not remain under God's wrath. Do not continue running headlong into eternal condemnation. In the gospel, there is a door of mercy open for you. There is a righteousness prepared for you, so that you might be freely accepted by God. Some of you are risk takers. You have decided to take the risk of living without being justified by faith. Others of you want to be justified before God, but you are seeking your acceptance with God in the wrong way. You are going to legalistic religions, trying to have your conscience quieted by their deceptive teachings. Or, you are looking to your own works and performance.

God tells you, give up all those things! Look for a true righteousness, better than any righteousness you yourself can produce! Christ says in the gospel, "Look to me, look to me." The kingdom of heaven is open. God freely offers you mercy and righteousness through Christ (Isaiah 55:6-7, Jeremiah 3:12). Repentance is being preached for the forgiveness of sins (Luke 24:47, Acts 2:38). Do not neglect "this acceptable time, this day of salvation" (Hebrews 2:1-3). Why?

- o **If you neglect God's salvation through Christ, you remain under the wrath of God (John 3:36).**

  You are under the curse of the law. If you remain under this curse, it will sweep you away like the flood swept away all of those who were outside Noah's ark. The curse of the law will sweep you away if you are not in the true ark, Jesus Christ.

- o **Your condemnation will be even greater if you neglect this great salvation in Christ (Hebrews 2:3).**

  You will have no cover for your sins if you refuse to accept the mercy of God (John 15:22). Do not think to yourself that you are ruined by your past sins. Do not think you are beyond recovery, and that there is no reason for you to strive for mercy. Look, the "forgiveness of sins" is being proclaimed to you right now (Ezekiel 33:10-11). The worst sin of all is if you despise the blood of the Son of God! (John 3:18,36).

Now, you may have some objections to the doctrine of justification by faith.

The Doctrine of Justification Explained and Applied

- o "If God justifies the ungodly (Romans 4:5), then why do I need to forsake my ungodliness at all? Why can I not just stay ungodly?

  My answer: you cannot truly seek justification unless you want to live in friendship with God. Justification is God's way of taking you into friendship with himself (Romans 5:1-2), and reconciling you to himself (II Corinthians 5:19). You must use justification by faith to seek friendship with God, and to enjoy God. Why would any man seek a pardon from the government, if he intended to continue in his rebellion and defiance against that government? (I Peter 2:24). You are seeking forgiveness in a mocking way if you have no intention of returning to obedience to God once you are forgiven (Galatians 6:7-8).

- o "My sins are so great, I am beyond all hope of recovery."

  My answer: Christ's righteousness is for all kinds of sinners! Christ's righteousness is for you no matter what your nationality is – whether Jew or Gentile. Christ's righteousness is for you no matter how great your sins have been. Great sinners, from both Jews and Gentiles, have been saved by the gospel (Romans 1-3). Those who killed and murdered the "Lord of glory" were forgiven (Acts 2:23, 36, I Corinthians 2:8). Grace was given to Paul, "the chief of sinners" (I Timothy 1:15, Acts 16). "Where sin abounded, grace abounded all the more" (Romans 5:20). Your sins are the sins of a human being. Christ's righteousness is the "righteousness of God" (John 6:37, Romans 10:3, 11, 13).

❑ **If you are currently a seeker. If you are thinking about turning to God:**

If you are thinking about turning to God, if you are looking to find his acceptance, make sure you turn the right way. Turn to faith in Christ for your justification and acceptance with God. Do not seek God's favor by your own works, as most people in the world do. Everyone is very prone to do this (Romans 9:31-32). The doctrine of justification by faith seems very foolish, and even destructive,

261

to the natural man. "Become a fool, so that you might become wise" (I Corinthians 3:18). If you do not, you will labor for nothing. You will wear yourself out for no gain. You will continually be loaded down with discomfort and discouragement.

Remember, you cannot do anything good while you are still in the flesh. You cannot obey God while you are under the law, and under its curse. You cannot serve God before he has received you into his favor. You must be justified before you can live in holiness in your heart and life (I Timothy 1:5, Hebrews 9:14). Faith is the greatest work. Faith is the mother of all obedience – it gives birth to all good works (John 6:29, Galatians 5:6, Isaiah 55:2). As long as you do not believe the gospel, you are dishonoring Christ and his death on the cross (Galatians 2:21, 5:2-4). Therefore, come boldly to Christ, even through you have been a great sinner (Acts 10:43). Seek righteousness in Christ first, and then seek holiness of life (Romans 8:1).

- o **You may be asking, "How can I get faith?"**

    My answer: faith is the "gift of God" (Ephesians 2:8). Faith comes through "the gospel" (Romans 1:15-17). "Faith comes by hearing" the gospel preached (Romans 10:17). Faith comes "not only in word, but in power" (I Thessalonians 1:5). Faith comes by something beyond what human beings can naturally do in their own strength (John 6:63). If you see no faith in yourself, the first thing to do is to listen to the gospel of Christ. Meditate upon two things: first, your own sin and misery; second, the excellence of Christ. If you do this, your heart will be inclined to believe the gospel (Galatians 2:16, Psalm 9:10). God uses the gospel to bring about faith (Isaiah 55:3). If you already desire to turn from yourself to Christ in your heart, if you already prefer Christ above anything else, then the Spirit is already working to produce faith in your heart. He will carry on the work. You may pray confidently for faith (Luke 11:13, Mark 9:24).

- o **You may be asking, "The Bible says, 'without holiness no man will see the Lord' (Hebrews 12:14). How can I get holiness? I cannot make myself holy. And, this confidence you are talking about may cause me to become lazy in seeking holiness**

  My answer: if you have received the righteousness of Christ by faith, God will make you holy. This confidence in the gospel is the only way you can receive holiness. You can only live a godly life if you have already received the righteousness of Christ (Romans 5:21). Christ has brought about the New Covenant. The New covenant promises you a new heart (Ezekiel 36:24-27). If your sins are truly forgiven, you will also be delivered from their power. Just as you have been justified by the death and resurrection of Jesus Christ, you will also be made alive to live in holiness by the death and resurrection of Christ (Colossians 2:12-13).

- ❑ **If you have already been justified by faith, there are several implications:**

  - o **Walk in humility**

    Remember, you have nothing in yourself. By nature, you are an enemy of God. Your sins before God are awful! However, you have been saved by the righteousness of another, not by your own righteousness. You had fallen so far from the favor of God that God's justice would have destroyed you if Christ had not satisfied God's justice (Psalm 121:16, Romans 3:27). Christ has satisfied the justice of God through his death. His righteousness is far greater than your sins (Ezekiel 36:31).

  - o **Praise and glorify God through Christ for his abundant grace**

    What abundant grace and love God has shown you! He has washed you and cleansed you with his Son's blood (Revelation 1:5, Galatians 2:20). God made his own son to be sin and a curse for you! (Romans 5:5,8, I John 3:16, 4:9-10, II Corinthians 8:9). What a glorious and excellent righteousness God has given you in Christ! (Isaiah 56:10).

o **Live in great comfort because of the righteousness you have in Christ (Isaiah 40:1-2)**

Triumph over sin and suffering (Romans 8:33,39). Be confident, and expect great things from God (Hebrews 10:22). True, you are unworthy, and yes, grace will continually show you how unworthy you really are. Yet, you stand upon the righteousness of Christ. Glory in the hope of God's glory. For, if Christ died to reconcile you when you were God's enemy, how much more will he save you by his life, now that you are reconciled to God (Romans 5:3,10).

Boldly ask for what you need. Christ, the God-man, is your mercy seat. Whenever your sins sting you, and doubts trouble you, look to Christ, the bronze serpent lifted up for you. Confess your sin, and trust God for his forgiveness. Meditate upon Christ's righteousness, and upon God's abundant grace in Christ (Romans 8:32). To be sure, you will find much ungodliness in yourself. You will find nothing in yourself that makes you acceptable by God. However, Christ is at hand for your comfort (Isaiah 50:10, II Thessalonians 2:16-17).

Whenever you sin, come to the fountain of the gospel (Zechariah 13:1, I John 1:7). If sin plagues your conscience, it will weaken your peace and your spiritual strength. Do not let your guilt weigh you down with slavish fear. Remember, you have a righteousness that delivers you from the guilt of your sin. Apply it to your heart by faith, so the condemnation of sin will no longer plague your conscience (Hebrews 10:2, Psalm 32). You have a better righteousness than any legalist or perfectionist will ever have by their own works!

o **Hold firmly to justification by faith, no matter how much opposition you face against it**

Remember, the world is very much against the doctrine of justification by grace alone through faith alone! The devil will try to scare you away from it, or steal it from you – just as he stole it from the Jews, from the Galatians, from the legalistic religions, and just as he is now stealing it from many Christians today (Galatians 1:6). The apostle Paul said that those who had the gospel stolen from them were "bewitched." Satan will always try to get you to trust in your own works for your acceptance with God. He will tell you, "If you truly want to live a holy life, give up free grace. Trust in your own efforts to make yourself holy." He will tell you to trust in your own works to gain Christ. He will tell you to make your own works the foundation for your spiritual life.

In the midst of all this opposition, remember this: if you lose the perfect righteousness of Christ, for whatever reason at all, you lose everything! (Galatians 5:2-3). Do not try to use your works to gain what you already fully have in Christ! If you do, you dishonor Christ! The gospel does not require you to be justified all over again by your own efforts. The gospel is not a legal covenant. The gospel is a declaration of the righteousness of Christ. If you have been justified by Christ, you are already an heir through adoption and through God's promise (Galatians 3:24-26, 4:7).

This doctrine of justification by grace through faith is the only doctrine that glorifies God and humbles you. This is its great characteristic. Be very aware of your own fleshly reasoning. It will always tend to go in a direction contrary to the grace of God in Christ. Your fleshly reason will always tend to make Christ's righteousness a stone of stumbling to you (I Peter 2:8, Romans 9:32-33).

o **Live as a person who enjoys the favor of God in Christ**

In your life, let Christ have all the honor and glory. Walk in holiness, because you know the price by which you have been redeemed (I Peter 1:17-18, II Corinthians 5:14-15, II Peter 1:5, 11, I Corinthians 6:20). Love the God who has loved you first (I John 4:19, Psalm 116:16). Believe that God will empower you to live a holy life (Romans 6:14). In particular, walk in love with other

Christians. Forgive your enemies. If you understand the depths of your own sins, and how much God has forgiven you, you will be able to compassionately forgive others. If you do not understand God's great forgiveness of you, you will not be able to pray or trust God for the forgiveness of your own sins (Ephesians 4:31-32, Matthew 6:14-15, 18:21).

Eagerly desire God's grace to be poured out upon others. Wait patiently for the full declaration of your justification at the great Judgment Day (Galatians 5:5, Acts 3:19). In this life, you know your justification only by faith. You still have to struggle against sin in your life. However, at that final Day, your righteousness will openly appear. God will deal with you according to this precious righteousness that you have received from Christ.